BEN JONSON
Studies in the Plays

BEN JONSON
Studies in the Plays

||||||||||||||||||||||||||||||||||||||||||||||||||||||||||||||||||||||||||||||||||||||||||||||||||||||||||||||||||||||||||||||||||

By C. G. Thayer

UNIVERSITY OF OKLAHOMA PRESS : NORMAN

The publication of this volume has been aided
by a grant from the Ford Foundation.

822.3
J81th

LIBRARY OF CONGRESS CATALOG CARD NUMBER: 63–8992

Copyright 1963 by the University of Oklahoma Press, Publishing
Division of the University. Composed and printed at Norman,
Oklahoma, U.S.A., by the University of Oklahoma Press.
First edition.

*This book is affectionately dedicated
to my wife Mary
and to two teachers,
Arthur Gilchrist Brodeur and John Marlin Raines*

Preface

THERE WILL BE NO END to Jonson studies, because the wealth of his genius is inexhaustible: the tenth rereading of *The Alchemist* reveals new, if not unexpected, pleasures, and the old pleasures never pall. In the present book I have dealt primarily with Jonson's arguments, secondarily with his art; to deal with both adequately would require more than one large volume. Strongly ethical in bent, very much the moralist, Jonson, like some other moralists, chose satirical comedy as his primary mode of dramatic discourse. What the discourse is about is the subject of the following pages.

Several of the conclusions independently reached here have also been suggested in other recent studies. I have acknowledged all conscious debts; the unconscious ones, perhaps not quite so great, cannot be enumerated, but they no doubt exist. The first debt of any student of Jonson is to C. H. Herford and Percy and Evelyn Simpson; all quotations in this book are from their edition, and I have profited further from their full and learned notes and commentaries. I have learned much, without always being able to use it here, from some excellent books, particularly L. C. Knights's *Drama and Society in the Age of Jonson,* Edward B. Partridge's *The Broken Compass,* Jonas A. Barish's *Ben Jonson and the Language of Prose Comedy,* and Madeleine Doran's *The Endeavors of Art.* And of course I have profited less directly from a large body of criticism and scholarship.

I should like also to record particular debts to friends, many of them former students: Elsie Adams, whose unpublished monograph on the theme of the comic artist in the early comedies is a major contribution to Jonson studies; Dennis Baumwoll, of Boston University, who read the manuscript and suggested many stylistic changes, and whose conversations on Jonson have been extremely helpful; Howard Starks, Wayne Dodd, and John L. Murphy, of the University of Colorado, and Paul McGinnis, of Sacramento State College, who virtually began the study with me; Margaret Haley, of the University of New Mexico, who wrote most of the chapter on *The Staple of News;* William Weaver, of the University of Oklahoma, who took a helpfully detached view of the whole project and saved me from several blunders; and Winston Weathers, of the University of Tulsa, who, if he reads the book, will perhaps realize how much I owe him. My colleagues, J. P. Pritchard, John M. Raines, and Victor A. Elconin, have read parts of the manuscript and offered helpful comments, as has Albrecht B. Strauss, of the University of North Carolina. My greatest personal debt is to Edward B. Partridge, who painstakingly read the entire manuscript and offered many pertinent remarks.

The chapters on *The Alchemist* and *The New Inn* appeared in radically different form in *ELH* and *The Oklahoma Quarterly,* respectively. The Faculty Research Committee of the University of Oklahoma provided funds for the typing of the manuscript, and the University arranged a temporary reduction in my teaching load, for which relief, due thanks. My obligation to the University of Oklahoma Library cannot be adequately described nor my gratitude adequately expressed.

C. G. Thayer

Norman, Oklahoma
January 4, 1963

Contents

xi

The Devil is an Ass
The Staple of News
The New Inn
The Magnetic Lady

BEN JONSON
Studies in the Plays

Chapter One

Prologue: The Age and the Men

THE DRAMATIC YEARS of the first two Stuart kings (James I, 1603–1625; Charles I, 1625–1649), saw, until the Puritans closed the theaters in 1642, a great wealth of literature for the stage, reflecting the intellectual, moral, and social dilemmas of a world confronted with new problems, new horizons, new orientations to reality and life, or at least a new sense of their urgency.[1] The Elizabethan age produced great drama in the plays of Marlowe and the young Shakespeare and the young Jonson; but the Jacobean and Caroline age, the age of the first Stuarts, had a greater Shakespeare and a greater Jonson, plus Chapman, Marston, Tourneur, Webster, Beaumont and Fletcher, Middleton, and Ford, and lesser playwrights who nevertheless outstripped the Kyds, Lylys, Greenes, and Peeles of the earlier age. The Jacobean Shakespeare is by reasonably common consent the greatest playwright the world has known, and the

[1] A few of the points made in this chapter coincide with some of the arguments offered by Robert Ornstein in the stimulating introduction to his *The Moral Vision of Jacobean Tragedy*. We have arrived independently at most points of agreement.

3

Jacobean Jonson is certainly one of the world's great comic writers. No doubt they would have been great in any age, but historical circumstances imposed an urgency on their art; if one can vaguely imagine an Augustan Jonson, a Victorian Shakespeare seems almost out of the question. For better or for worse, the Jacobean and Caroline age demanded, and got, the drama it needed as perhaps no other age has ever done.

Whether the drama in fact reflected the preoccupations of the age's Everyman, or even of its every thinker, is another question. If the average man, whoever or whatever he may be, was not obsessed by philosophical, ethical, or social problems, he was perhaps not much different from today's average man and could still be interested, even enthralled, by a drama whose intellectual core was beyond his grasp, but whose entertainment value was tremendous. And if, as is sometimes said, theologians and scientists were not too much disturbed by a conflict between science and religion, the playwright, neither scientist nor theologian, often was. If the middle class, understandably enough, was uncritically pleased with the new capitalism, the playwrights, or some playwrights, viewed it with a singular lack of enthusiasm. If politicians, as they sometimes are, were ruthless in their drive for power, playwrights could savagely decry the Machiavellian ethic and the Machiavellian state. Not to multiply instances, if the age rushed headlong to its perhaps inevitable destruction, the playwright, if he was a meliorist, argued that it could do better, if he was a tragedian, that it could hardly do worse.

The Jacobean age[2] reaped the whirlwind. The Tudor age[3] was the age of great revolutionary change. The Jacobean was the re-

[2] For so one may conveniently term the years from 1600 to the closing of the theaters in 1642.

[3] 1485–1600. Elizabeth died in 1603, but the distinctly "Jacobean" qualities may be observed from about 1600.

action and the logical culmination. The Tudor age saw the enrichment of the crown in both economic and political power at the expense of the old aristocracy; but it also saw the rise of a powerful and prosperous middle class, a rise that was to have fatal consequences for Stuart ambitions and Stuart principles. It saw the long-heralded but nevertheless convulsing break with Rome; it saw the Reformation and the Counter-Reformation, and the bitter beginnings of a religious conflict and hatred not to be *legally* cleared up until the nineteenth century, not to be *really* cleared up at all. It saw the rise of capitalism and the end of a feudal-agrarian economy and culture. It saw the new Copernican cosmology slowly replacing the older Ptolemaic, and the new empirical science slowly replacing the Scholastic-deductive approach.

But while in certain areas certain kinds of men resisted the changes that were coming about, particularly in science and religion, while others attempted to hurry them forward, it would be inaccurate to say that the common man was aware of the implications of the world in which he lived. He was no doubt fervently patriotic at the time of the Armada; he loved the Queen; he clung dangerously to the old religion if he could afford it and had the fortitude, or accepted the new with misgivings, with equanimity, or with enthusiasm. In general, he went about his business. He did not concern himself with science, with the larger implications of changing winds of doctrine, with the structure of the cosmos, with the moral implications of big business.

Against this background Ben Jonson began his career. Born in 1572–73, he gained his early education and did his early writing— and fought against the Spanish in the Low Countries and became a master bricklayer—during the closing years of the Tudor age. Living until 1637, he rose to eminence in the reign of the first Stuart, an eminence he was hard pressed to maintain during the reign of the second. His life and his career began in the earlier

5

age and his greatness came in the later age. He was thirty when Elizabeth died.

By the 1590's, if the average man was going about his business in the old casual way, Marlowe and Shakespeare were considering things very thoughtfully indeed, and Ben Jonson, nine years their junior, was beginning to examine, perhaps with amused alarm, the follies and vices of men in organized society. The playwrights were not the only men concerned, of course, but their work has proved, on the whole, to be even more enduring and more attractive than that of most of the great nondramatic poets. The age of disenchantment was already well under way when in 1587 Marlowe produced the first part of *Tamburlaine,* that stunningly savage attack on the power drive. *Tamburlaine* seems almost to be a retort to what Sackville and Norton had been doing in *Gorboduc* in 1561, a justification of the major aims of Tudor absolutism.[4]

Marlowe continued his attacks, and his disillusionment grew. *The Jew of Malta, Faustus, The Massacre at Paris,* and *Edward II* explore with unparalleled bitterness the corruption at the heart of almost all the familiar objects of Renaissance aspiration: political power, economic power, intellectual power, artistic power. Marlowe's protagonists, with the possible exception of Faustus, are totally and uncritically committed to the realization of their ambitions, the ambitions of what a later writer has called "the power elite." And Marlowe was totally committed to stripping the façade from such ambitions, to show them for what they really are.

Shakespeare, on the whole, is more expansive, more sympathetic, perhaps even more detached. In some of the early comedies he stresses the possibility of man's improvement, and in the history plays from *Richard II* through *Henry V* he works toward the con-

---

[4] It has been said that there was no such thing as Tudor absolutism, but Sackville and Norton were not aware of this extraordinary notion, nor were the politicians and the writers of the Tudor homilies of 1570–71.

ception of an ideal prince and an ideal state significantly at odds with the established order of his own time. But in *Titus Andronicus,* his first tragedy, he is neither expansive, sympathetic, nor detached. He is angrier than Marlowe, less in control of his art, more concerned with presenting a one-sided, one-dimensional image of the times disguised in a trumped-up ancient Roman historical setting where the hero is accused of having "Popish tricks" at his disposal, and the villain may be found lurking by the wall of a "ruinous monastery." By 1599, when he wrote *Julius Caesar,* he had calmed down considerably—albeit temporarily—and was better equipped to explore the human and philosophical implications of political events.

Marlowe raged and scoffed; Shakespeare, on the whole, pondered compassionately. The early Jonson also raged, scoffed, and pondered, but he also laughed, more than Shakespeare. The early plays[5] deal with the follies and vices of men in a familiar if topsy-turvy society. And, as we shall see, they contain a significant new dramatic personage, a kind of ironic *raisonneur,* the poet's mask, who exerts a controlling point of view for each of the plays. Even in the most sparkling Shakespearean comedies, the laughter is balanced by genuinely serious and sometimes painful situations. In Jonson, for the most part, the *implications* are serious, but what we see on the stage is purely laughable—although admittedly there are different kinds of laughter in different plays. And it is laughable largely because it is familiar. Jonson, like Shakespeare and Marlowe, was deeply concerned with the problems of his time, and it is, I think, a measure of his human greatness that as a comic playwright he was able to express his concern in a series of very great plays that, in true classic form, mix profit with pleasure, instruction

---

[5] *Every Man in his Humor,* 1598; *Every Man out of his Humor,* 1599; *Cynthia's Revels,* 1600; *Poetaster,* 1601.

with delight. To the problems of his time he brought to bear, as L. C. Knights finely puts it, a "steady, penetrating scrutiny of men and affairs."[6]

But it is only in the Jacobean drama that the "steady, penetrating scrutiny of men and affairs" becomes almost the dramatic rule. Then, very suddenly, it seems to me, we have a large body of great drama concerning itself more or less directly with basic questions, problems of being and existence, problems of knowledge (that is, ontological and epistemological problems in a really serious sense), ethical problems, social problems. Indeed one might suggest that the term "problem play," as applied to a few Shakespearean plays that have puzzled critics more than is necessary, might better apply to a majority of the serious dramas produced during the time of the first Stuarts.

Drama was the dominant literary mode from 1590 to 1642. It had never been so before—not in England—and would never be so again. It would seem that a series of moral crises presented themselves at a time when a literary tradition was reaching maturity of form or proliferation of forms—Polonius' catalogue of dramatic types is, in number, only slightly exaggerated. Or perhaps it would be more accurate to say that the playwrights of the early seventeenth century were singularly perceptive as observers and enormously gifted as artists and were thus able to render in art what otherwise would have been rendered only in the tamer volumes of the philosophers, historians, and psychologists, interesting and valuable as they may be in their own right. Then we might have had at one end a Montaigne, at the other a Hobbes, but no Shakespeare, Webster, or Tourneur in the middle; a Burton without a Ford; an Erasmus—thank heaven—but no Jonson. This is not to imply direct connections, although Webster certainly read Mon-

6 *Drama and Society in the Age of Jonson,* 199.

taigne, and Ford certainly read Burton. It does suggest though that the playwrights rendered in art those matters that concerned other serious men as well—and in what is probably the most immediate, the most public, and the most appealing of all arts.

II
The new Philosophy calls all in doubt,
The Element of fire is quite put out.
(Donne, *First Anniversary*, 205–206.)

The Jacobean age was confronted with a series of accomplished, or almost accomplished, facts. What had been happening for the Elizabethans had happened for the Jacobeans—even though many of them may not have known it. From top to bottom things had changed. Man's conception of his universe, once theological and teleological, was now essentially empirical. The ontology of the Tudors, essentially the ontology of the Middle Ages, was shaken and confused: if divine vengeance would assuredly overtake a Cambyses, or even a Tamburlaine, Tourneur's Vendice (*The Revenger's Tragedy*) could ask if the heavens would no longer thunder against the impieties of a Lussurioso. Indeed, ontology, as one might expect, was being challenged by epistemology, even in tragedy, so that Webster's Flamineo could say, in something like despair, "While we look up to heaven, wee confound/Knowledge with knowledge."[7] (*The White Devil*, Lucas, ed., V, vi, 259–60.) What *could* one know? A central paradox occurs at the outset of the age: Othello, losing his faith in the divine Desdemona, demands of the Satanic materialist Iago "ocular proof" of her falseness: the wrong epistemology applied to the wrong ontology. And by the time we come to the tragedies of John Ford, in the late 1620's and

---

[7] In spite of this, Webster's tragic arguments are primarily ontological, even those presented by Flamineo.

early '30's, the primary interest is psychological, as though one could understand the universe only in terms of neurosis—"melancholy."

If one is inclined to see some of the great Tudors as madmen (the Dudleys, most of the Howards, many of the Seymours, not to mention Henry VIII), it seems even more appropriate to speak of a Jacobean neurosis. I speak here of what we find in the plays, but one might consider the age's malady in connection with a few of its more striking figures: James I, Lady Arabella Stuart, Buckingham, Overbury, and Somerset, plus the anguish and disillusionment displayed by a Raleigh or a Donne.

What the age in general may have felt as an uneasy sensation that all was not well, the playwrights rendered specifically. They were, most of them, very different from each other, but a few qualities they had in common. They shared an astonishing clarity of vision as they looked at the social, spiritual, and psychic problems of the age. But they looked in different ways, saw different problems, and interpreted them in different terms.

Marlowe had been the great iconoclast; Chapman was the philosopher, so much so that he sometimes seems hardly to have been writing plays; Jonson was the philosophical social satirist and meliorist; and much more; Tourneur was the great visionary of the world as cesspool and the savagely jesting champion of a rather shallow orthodoxy; Webster was the tortured Manichean ironist, Beaumont and Fletcher the supersophisticated critics of the newly established Jacobean order; Middleton in his comedies was the amusing if artistically irresponsible social satirist, and in his tragedies the great ironic moralist; Ford was the philosophical psychologist, summing up the self-destructive tendencies of a dying world. Shakespeare is almost everything, one reason why he is so hard to interpret. He is the supreme pessimist and the supreme optimist, as aware as anyone was of the great issues of the age and more willing than most to deal with them head-on. His actors were indeed "the abstract and brief chronicles of the time," and perhaps the most philosophical chronicles of any time.

These remarkable playwrights were concerned with the impact of new religion, new philosophy, new science, new modes of thought, new politics, new economics, and new morality on a once reasonably settled but now grossly disturbed way of life. With Donne, they saw all coherence gone, the anatomy of the world shattered. Faustus had "gone to prove cosmology," as well he might in an age that pondered the metaphysical implications of Copernican discoveries. Bacon was the gifted press agent of the new empiricism, sweeping the remnants of scholasticism under the intellectual carpet—where, to be sure, it left an unsightly and embarrassing bulge. Against the background of tension, neurosis, disturbed order, the playwrights made their ontological and psychological statements, proposed the various responses that men could make to reality.

What were the responses? A major character in Jacobean drama is the Machiavellian protagonist. Following the example of Marlowe in *Tamburlaine,* some of the playwrights discussed that type of almost diabolical, though in ways extremely rational, character who, aware of the neurotic folly of the world in which he lives, seeks to climb to some position of power or pleasure. Not always inherently evil, the Machiavellian protagonist simply tries to profit in a disturbed world.

Chapman's *Bussy d'Ambois* is a good example. Chapman, obviously influenced by Marlowe, paints a portrait of a charming, colorful malcontent, a dissatisfied boy scout, who knows that fortune, not reason, governs all and who knows that wealth is success and poverty a crime. Given social and monetary opportunities by the Monsieur, Bussy rises to those worldly heights that seem to represent the highest human achievement. But unsupported by any real learning or awareness, supported only by sensory capacity and the phallic sword, Bussy is destroyed by his own moral stupidity. More a very foolish person than a wicked one, Bussy's tragedy is that of the Machievellian approach to life. Such characters as the Monsieur in *Bussy d'Ambois,* Mendoza in Marston's *The Malcontent,* the Cardinal in Webster's *The Duchess of Malfi,* and Jonson's Sejanus, Macro, and Catiline represent the age's awareness of the power- and pleasure-seeking man who attempts to take his short cut to some sort of temporal paradise.

Another important Jacobean character is the malcontent. Of two sorts—the corrupted player of the world's game and the melioristic reformer—the malcontent is on the whole more perceptive, more sensitive than the simply Machiavellian figure. The malcontent, who sees life in all its horror, may decide to follow his conception of the universal ground rules: he joins in the evil game, assuming there is no other way. Borachio in *The Atheist's Tragedy,* Flamineo in *The White Devil,* and De Flores in *The Changeling* represent this type. On the other hand, Marston's Malevole, in *The Malcontent,* is a reformer at heart, who contributes to a conversion and transformation of society. Between these types is Tourneur's Vendice, in *The Revenger's Tragedy,* who, seeking to reform and change, only succumbs to the very horror against which he is reacting; he becomes immoral in his response to immorality.

Another response is implied by the Stoic. Chapman especially, in *Chabot, The Revenge of Bussy d'Ambois,* and *Caesar and Pompey,* portrays the man who does not succumb to evil, does not engage in the Machiavellian power game, does not even seek to reform or change his environment, but resists passively, sits and waits. Though sometimes led to suicide, like Chapman's Cato, the Stoic has his chance for survival in a difficult world.

In addition to the tragic, or potentially tragic, responses, two basic comic responses exist—that of the fool and that of the comic manipulator. The fool and the manipulator are fully developed in the comedies of Jonson and will engage our attention shortly. They appear, with much less art, in Middleton, occasionally in Shakespeare, frequently in the excellent comedies of Chapman, and in several of the lesser comic writers. The fool, of course, does not represent a conscious response but a comic symptom of the age's bewilderment. Thus the greatest fool in Jacobean comedy is Jonson's Sir Epicure Mammon, in *The Alchemist.* Irrelevantly learned, fatuously erudite, he knows all and understands nothing. The manipulator—Jonson's Subtle, for example—is the comic Machiavel as well as the prototype of the comic playwright, the poet's mask. He is almost always immoral and justifies his comic existence by satisfyingly exploiting the follies and vices of the fools.

The responses thus sketched make it possible to see something of the playwright's own vision of his world. Some artists present more than one view, although the diverging views of a single artist are seldom antithetical. Shakespeare's comedies may represent a hope, his tragedies an intensified vision of reality. Jonson's comedies and tragedies represent different ways of examining essentially similar phenomena. Webster's *Duchess of Malfi* implies a ray of hope absent from *The White Devil,* and his late and sadly underrated tragicomedy, *The Devil's Law Case,* implies a divinely sanctioned escape from the materialistic shackles of the Manichean world.

Whether their modes are comic, tragic, or tragicomic, however, the playwrights address themselves to what they regard as the central problems of their world. It is significant, though, that as the age draws on, the sense of urgency and of immediacy seems to weaken. Chapman, after *Bussy d'Ambois,* seems to be increasingly attracted to the possibility of a Stoic retreat from direct involvement in affairs. Nothing is so intense and immediate as Shakespeare's middle tragedies—*Hamlet* through *Macbeth*—but Macbeth has "supped full with horrors," and Antony and Cleopatra triumphantly escape from the world, leaving it to Caesar and to us. His last plays—*Cymbeline, A Winter's Tale,* and *The Tempest* —are wonderfully wrought romantic tragicomedies, presenting a vision of what might have been or what should be, but not of what is. They are very great plays but their impact is far different from that of *Othello, King Lear,* and *Macbeth.*

Webster and Tourneur, in their tragedies, are raging and intense, raising the great ontological questions without really answering them. Significantly, the *second* of the two tragedies of each *attempts* an answer. They display more suffering and less violence, and *The Atheist's Tragedy* even implies a shallow and orthodox optimism. Beaumont and Fletcher, writing early in the century, anticipate clearly what is to come. A consuming paralysis of the will, far more debilitating than Hamlet's, imposes itself on most of the principal characters of *Philaster* and *The Maid's Tragedy.* A new and disheartening masochism appears, a brilliant but unnerving understanding of psychic aberration, and a sensational but perhaps shallow theatricality.

If Beaumont and Fletcher clearly anticipate what is to come, the full realization appears in John Ford; yet Ford is more serious and hence more affecting, more dramatic and less theatrical. He is the last great tragic playwright of the great age, and in his pondering of the psyche, in his sense of man's helplessness, in his poignant use of aberration as a substitute for asking the larger ontological questions, he seems to say that man can no longer rage against a hostile or indifferent universe but only succumb to its dismal imperatives. In *The Broken Heart,* Ithocles, strapped in a chair, welcomes the dagger of Orgilus; Penthea, wed to a brutal and ridiculous husband, goes pathetically mad; Orgilus bleeds to death; and Calantha, after a brilliant dramatic evocation of the Dance of Death, dies of a broken heart. Earlier in the age stabbing and poisoning were characteristic modes of tragic death. Now the dagger or rapier is welcomed—as by Aspatia, in *The Maid's Tragedy*—and the poison is likely to be psychic.

Even in Jonson one sees the change coming about. The early and middle comedies, containing, to be sure, their "built-in" allegories are strongly realistic ("the deeds and language such as men do use"); *Cynthia's Revels,* with its masques and allegorical personages, satirizes realistically the vices and follies of courtiers. But the superb realism of *Bartholomew Fair* is tempered by a newly-integrated mythic element. *The Devil is an Ass* (1616) and *The Staple of News* (1626), with brilliantly realistic scenes of sweeping social satire, are strongly influenced, structurally and conceptually, by the overt allegorical techniques of the old morality plays; and *The New Inn* (1629), with a few frankly realistic passages, is primarily allegorical and idealistic. The unfinished *Sad Shepherd* (1637), with its pastoral scenes and figures and supernatural and mythic overtones, is again allegorical and idealistic. Furthermore, most—but not all—of the earlier plays, with their wealth of familiar detail, were designed to appeal to a relatively wide audience, on the familiar Jonsonian assumption that men and society could correct their vices and follies through laughter. But men and society were changing, and the last plays are directed—unsuccessfully, it would seem—at a much smaller segment of the population.

Jonson died in 1637, the theaters closed in 1642. The silence came. The Puritans triumphed for a while and left their mark for a long time. The new science triumphed, too, without consciously divorcing itself from the old religion. Except for the "Popish Plot," the horrid product of a sick mind, the religious troubles were almost over, and the Glorious Revolution was also a bloodless one. By the reign of Queen Anne men thought they had solved the ontological question, the social question, almost all questions.

The brilliant battle that the Jacobean dramatists had fought upon the stage—the battle with the universe, with the psyche, with society—seemed forgotten almost in the neo-classic and Augustan certainties. The questions that the Jacobean playwrights had asked —Who are we? In what sort of world do we live? Why do we do what we do?—though never really answered, were laid aside in the more optimistic, less disturbed clime of the Stuart end and the Hanoverian ascent.

Even more lost, it seemed, were the topical concerns of the early seventeenth century. The debate between an orthodox Catholicism and an evolving Protestantism (*Cymbeline* and *Philaster, Hamlet* and *The Atheist's Tragedy,* even *Henry IV* and *Sir John Oldcastle* from an earlier era), or Jonson's attacks on the rising capitalism and Puritanism—these no doubt seemed less than vital issues to the centuries that followed. The literature of the eighteenth and nineteenth centuries went on, or so they thought, to more modern issues.

Yet from the perspective of the twentieth century we suddenly realize that what the Jacobeans discussed is what we are discussing still. Both on the philosophical level (man in the universe) and on the psychological level (why man does what he does); both on the religious level (orthodoxy *vs.* liberalism and relativism) and on the social level (social order *vs.* individual need), the Jacobeans touched upon the abiding issues that we still must discuss, still must argue out. In that sense, the Jacobean and Caroline dramatists are modern, speak to our condition. Webster and Tourneur yet rage for us; John Ford ponders the psyche for us; Jonson yet laughs for us. Just as Shakespeare is "timeless and universal," so his fellow dramatists are not lost in a point of time some three hundred years ago: their subjects are ours; they remain a vital voice even in our lives today.

Chapter Two

The Early Comedies

||||||||||||||||||||||||||||||||||||||||||||||||||||||||||||||||||||||||||||||||||||||||||||||||||||||||||||||||||||||||||||||||||

EVERY MAN IN HIS HUMOR

Every Man In and *Every Man Out* provide the introduction to
an important aspect of Jonson's work.[1] In these two plays, the
earliest that he wished to preserve, he presents almost the entire
range of character and argument that will appear, more richly developed, in the plays that follow. It seems to me that Knights is
wrong in his assertion that the early humor comedies are "mere
experiments."[2] Taken together they constitute Jonson's statement
on the correct principles and limits of comic drama.

The Prologue to the Folio version of *EMI* contains a characteristic Jonsonian statement about comedy. The poet will not "serue

---

[1] For the present discussion I use the revised version of *Every Man In,* as it
appeared in the Folio of 1616. The characters are virtually the same as they were
in the Quarto of 1599, although the names are different; and the plot is in all
essentials the same. The Folio version was the one by which Jonson wished to
be judged.

[2] L. C. Knights, *Drama and Society in the Age of Jonson,* 180.

17

th' ill customes of the age"; battles on the stage are ridiculous; popular drama is wildly improbable; tricky stage effects are dramatically irrelevant. Instead of the usual kind of play there will be "an Image of the times," "Humane follies," which can become crimes only if we love them and practice them ourselves. This gets us at once to a critical and frequently misunderstood aspect of Jonsonian comedy, which will "sport with humane follies, not with crimes"—although why this should have been misunderstood in view of Johnson's very precise statement is not altogether clear. Critics have asserted that in *Volpone,* for example, he departs from his practice, for surely Mosca and Volpone, not to mention the gulls, are more criminal than foolish. This ignores the difference between drama and real life. The passage in question promises

> . . . deedes, and language, such as men doe vse:
> And persons, such as *Comoedie* would chuse,
> When she would shew an Image of the times,
> And sport with humane follies, not with crimes.
> Except, we make 'hem such by louing still
> Our popular errors, when we know th'are ill. (21–26.)

From this it would seem to follow that what is mere laughable folly on the stage can become genuinely criminal if it takes the same form in the real life of the times outside the theater. When he represents idealized folly on the stage, Jonson produces comedy. But when he presents on the stage actions which have actually occurred in history, he produces tragedy. A significant difference between the comedies and the tragedies is that the follies of the comedies exaggerate or caricature human motives, speech, and actions; the crimes of the tragedies duplicate historical fact. Thus Volpone and Mosca in the comedy are like the tragic characters Tiberius and Sejanus made ridiculous.

It is Jonson's explicit intention to sport with follies on the stage so that they will not become—or remain—the crimes of real life. This does not mean that Jonson is not "realistic"; it does mean that he is not naturalistic. The characters that he presents on the stage are *like* characters one might meet in real life, but they are not the same. Jonson's typical use of psychologically oversimplified characters—the "humor" characters—implies a deliberate limitation on characterization that is both artistic and didactic, qualities which for Jonson are inseparable. And even in such a generally pleasant and indulgent spectacle as that provided by *EMI*, one can see that society could be corrupted and ruined if it included a sufficient number of Stephens, Kitelys, Matthews, and Bobadills.

In its general tone, in most of its characters, and perhaps in its situation, this play has something in common with the version of Roman new comedy represented by Plautus—the father-son-crafty servant combination being especially reminiscent of Plautus. However, the intention of reforming society, central to Jonsonian comedy, is a seemingly minor concern in Plautus and Terence. Jonson makes it perfectly clear in his prologue that he has a specifically didactic intention, which is to prevent or ameliorate crimes in or against society by presenting them on the stage as follies, that is, as actions which are absurd and laughable and hence not to be imitated in real life.

The education of Plautine and Terentian characters generally occurs in the plays themselves, in the action. In Jonson, however, the situation is sometimes different: the audience is educated by watching the comic characters remain essentially *uneducated*, even though the material for their moral and intellectual improvement is implicit in the action and language of the play. There is, therefore, an implied moral norm, which exists outside the action of the play. In Jonson, until the last four plays, the intelligent audience is instructed by observing folly amusingly presented, occasionally by seeing it jolted into something like sanity. For Plautus, and particularly for Terence—with the expected exceptions—the audience is theoretically led to wisdom—when this actually is part of the author's intention—by observing the education of the characters in the plays. Furthermore, in Jonson, even in *Every Man In,* the social criticism seems much more trenchant than it ordinarily is in Roman comedy. It resembles more closely what we find in Aristophanes, and it seems to me that the prologue to *EMI* constitutes an essentially Aristophanic, rather than Plautine or Terentian, statement of the ends and principles of comedy. The idea of "popular errors"—since popular errors suggest something public rather than private, social rather than domestic—seems to go beyond the accidents of domestic comedy that we associate with both Plautus and Terence.

But it is not until *Every Man Out* that the parallel with Aristophanes becomes really clear. *Every Man In,* in its original form, was the earlier play, and, although the Prologue was produced for the folio version, the play, even in its revised form, represents a transition between the very Plautine *The Case is Altered* and the essentially Aristophanic *Every Man Out.* The characters in *EMI,* as already suggested, are basically Plautine; and the situation—with the predictable reforms of Kitely and the Knowells, with Brainworm acting as the clever agent of moderately painful education, with the invitation to a pleasant dinner at the end—is the sort of thing commonly found in Plautus.

And yet Jonsonian comedy is on the whole closer to Aristophanes than it is to either Plautus or Terence. Why, then, did he choose to rewrite and preserve *Every Man In?* The title itself suggests the answer. *Every Man in his Humor* represents a compendium of comic humors—it is a display of the relatively pleasant foibles which contribute to the comic way of the world. Jonson was not concerned with a cataloguing of the medical humors and their psychological counterparts. The ancient theory of the four humors

20

provided Jonson with a metaphorical theory of human behavior that lent itself very well to the purposes of comedy, for it tends inevitably to oversimplify motives, a process essential for the Jonsonian presentation of comic character.

But what *humors* finally means for Jonson is *manners,* as he himself often indicates. Indeed, in the Prologue to *The Alchemist,* he specifies that humors is simply a fashionable term for manners: "... whose manners, now called humours feed the stage...." The humors are the simplified, often caricatured, manners of men; from this it would follow that the comedy of humors is for all practical purposes a comedy of manners, specifically, a comedy concerned with the manners of men in society. One might say that *Every Man In* combines a Terentian conception of character—although not of character development—with an Aristophanic concern for the behavior of men specifically as members of society, with, however, the emphasis more strongly here than in the later plays centered in some kind of educative process experienced by the principal characters. Kitely, like any old man in Plautus, has learned his lesson: on one particular subject—in this case, his wife's fidelity—he will presumably not make any more mistakes. But Kitely is still a fool at the end.

If *Every Man In* is a pleasant version of New Comedy with Aristophanic overtones, in which everything finally is set right by the amusing and not misnamed Justice Clement, it is also something else; and since this "something else" reappears in play after play, it must be recognized. The *action* of this play is concerned with establishing a kind of rapport between parents and children and husbands and wives, and with the exposing of an appropriate number of gulls. But this same action, and the language in which it is presented, also carries another and very different kind of statement—a metaphorical commentary on the function and nature of art. Knowell expresses pride in his son but fears that the young man may be so immature and ill-advised as to pursue too seriously his study of poetry:

> My selfe was once a student; and, indeed,
> Fed with the selfe-same humour, he is now,
> Dreaming on nought but idle *poetrie,*
> That fruitlesse, and vnprofitable art,
> Good vnto none, but least to the professors,
> Which, then, I thought the mistresse of all knowledge:
> But since, time, and the truth haue wak'd my iudgement,
> And reason taught me better to distinguish,
> The vaine, from th'vsefull learnings. (I, i, 15–23.)

Knowell is in most respects the devoted and indulgent father, a milder version of Ovid Senior; and though he is wrong, Jonson makes his point of view *seem* reasonable enough. He is brought around only by Justice Clement's words toward the end of the play, words that save Edward Knowell the trouble of making the impassioned defense of poetry made by Lorenzo Junior in the quarto version. Since Knowell's speech about idle poetry comes at the beginning of the play, we can assume that it has thematic importance. Yet if this speech establishes the poetic theme which is a constant undercurrent in Jonsonian comedy, young Knowell is not like Ovid, in *Poetaster,* defying a foolishly unreasonable father. Though on the second level the play is about poetry, it is still not like *Poetaster*: it does not present an impassioned argument, it merely shows us something.

And in the development of the poetic theme the principal figure is not Edward Knowell but Brainworm, who seems to represent the comic poet. Brainworm's career in the play is revealing, but in describing it I do not wish to suggest that Brainworm as comic poet eclipses Brainworm as clever servant. He is patterned after Tranio and other clever slaves in Plautus, but in helping Edward Knowell outwit his father and marry Bridget he also has a symbolic function. Brainworm's talents are rather like those of Face in *The Alchemist;* it is his function in the play to bring out the most absurd and ridiculous in the various characters with whom he is involved, a function very much like that of the comic poet.

Brainworm becomes involved in conspiracy when Knowell, having read Wellbred's letter to Edward, seals it up again and tells Brainworm to deliver it to Edward, enjoining him not to tell his young master that he has read it—something Brainworm had not known until Knowell revealed it to him. Brainworm's comment is, "O lord, sir, that were a jest, indeed!" (I, ii, 121.) In I, iii, he delivers the letter, reveals the information he had been ordered to conceal, and thus automatically becomes involved in a plot against his old master. Then he directs his attention to the idiot Stephen, offering him his gelding to follow the servant whom Stephen pretends he would like to beat. The dialogue that follows suggests Brainworm's function as comic spirit:

STEP. But, I ha' no bootes, that's the spight on't.

BRAY. Why, a fine wispe of hay, rould hard, master STEPHEN.

STEP. No faith, it's no boote to follow him, now: let him eene goe, and hang. 'Pray thee, helpe to trusse me, a little. He dos so vexe me—

BRAY. You'll be worse vex'd, when you are truss'd, master STEPHEN. Best, keepe vn-brac'd; and walke your selfe, till you be cold: your choller may foundre you else. (I, iii, 30–39.)

This is followed by observations on Stephen's "leg," concluding with Brainworm's delightful, "You haue an excellent good legge, master STEPHEN, but I cannot stay, to praise it longer now, and I am very sorie for't." (51–53.)

In II, v, the actual gulling of Knowell begins when he is accosted by Brainworm disguised as the impoverished veteran Fitzsword,

23

who wishes to enter Knowell's service. The idea of Brainworm as a kind of metaphorical spirit of comedy reminds one of Face and his highly suggestive changes of identity in *The Alchemist*. The point is that Brainworm, like Face, can assume many identities that serve to baffle, challenge, and render ridiculous the characters to whom they appear in their various forms. Brainworm's comic identity has already been strongly suggested when, in his soldier's disguise, he sells the worthless sword to Stephen. In that passage neither Stephen nor Edward recognizes him, and it must be re-membered that, though Brainworm is on Edward's side, Edward lacks Brainworm's perceptiveness and is thus, in his own affairs, also guided by the spirit of comedy.

When comic characters like Edward begin to understand their own motives, they tend to lose their comic significance. Comedy is not the place for serious soul-searching or moments of truth in the ordinary sense. From II, v, 133, to the end of the scene, Brain-worm regales himself with the idea of his own cleverness: "S'lid, was there euer seene a foxe in yeeres to betray himselfe thus?" (135–36.) This is of great importance, because Brainworm is the comic agent of deceit, not the thing itself. His appearance and talk have indeed deceived Knowell, but, more important, he has also caused the "foxe" "to betray himselfe."

From this scene until late in the play Brainworm is involved in various situations in which he forces other characters to reveal their absurdities. He thus has a double function: in the realistic action he helps his young master outwit his father and get the girl—who in this play is of no more significance than most of the girls in Plautus; but while doing this, he manipulates and deceives other characters to emphasize his symbolic identity as comic poet. At the end of the play, however, he is trapped in a situation that re-quires him to reveal his identity to everyone and then to revert to his former realistic status as the elder Knowell's servant. Overstepping his assumed authority as a sergeant, he has been forced to arrest Downright and take him to Justice Clement's house, where, after a salutary reign of terror, the justice burns some stolen poems and drinks a toast to Brainworm.

If Brainworm is the comic poet, Justice Clement represents the guiding hand of a particular kind of comedy, a comedy quite consistent with the title, *Every Man in his Humor*. The humors represented place no intolerable burdens on the body politic—at least not as they are conceived for the purposes of this play. Therefore Clement is not merely a character; he also represents a quality that establishes the tone of the play. Brainworm has the true satirist's bent, but the Justice appropriately tempers satire with clemency.

Every Man in his Humor is an altogether engaging play, containing almost nothing extraneous to its purpose. Even Cob and his malodorous lineage are so amusing that the essential irrelevance of some of his speeches can hardly be objected to. Yet, if such a distinction is valid, one might say that this play is in all respects an admirable comedy without being either great or profound. The only real subtlety of thought, anticipating the later plays, lies in Justice Clement's very interesting quibble over what he *must* do and what in fact he *will* do as he brandishes his long-sword over the terrified Brainworm. This is surely a commentary on the relationship between the humor on the one hand and reasonableness on the other, and it suggests that the old man's merry humor is very close to reason itself.

EVERY MAN OUT OF HIS HUMOR

In the discussion of *Every Man In* it was not necessary to give much attention to the theory of humors. But with *Every Man Out,* Jonson and his critics, in characteristically different ways, force us to consider the subject. The physiological theory of the four humors, whose proper balance controlled physical and mental health, was first advanced by Hippocrates, amplified by Galen, and given more or less definitive form in Sir Thomas Elyot's *Castle of Health*. This medical theory lies back of the comic theory of the humors, to be sure, but scholars have, I think, tended to exaggerate its importance as a prerequisite for understanding the plays of Ben Jonson. Actually, Jonson himself tells us all we need to know on the subject:

> Why Humour (as 'tis *ens*) we thus define it
> To be a quality of aire or water,
> And in it selfe holds these two properties,
> Moisture, and fluxure: As, for demonstration,
> Powre water on this floore, 'twill wet and runne:
> Likewise the aire (forc't through a horne, or trumpet)
> Flowes instantly away, and leaues behind
> A kind of dew; and hence we doe conclude,
> That what soe're hath fluxure, and humiditie,
> As wanting power to containe it selfe,
> Is Humour. So in euery humane body
> The choller, melancholy, flegme, and bloud,
> By reason that they flow continually
> In some one part, and are not continent,
> Receiue the name of Humours. Now thus farre
> It may, by *Metaphore,* apply it selfe
> Vnto the generall disposition:
> As when some one peculiar quality
> Doth so possesse a man, that it doth draw
> All his affects, his spirits, and his powers,
> In their confluctions, all to runne one way,
> This may be truly said to be a Humour.
> But that a rooke, in wearing a pyed feather,

> The cable hat-band, or the three-pild ruffe,
> A yard of shooetye, or the *Switzers* knot
> On his *French* garters, should affect a Humour!
> O, 'tis more then most ridiculous. (Grex, ii. 88–114.)

A humor is simply an imbalance in favor of "some one peculiar quality," a gross exaggeration of a normal trait of character, an affectation that significantly departs from the normal. We must distinguish, then, between the medical theory and Jonson's metaphorical application of it. We will never understand a Jonsonian character if we try to decide which of the four humors is out of balance in his system; we would arrive only at a singularly tiresome view of his comic art. The humor theory metaphorically applied to personality, as Jonson explains it in *Every Man Out,* involves considerable psychological oversimplification. Needless to say, Jonson was aware of this fact: the process is quite deliberate. Indeed, one of the most impressive characteristics of Jonson's comic art, here and elsewhere, is his rigid exclusion of potentially attractive character traits if they are not consistent with his literary aims.

He is not, as has been often charged, deficient in sympathy, compassion, and human understanding; but more often than not he finds them irrelevant to his particular kind of comedy. Jonson's comic aim, as stated in the prologue to the Folio *Every Man In,* is "to shew an image of the times,/ And sport with humane follies, not with crimes." Although his comedies differ from each other, his aim is consistent. The humor itself means "the manners of men." Manners as a gloss on humors suggests the range of the comedy of humors, and it also strongly implies the comic context. One scarcely needs to worry, then, about the cubic centimeters of black bile in a humor character's make-up; what *is* important is to see the humor characters as members of a vast social panorama, as possessors or practitioners of absurd follies which, unchecked, would threaten or destroy the social order. The deliberate psychological oversimplification means that none of these characters is special, that all are typical; thus the morality of Jonsonian comedy is social.

The two humor plays suggest the range and scope of the comedy of humors. In *Every Man In* Jonson has conceived a kind of domestic panorama showing typical practitioners of recognizable follies, presenting an engaging picture of the relatively harmless side of human folly and absurdity. *Every Man Out,* which depicts the vicious side of human folly and absurdity, is exactly the opposite. As Jonson's descriptions of them indicate, the humor characters here are not amiable and harmless. Furthermore, to accentuate this side of folly, he concentrates on the characters and supplies only the most rudimentary plot.

Why is there this sudden and radical change in dramatic technique from the easygoing domestic comedy of manners to the scathing satire of *Every Man Out?* Many critics have assumed that Jonson was motivated by a personal resentment at not being sufficiently appreciated as a playwright, at the fact that lesser writers were more popular. The satirist is often enough accused of this sort of envy, but a much simpler and more reasonable answer is available, namely, that Jonson is exploring the possibility of applying to stage comedy some of the techniques of pure satire. The violent and abusive satire of *Every Man Out* suggests both Aristophanes and the Roman satiric poets. O. J. Campbell has clearly demonstrated that Jonson is here adapting the methods of satiric verse to drama.[1] The relative plotlessness of the play underlines the point. Jonson is for all practical purposes inventing a new form, and the purely formal aspects of his work must never be overlooked. The genre is established in the reference, in l. 232 of the Induction to *Vetus Comoedia,* the "Old Comedy" of Aristophanes. This ref-

[1] *Comicall Satyre and Shakespeare's Troilus and Cressida,* San Marino: The Huntington Library, 1938.

erence tells us a good deal about the kind of play we are going to have, and we are told even more by Asper, "the presenter."

> ASP. Away.
> Who is so patient of this impious world,
> That he can checke his spirit, or reine his tongue?
> Or who hath such a dead vnfeeling sense,
> That heauens horrid thunders cannot wake?
> To see the earth, crackt with the weight of sinne,
> Hell gaping vnder vs, and o're our heads
> Black rau'nous ruine, with her saile-stretcht wings,
> Ready to sinke vs downe, and couer vs.
> Who can behold such prodigies as these,
> And haue his lips seal'd vp? not I: my language
> Was neuer ground into such oyly colours,
> To flatter vice and daube iniquitie:
> But (with an armed, and resolued hand)
> Ile strip the ragged follies of the time,
> Naked, as at their birth: COR. (Be not too bold.
> ASP. You trouble me) and with a whip of steele,
> Print wounding lashes in their yron ribs.
> I feare no mood stampt in a priuate brow,
> When I am pleas'd t'vnmaske a publicke vice.
> I feare no strumpets drugs, nor ruffians stab,
> Should I detect their hatefull luxuries:
> No brokers, vsurers, or lawyers gripe,
> Were I dispos'd to say, they're all corrupt. (Grex, II. 3–26.)

In this passage Jonson, as Asper, seems to assume the mask of the Roman satirists, particularly Juvenal. We are being prepared for something radically different from *Every Man in his Humor,* where there are certainly no wounding lashes, nor iron ribs to imprint them in. This is the other side of the comic mask, and its face is not nearly so genial as that which presides over the earlier play. Asper tells us plainly that here we are to be confronted with follies that are devastating in their effect on the body politic and must therefore be extirpated.

The figure of Asper requires special comment: he has been described as "Jonson to the life."[2] This is simply not true, even though Asper is later referred to as the author, because the Grex, after all, is part of a stage representation, and Asper, as a character in the play, represents only one aspect of Jonson's artistic personality. And if Asper is really Jonson, who wrote *Every Man In?* The author of *that* play surely was not concerned with stripping naked the ragged follies of the time, so that he could, "with a whip of steele,/ Print wounding lashes in their yron ribs." No: Asper is an Elizabethan Juvenal, the austere satiric poet, and Jonson, like Swift, assumes a mask for the occasion. That he is not himself when he assumes the mask is explicitly stated when Cordatus observes "that a madman speakes." (l. 150.)

The author of *Every Man In,* on the other hand, was much more like an Elizabethan Plautus. Actually, Jonson assumes several masks in *Every Man Out.* Cordatus, explaining the action and the author's comic theory, also represents a side of Jonson's public personality; and the envious Macilente represents an Asper-like character stripped of the artist's moral point of view and injected into the action of the play. The identification of Macilente with Jonson reflects little credit on the critic who assumed that Jonson would represent himself as a poisonously bitter and wretchedly envious man. Percy Simpson denies, quite correctly, that Macilente is Jonson,[3] but his essential function, exposing the follies of the other characters, is precisely the function of the satiric poet. Macilente is Asper as he would be if he were transferred from the Grex to the play proper,[4] just as Asper is the Juvenalian mask assumed by

---

[2] Herford and Simpson, Vol. IX, 402.

[3] *Ibid.,* 402.

[4] Alvin Kernan makes a similar point in *The Cankered Muse.* See particularly 158–62.

Jonson as "Presenter" of *Every Man Out*. The mad Asper leaves the scene early in the play to return as the envious Macilente.

Jonson, therefore, does not appear as himself at any point in the play; instead, various functions of the writer of comical satire are performed in different ways by Asper, Macilente, Cordatus, and even the jeering Carlo Buffone. This typically Jonsonian use of the multiple point of view occurs in several other plays and always functions as a peculiarly coherent way of presenting the various facets of human experience relevant to a particular dramatic context.

Every Man out of his Humor appears to be a comical satire on the *subject* of comical satire in which the sharp and bitter Asper assumes the guise of the barren, gaunt, thin Macilente to comment enviously on the follies of the other characters, and in which the clownish Buffone jeers for the sake of jeering. The fact that Jonson changes to Asper and Asper changes to Macilente is an exceedingly meaningful aspect of Jonson's comic technique. Since this is in effect a play about a play, or at least about something about a play, we would do well to consider this complexity of representation. No one in the play itself is identified as a playwright or specifically as a literary satirist, but two characters in the play proper function somewhat like one or the other of these.

Macilente is of primary importance, and he, I believe, is intended to suggest what a man like Ben Jonson would be if he were translated from real life to the stage as a character in a humor play. Jonson's austere view of society and the world thus gives way to Asper's *furor poeticus,* his rage at the world; this yields to Macilente's gnawing envy, which has its purely absurd counterpart in the irresponsible and insane jeering of Carlo Buffone. The presentation of multiple viewpoints takes on added importance as we realize that the characters in this essentially plotless play are put through their paces, in various ways and on different levels, by

Jonson, Asper, Macilente, and Buffone, and that the play is explained by another Jonsonian mask, Cordatus.

This is a formidably literary work, an adaptation of certain aspects of Roman satire to the stage at a time when verse satire had been officially banned. Its origins in verse satire help to explain its plotlessness, which is of course quite deliberate, and its apparent origin in a particular kind of satire help explain its tone. Jonson never tried anything like it again, and he did not need to, because in these two humor plays he established, tentatively at least, almost the entire range of character and of comic presentation that he was to use until late in his career. I have avoided a detailed discussion of the characters in these two plays, because in the former play they represent something quite familiar and in the latter they are all carefully described by Jonson himself—who does it better than anyone else could—and because in describing the plays I have suggested the kind of characters appropriate to each. The humors in the one are tolerable, in the other intolerable.

CYNTHIA'S REVELS

Cynthia's Revels continues and expands the techniques of *Every Man Out,* placing allegory at the service of comical satire, and suggesting an idealized rather than violently satirical reformation of manners. Socially the scope of *Every Man Out* is greater than that of its successor, but artistically *Cynthia's Revels* is more expansive and ambitious, introducing the masque into the comic action. Like the other plays in the group (*Every Man Out* and *Poetaster*), it is designed not only to satirize facets of society—courtiers in the present play—but to show how the artist can effect salutary changes in society. Yet *Cynthia's Revels,* through its allegorical superstructure, extends beyond the customary scope of satire, involving in its action the gods, the poet, society, and the somewhat ambiguous Cynthia.

Cynthia's Revels reads almost like an experimental version of *The Staple of News,* far less complex than the later play and on the whole less successful artistically. It also anticipates *The Devil is an Ass,* although in that play the argument rather than the technique of the masque is subtly and effectively introduced. *Cynthia's Revels,* then, is an experimental work—a point suggested by the Prologue—in which comical satire is joined with allegory and the masque to do two separate but related things: to satirize courtly society and to show how the artist can effect changes in that society.

At first glance the play seems structurally incoherent, with such disparate elements as realistic satire and ideal metamorphosis. *Every Man Out* and *Poetaster* remain within the more or less conventional bounds of satire: in the first the characters are rudely jolted out of their humors through the actions of other satirized characters; in the second they are reformed through the actions of a satiric poet and a just prince. But in *Cynthia's Revels* their peccant humors are subtly altered through the roles they play in Crites' masque; when Cynthia discovers who the masquers actually are, they are made to repent their follies and abandon their self-love, and are presumably reformed.

What this means, in brief, is that the characters who have behaved with absurd folly when pursuing their own natural bent are subject to change through their appearance in a highly idealized form of art. The changes are logical ones, for Crites chooses the roles carefully, and they represent alterations in degree, not in kind. Thus, in the masque, Amorphus becomes the neat and elegant Eucosmos; Hedon becomes Eupathes; Phantaste becomes Euphantaste; Gelaia becomes Aglaia, etc. The masque identity represents the extension of a vice into a parallel virtue. But the courtiers

have all drunk of the fountain of self-love; they are not yet prepared to assume permanently their new identities. They must be
unmasked by Cynthia, recognized, and purged of their guilt, a
guilt that in the presence of Cynthia they cannot deny.

Crites, like Horace in *Poetaster,* administers the purgative sentence—less literally purgative, of course. The important and idealistic point is made, however, that vice is its own punishment:

> But there's not one of these, who are vnpain'd,
> Or by themselues vnpunished: for vice
> Is like a furie to the vicious minde,
> And turnes delight it selfe to punishment. (V, xi, 130–33.)

The penance imposed is a ritual purgation of the recognized and
acknowledged vices and follies; the effects of the water of the fountain of self-love must be offset by the waters of Helicon.

Yet, as has been suggested, between the fountain of self-love and
the waters of Helicon lies the pseudorealistic court with its realistically conceived courtiers and their symbolic names. As every
critic has realized, the chief problem of the play is to reconcile
the apparently jarring artistic elements—what the play "means" is
reasonably clear. We have a partly realistic play whose dramatis
personae includes, *inter alia,* Cupid, Mercury, Echo, Arete, Crites,
Argurion, and Cynthia—also called Delia and Diana. Perhaps the
experiment has not succeeded fully, but some of its theory can certainly be explained.

The presence of the gods and the goddess serves to expand the
significance of the realistic elements represented by the foolish and
ridiculous courtiers, just as the symbolic names of the courtiers provide a larger than individual significance for each of them. The system works both ways: Mercury and Cupid have their normal mythological import, but Cupid particularly becomes an object of semi-
realistic satire under the verbal disapproval of Cynthia. Hedon,
Anaides, and the others may or may not symbolize real people, but

34

surely they are shrewdly chosen so that the virtues corollary to their vices can be symbolically evoked in the masques in the last act. And Cynthia, no matter how many echoes of Elizabeth she may evoke, certainly represents a moral and intellectual ideal as well as the virgin queen. In calling forth the virtues of an ideal Cynthia, Jonson is not so much flattering the queen as instructing her, as he was to do implicitly in *Poetaster*.

That one should be cautious in identifying Crites with Jonson himself is a point made long ago by C. H. Herford, but it bears repetition. No doubt Crites is Jonson as Jonson ideally wanted himself to be; but this is only to say that Crites is the ideal critical poet—the writer of moral satire who can castigate the follies of the court and suggest the way to their correction.

Echo is a purely mythological figure, yet it is she who seems to establish the artistic basis of the play. As the archetypal sufferer from the follies of self-love she is granted the power of speech long enough to inveigh against self-love and describe its effects. Through her own identity and through her association with Narcissus she expands the significance of the ensuing realistically presented theme of self-love in the courtiers and prepares the way for the later masque-theme of metamorphosis.

And if Echo establishes the artistic basis, Argurion is its prime concrete example; for she, more than any of the other courtiers, has a clearly defined dual nature, even before the formal masques of Act V, and she directly anticipates the more complex figure of Aurelia Clara Pecunia. She is, on the one hand, money pure and simple, and descends from the citizen father to the fatuously ambitious son; and, on the other hand, she is a more or less realistically conceived foolish lady of the court. The emphasis, therefore, seems to be on the double materialism with which her double identity is viewed, and the love of money is symbolically opposed to the love of virtue and associated with the love of trivial vice.

It will not do to say merely that there is an artistic confusion present in the conception of this character. Jonson, all through this essentially masque-like comedy, is insisting on the existence of universal ideals as well as temporal absurdities. Points of view are distinctly involved, and we are asked to examine things as they are and as they ought to be. A careless light wench about the court is called Argurion because such a person is subject to the same kind of misuse that money is, both being temporal and material. In the conception of such a character we can see as clearly as we can anywhere the idealism which is central to Jonsonian comedy, because the existence of such a character suggests elaborate interrelations between appearance and reality, interrelations which are clarified in the masque itself.

The clarification is implied in the figure of Arete, the pure virtue, detested by the courtiers, under whose immediate domain Crites conceives the masque which will relate vices to virtues in a balanced order and prepare the way for the final resolution under the influence of the divine Cynthia. The resolution occurs in the sentence passed by Crites as he lances the ulcer of the corrupt courtiers, who are ordered to go

> to the well of knowledge, *Helicon;*
> Where purged of your present maladies,
> (Which are not few, nor slender) you become
> Such as you faine would seeme: (V, xi, 153–56.)

When knowledge replaces self-love, reality will supplant appearance, and this desirable alteration will occur only when an ideal monarch, representing also a moral ideal, gives free license to the moral satirist.

The point is worth examining: we have here nothing like the "self-contained" comic action of *The Alchemist,* or even of *Every Man Out.* Crites alone—or even aided by Mercury and Arete—cannot reform the foppish courtiers, although he can embarrass or humiliate them. As in *Poetaster,* so in *Cynthia's Revels,* the lessons of the satirist will achieve their desired end—"the amendment of vices by correction"—only through the participation of the ruler. While *Cynthia's Revels* and *Poetaster* concern themselves to a considerable extent with the nature of the good poet, they are primarily concerned with the relationship between the poet and the prince. But the present play is not simply a work *de regimine principum,* because Cynthia is not merely the queen. In *Poetaster* there is no question whatever about the identity of Augustus Caesar, since he is called by his name. But, though Elizabeth was often called Cynthia, and is certainly involved in the identity of *this* one, *Cynthia* also represents an exalted moral and spiritual ideal, which reappears, strangely and tellingly transformed, in a far riper and far greater play, *The New Inn.*

On one level, then, Crites is the satiric poet writing under the aegis of an enlightened prince whose handmaiden is virtue; on another level he is the satiric poet inspired by an ethical idealism which, whether specified (as in the dedication of *Volpone* to the two universities) or not, was always present for Ben Jonson. The allegorical superstructure, therefore, not only expands the kind of action possible in a play like *Cynthia's Revels* but also the kind of argument possible, by representing the higher impulse of the satiric poet.

In a way the comical satire of *Cynthia's Revels,* with its explicitly stated moral idealism, its heavily mythological and allegorical superstructure, and its idealized resolution, resembles the fully developed masque, a form which Jonson was not to perfect for several years. The emphatic contrast between the realistic and the allegorical suggests also the masque-antimasque arrangement, although often the two opposing parts of the masque could be allegorical or symbolic as well. Finally, the use of the dance, the pattern of divinely inspired order, which occurs in the last act, is suggestive of the masque. In addition to being a logical predecessor of the later comedies, *Cynthia's Revels* seems to anticipate the other dramatic form in which Jonson excelled, and it may be that at this stage of his career, before the great period of masque-writing had begun, Jonson was considering the possibility of a heavily symbolic comic drama which would combine realistic comedy with the allegorical and symbolic techniques of the masque. If this is true, he was prevented, or saved, from such a course by the coronation of James I.

For all of its masque elements, *Cynthia's Revels* is a comical satire, and, though references to the masque may help to clarify a few points and cast light on the idealistic nature of the play, it must be seen as a comical satire and not as something else. To put it succinctly, *Cynthia's Revels* is a comic play in which the satirist Jonson hopes to amend the vices of courtiers by having the other satirist Crites, under the influence of the divine Cynthia, correct the vices of the comic courtiers by dissipating the effects of the waters of the fountain of self-love through the influence of the waters of Helicon. To the extent that comic vices are rigorously corrected by the satiric poet, *Cynthia's Revels* is a comical satire.

POETASTER

Poetaster is the best of the comical satires. Its significance as a work of art has been clouded by its having been viewed almost exclusively as a document in the so-called War of the Theaters, although if it were nothing but that we should reasonably expect to see a good deal more of Crispinus and Demetrius, for, representing Marston and Dekker, they represent Jonson's two chief antagonists in that farcical rivalry.

However, even if there had been no such thing as the War of the Theaters, this play would hardly lose its significance, because, while it does attack Dekker and Marston, particularly the latter, this attack is very far from being its main function, limited as it is to a handful of very amusing scenes. I do not, therefore, wish to discuss this play in the usual context, although one point, generally overlooked, might be made here: the play, vastly superior to any of the others which figure in the controversy, had one very salutary effect on one of its victims—after Crispinus was forced to vomit up his uncouth words, John Marston improved his style. That interesting detail in the War of the Theaters is not always recognized, but it is an excellent example of the rarely successful use of satire to amend vices by correction. It seems possible that without the salutary effects of Jonson's not entirely unfriendly chastisement Marston would have been unable to produce that masterpiece, *The Malcontent*. And he certainly would not have collaborated with Jonson and Chapman in another masterpiece, *Eastward Ho*.

Since none of the commentators seems to have called attention to it, it is probably worth noting that the Elizabethan War of the Theaters was not unique. Something very similar happened in Athens, for example, between Aristophanes and Cratinus, and Aristophanes' attacks on Euripides are in the same vein.

But if *Poetaster* is not to be viewed as simply the last shuddering gasp in the War of the Theaters, it is still directly concerned with literary problems, and, as is usual with Jonson, the literary problems are also moral problems. In spite of the title, which reflects the author's differences with Dekker and Marston, the subject of the play is not bad poets, but the good poet and the education of the poet. Jonson was no doubt led directly to this subject because he had been attacked by some bad poets; yet it is characteristic that in returning the attacks he should go much further and instead of merely presenting Marston and Dekker as asses—which he certainly does—he should dwell more intently on the nature and function of the good poet and on the educaton of the poet.

Poetaster, partly no doubt because of its connection with the War of the Theaters, reverses Jonson's usual procedure. Ordinarily, as

I have suggested earlier, when he is concerned with literary problems, he presents them not on the realistic level of action but on a symbolic level implied in the realistic level. *Poetaster* is frankly a play about poets; the primary action is about poets and their problems. The social satire, which is always such a strong element in Jonsonian comedy, is here secondary, although it is of course present. It is secondary in the relatively small number of scenes devoted to it, and also because the gulls in this play present a more or less constant threat to the poets, whereas in many other plays the poet-figures present a kind of constant pleasant threat to the gulls. And here the controlling figure is not an artist at all, but Caesar.

In this respect *Poetaster* has greater scope than most of the other plays which combine a realistic action with a symbolic commentary on art, and one is inclined to wonder whether Jonson had more reasons than the ones given in the prologue for shifting his scene from London to Rome. He had been criticized for bringing in the queen herself at the end of *Every Man Out* and *Cynthia's Revels*. Is Augustus Caesar's perfect sympathy with the good poets intended here as a comment on the rebuffs Jonson had apparently received in consequence of the two preceding plays? And did he perhaps anticipate that Elizabeth would be succeeded by the man he was to admire so genuinely and so intensely?

In any case, *Poetaster* presents a wise ruler availing himself of the services of wise poets in governing the affairs of state. Elizabeth, like Walpole, could get along without them, although she was obviously not averse to having a few very great ones throw themselves fruitlessly on her penurious mercy. The idea of a Caesar deferring to the judgment of Horace and Virgil had an understandable appeal to Jonson, and it is important to remember that his own career as a writer of masques was largely devoted to supplying, in highly artistic terms, moral instruction for his king. Moreover, it is pleasant to think of James himself, tyrannized over in his youth by George Buchanan, complacently receiving instruction from the greatest poets and playwrights of the age, including Shakespeare.

Perhaps we should begin at the beginning, instead of at some time past the end. Percy Simpson asserted that some difficulty attends beginning a play called *Poetaster* with a representation of Ovid's troubles with his unsympathetic father.[1] Yet Ovid is, after all, a central figure in the play, and with his affairs we must concern ourselves first. There is no question that the figure of Ovid presents difficulties of interpretation, but these problems are lessened somewhat when we recall that Ovid is not precisely a good man and thus, for Jonson, cannot be precisely the good poet.[2] This idea, which Jonson was to specify so clearly in the dedication of *Volpone,* was certainly in his mind when he conceived the comical satire about poets.

Two things about Ovid are, it seems to me, perfectly clear: he is an extremely talented poet, and his character as a poet is sullied by his illicit relationship with Julia. In this respect he seems to anticipate the figure of Wittipoll in *The Devil is an Ass.* Wittipoll is in a sense a symbolic poet-figure himself, but an impure one because of his love for Mistress Fitz-Dottrell. Jonson succeeds in making Wittipoll both sympathetic and morally imperfect. His wooing of Mistress Fitz-Dottrell is tremendously eloquent; at the same time it is morally wrong, since she happens to be married and he happens to be intent on adultery. Wittipoll is purified, as it were, when his adulterous love gives way, in a highly Platonic denouement, to virtuous friendship. In *Poetaster* Ovid is presented with great sympathy, but also in a way that shows his love for Julia is not morally perfect.

Indeed Jonson seems to go somewhat further and to suggest that

[1] Herford and Simpson, Vol. IX, 538n.
[2] A point made by Simpson: *Ibid.,* 533.

Ovid's sullied love is an aspect of a generally imperfect under-standing of his own life. After Caesar passes the sentence of banish-ment, Ovid's lament reveals a complete lack of moral independ-ence and fortitude:

> Banisht the court? Let me be banisht life;
> Since the chiefe end of life is there concluded:
> Within the court, is all the kingdome bounded,
> And as her sacred spheare doth comprehend
> Ten thousand times so much, as so much place
> In any part of all the empire else;
> So euery body, moouing in her spheare,
> Containes ten thousand times as much in him,
> As any other, her choice orbe excludes.
> As in a circle, a magician, then
> Is safe, against the spirit, he excites;
> But out of it, is subiect to his rage,
> And loseth all the vertue of his arte:
> So I, exil'd the circle of the court,
> Lose all the good gifts, that in it I ioy'd. (IV, viii, 1–15.)

The principal "good gift" was Julia, and this gift Ovid misused, a fact made reasonably clear in the banquet of the gods, a scene which I assume has two levels of significance. On one, it is, as Horace says, ". . . innocent mirth,/ and harmelesse pleasures, bred, of noble wit." (IV, vii, 41–42.) On another, it is presumption, as Ovid and his merry friends rise symbolically beyond their proper identities and ape the gods at their jolly worst. In a sense we can say that Ovid has been heading for this since we first saw him with his misapplied love and his misapplied poetry.

But the banishment is not only punishment, it is also education. In IV, ix, Julia wishes to commit suicide so that her soul may join with Ovid's; but he dissuades her by arguing that their souls may not experience this desired union at all, that,

"No life hath loue in such sweet state, as this;
"No essence is so deare to moodie sense,
"As flesh, and bloud; whose quintessence is sense.
"Beautie, compos'd of bloud, and flesh, moues more,
"And is more plausible to bloud, and flesh,
"Then spirituall beautie can be to the spirit. (IV, ix, 36–41.)

Julia, having been thus improperly corrected, arrives at a truer notion of an idealized if not quite Platonic love:

Farewell, sweet life: though thou be yet exil'd
Th'officious court, enioy me amply, still:
My soule, in this my breath, enters thine eares,
And on this turrets floore, will I lie dead,
Till we may meet againe. In this proud height,
I kneele beneath thee, in my prostrate loue,
And kisse the happy sands, that kisse thy feet.
"Great IOVE submits a scepter, to a cell;
"An louers, ere they part, will meet in hell. (IV, ix, 68–76.)

There follows the affecting passage in which neither can bear to turn away from the other first, but in which Ovid finally leaves the scene with a speech revealing that the follies which produced his morally imperfect poetry have finally, under stress, been corrected:

OVID. Ay me, there is no stay
In amorous pleasures: if both stay, both die.
I heare thy father; hence, my *deitie*.
Feare forgeth sounds in my deluded eares;
I did not heare him: I am mad with loue.
There is no spirit, vnder heauen, that workes
With such illusion: yet such witchcraft kill mee,
Ere a sound mind, without it, saue my life.
Here, on my knees, I worship the blest place

43

That held my goddesse; and the louing aire,
That clos'd her body in his silken armes:
Vaine OVID! kneele not to the place, nor aire;
Shee's in thy heart: rise then, and worship there.
"The truest wisdome silly men can haue,
"Is dotage, on the follies of their flesh. (IV, ix, 95–109.)

I take it that this passage, unless I have wholly misjudged Jonson's intention, completes the education of one who could not be a good poet without first being a good man.

But we have been examining Ovid's career in isolation from the rest of the play, and, as Jonson presents it, it is not to be seen in such relatively simple, black and white terms. Ovid is, as we have seen, sympathetically portrayed, even though he is morally deficient. He is superior, for example, to the very movingly presented figure of Sextus Propertius, who, we are told by Horace, "Hath clos'd himselfe, vp, in his CYNTHIAS tombe;/ And will by no intreaties be drawne thence." (IV, iii, 5–6.) Ovid at least will learn how to live without the living Julia, while Propertius will not live without the dead Cynthia. Jonson himself respected the historical Ovid and the historical Sextus Propertius, but if we recall the infinitely affecting fortitude and tenderness with which he was to reconcile himself to the deaths of his own two children, and the superb poems with which he commemorated those events, we will recognize that he thinks that Propertius has taken the wrong course and Ovid, finally, the right.

On yet another level Ovid is thrown, at the very beginning of the play, into sharp and exemplary contrast with the people who really don't care for poetry at all—his very well-meaning but dull-witted father and the almost incredibly funny, stupid, and boorish Captain Tucca. Again, we realize that a nation composed of minds like that of Tucca would simply collapse of its own inanity; yet, as we watch the character floundering on and off the scene in this play, we are seeing one of Jonson's greatest comic creations. Captain Tucca is one of those great satiric triumphs that, like Lady Booby or Mistress Slipslop, are at once vain, stupid, ridiculous, and infinitely amusing. He is even funnier, although less significant, than Sir Epicure Mammon, and our laughter is evoked, I think, by the unerring precision of the language with which Jonson presents him. A person the like of whom we will never meet in real life suddenly appears before our startled eyes, answering Ovid Senior's question, what was Homer— "... what was he? what was he?" (I, ii, 83.)

> TVCC. Mary, I'le tell thee, old swaggrer; He was a poore, blind, riming rascall, that liu'd obscurely vp and downe in boothes, and tap-houses, and scarce euer made a good meale in his sleepe, the whoorson hungrie begger. (I, ii, 84–87.)

Again, for precision of utterly fatuous language, it would be hard to find anything more effective than his observations to the player, in what must certainly be the funniest single scene in the play:

> TVCC. And what new matters haue you now afoot, sirrah? ha? I would faine come with my cockatrice one day, and see a play; if I knew when there were a good bawdie one: but they say, you ha' nothing but *humours, reuells,* and *satyres,* that girde, and fart at the time, you slaue. (III, iv, 187–92.)

This brings us to a very nice and a very interesting balance in *Poetaster.* Ovid is presented in opposition to enemies of poetry, while Horace is presented, significantly, in contrast both to enemies of poetry and to enemies of the state who have no love for poetry; and what Jonson is finally concerned with in this play, as the last act indicates, is the relationship between poetry and the body politic, poetry and the state. Ovid's poetry is related to the state only when its non-moral basis becomes a threat to the morality of the

body politic; but the poetry of both Horace and Virgil is concerned directly with the health of the body politic. Horace particularly is presented in contrast to the zealous misapplication of
Lupus, the stupidity of Tucca, and the absurdly bad poetry of
Crispinus, the poetaster.

In presenting Horace on poetry, Johnson proceeds with great
care and intelligence, from the private, as it were, to the public
aspects of Horace's career, in a manner similar to that of Pope's
Epistle to Arbuthnot. Jonson's Horace is introduced in III, i, in a
dramatized adaptation of the ninth satire of the first book. The
whole passage reveals, in extremely amusing terms, some of the
more private vicissitudes of the poet. Horace would like to get on
with his business, but Crispinus, anxious to become friends with
the great man, won't let him. Yet the scene has a more important
function than that already outlined, for at the end, when Crispinus has suggested that he and Horace might join forces and
banish Virgil and Varius from the graces of Maecenas "and enioy
him wholy to our selues" (III, i, 245), Horace introduces Crispinus
to the republic of letters in very specific terms:

> HORA. Gods, you doe know it, I can hold no longer;
> This brize hath prickt my patience: Sir, your silkenesse
> Cleerely mistakes MECOENAS, and his house;
> To thinke, there breathes a spirit beneath his roofe,
> Subiect vnto those poore affections
> Of vnder-mining enuie, and detraction,
> Moodes, onely proper to base groueling minds:
> That place is not in *Rome,* I dare affirme,
> More pure, or free, from such low common euils.
> There's no man greeu'd, that this is thought more rich,
> Or this more learned; each man hath his place,
> And to his merit, his reward of grace:
> Which with a mutuall loue they all embrace. (III, i, 247–59.)

The larger implications of this ideal situation are realized in the last act, and the republic of Maecenas expands, with Virgil advising the emperor and Horace administering justice. Between the marvelous dialogue with Crispinus and the lofty conclusion, however, there is an intermediate point (III, v) in which, in an adaptation of the first satire of the second book, Jonson has Horace explain why he is a satirist. Horace loves virtue and scorns and detests vice and folly. He will continue to uphold the one and attack the other in his customary way: "What hiew soeuer, my whole state shall beare,/ I will write *satyres* still, in spight of feare." (III, v, 99–100.) He will continue to ". . . spare mens persons, and but taxe their crimes" (III, v, 134), to which his friend Trebatius replies:

> Nay, I'le adde more; if thou thy selfe being cleare,
> Shalt taxe in person a man, fit to beare
> Shame, and reproch; his sute shall quickly bee
> Dissolu'd in laughter, and thou thence sit free. (137–40.)

In effect Jonson himself reserves the right to engage in personal satire so long as the satire is genuinely deserved. The scene between Horace and Trebatius, which did not appear in the quarto version and was apparently added for the folio text, defines satire as a valid instrument for correcting vice and commending virtue and also provides justification for Jonson's departure from his usual custom in directly satirizing a particular person—Marston as Crispinus. Horace's problem in the first encounter with Crispinus is essentially a private one with public implications. The dialogue with Trebatius establishes the public function of satire and thus prepares us directly for Horace's role in the last act.

Act IV ends with the final details of the education of Ovid, and Act V begins with Caesar's words in praise of poets and poetry, followed immediately by the sustained passage in praise of Virgil, who among other things is notably free of the moral defects of Ovid. The most revealing comment, probably, comes from Tibullus:

> But, to approue his workes of soueraigne worth,
> This obseruation (me thinkes) more than serues:
> And is not vulgar. That, which he hath writ,
> Is with such iudgement, labour'd, and distill'd
> Through all the needfull vses of our liues,
> That could a man remember but his lines,
> He should not touch at any serious point,
> But he might breathe his spirit out of him.

> CAES. You meane, he might repeat part of his workes,
> As fit for any conference, he can vse?

> TIBV. True, royall CAESAR. (V, i, 116–26.)

This establishes the high office of the poet and is entirely consistent with the view expressed in the dedication of *Volpone* that the poet ". . . can alone (or with a few) effect the business of man-kind."

The subject of this lofty discourse then appears and is persuaded by Caesar to read a passage from Book IV of his newly completed *Aeneid*. The passage Jonson translates here has been shrewdly chosen, because it extends both the Ovid and the Horace themes in the play. It is concerned with the love-making of Dido and Aeneas and the scandal-mongering which follows and thus glances at the relationship between Ovid and Julia and, in view of Horace's role in the play, suggests a situation—irresponsible gossip—which the satiric poet may correct. Virgil thus is introduced as the ideal poet, free even of the petty distractions which beset Horace, and the most appropriate counselor for Caesar himself. Poetry, in the figure of Virgil, is described as having the highest moral function and at the same time the highest social function.

But the play is after all a *comical* satire, and, to avoid an inconsistency of tone, Jonson does not end it here but reintroduces the various malefactors, Lupus, Tucca, Crispinus, Demetrius, and the actor. In V, iii, then, the function of the satiric poet is established in a wonderfully satirical scene, as Horace the satirist, now appropriately acting as judge with the authority of Caesar, first clears himself of Lupus' absurd charges and then passes sentence on the poetaster. The Virgil passage perhaps reveals Jonson's conception of the full and exalted function of the perfect poet, while the ensuing Horace passages reveal metaphorically his conception of the judicial function, as it were, of his own art in this play that of the satirist. Virgil is clearly greater, but in effecting the business of mankind Horace's role is more direct, immediate, and applicable.

In view of its subject, *Poetaster* seems to be related to *The Frogs* of Aristophanes, although it is perhaps slightly less coherent as a work of art. Certainly, in its far-reaching social satire, it has something in common with Old Comedy as well as being directly associated with Horatian satire, and in the implication that a good poet is a potential savior of the state, Jonson seems to be repeating in effect the implication of Dionysus' search for a poet who will save the city. Tucca's irreverent jests about Homer are, on a very small scale, faintly reminiscent of the gloriously funny contest between Euripides and Aeschylus, while the exaltation of Virgil is roughly parallel to the accidentally correct decision of Dionysus to take Aeschylus back to Athens with him. Ovid's banquet of the gods in *Poetaster* may reflect the similar diminution of their importance which occurs in Aristophanes. And Crispinus vomiting up his big words may have been suggested by that part of the contest between Aeschylus and Euripides in which the weightiness of their words is tested in a scale. There does appear to be some connection, the general terms of which are quite consistent with Jonson's comments in *Every Man Out* about his artistic independence combined with his partial reliance on the tradition of *Vetus Comoedia*.

Chapter Three

The Middle Comedies

||||||||||||||||||||||||||||||||||||||||||||||||||||||||||||||||||||||||||||||||||||||||||||||||||||||||||||||||||||||||||||||||||||||||||||||||||||

VOLPONE

WITH THP POSSIBLE EXCEPTION of *Sejanus, Volpone* is the best play Jonson had produced by 1606. Virtually every critic of Jonson agrees that it is a masterpiece, yet some still profess themselves troubled by it. It is a great play, but is it really a comedy? So runs the usual question. It is apparently a comedy, but it seems to move perilously close to tragedy. So goes the usual answer. But can a play really be a masterpiece if it is not really comic, not really tragic, and of course far from tragicomic? I would say no, but then I find the play very entertaining. I understand why many critics have felt that it borders on the tragic, but I think this is a mistaken view. *Volpone* contains some of the most entertaining scenes Jonson ever wrote, and it contains no scenes that are even remotely tragic.[1] The common view, therefore, seems to me to be based on a partial misreading of Jonson's intention and of his play.

---

[1] *Cf.* on this point the studies of Nash and Putney.

But these are rather flat assertions. Why have so many critics said the play comes close to tragedy? Because Volpone is really a wicked man who wants to rape a radiantly beautiful creature named Celia; because her husband's avarice leads him to give his consent; and because at the end of the play stiff sentences are passed on Volpone and Mosca. Less momentous reasons are that the subsidiary characters, except for Sir Politic Would-Be and his lady, and Celia and Bonario, are not nice either. A further objection might be that legacy-hunting is too repugnant to be comic—as though avaricious fools and rogues did not practice it constantly.

Before taking up some of these matters in detail, we might consider a fairly specific statement by the poet:

> All gall, and coppresse, from his inke, he drayneth,
> Onely, a little salt remayneth;
> Wherewith, he'll rub your cheeks, til (red with laughter)
> They shall looke fresh, a weeke after. (Prologue, 33–36.)

Jonson's prologues are notable for their seriousness, and there is nothing in the tone of this one to suggest a departure from the general rule. Therefore only two alternatives are possible: the play is approximately as amusing as the author says it is, or the play does not live up to the promise of the prologue and is a failure. So far from calling it a failure, however, almost everyone agrees it is a masterpiece, but apparently not the sort of masterpiece the author intended, for the reasons given above; hence it must be a masterpiece by accident, unless Jonson was right and his critics wrong.

I think the critics are unquestionably wrong and, since the matter is important, we must at the outset examine the objections. Corvino's willingness to prostitute Celia to the lust of Volpone violates all comic principles (except, perhaps, those in other comedies—the *Mandragola,* for example). But does it, really? It seems to me Jonson has kept this whole business well within reasonable comic bounds—not, however, the bounds of Terentian comedy. Corvino is both jealous and avaricious. Through Mosca's ingenuity his avarice is made to take precedence over his jealousy. The situation itself is not at all improper to comedy. When Corvino observes Celia dropping her handkerchief to be picked up by Volpone disguised as Scoto of Mantua, he flies into a jealous rage. But when he learns that he may still inherit Volpone's fortune by packing Celia off to bed with him, he is willing to do so. When she refuses, he is as furious at her chastity as he had been before at her imagined turpitude.

The spectacle of one absurd vice giving way to another is amusing enough in itself, but the circumstances under which this happens are thought to be too dreadful to be funny. And perhaps they would be if Celia were different from what she actually is. The critic who immortalized himself by his reference to the "radiantly beautiful Celia" was, I think, typical in his ludicrous misreading of the character. So far as I can see, there is nothing in Jonson's presentation of this character to indicate that she is anything but an idiot, an eloquent Dame Pliant. Almost every passionate speech she utters is parody of the sort of thing one might expect from a young woman named Celia. What are we to think of a character who gives Celia's reply to Volpone's sublimely lustful wooing speech in III, vii, when the divine afflatus approaches that of Sir Epicure Mammon?

> Good sir, these things might moue a minde affected
> With such delights; but I, whose innocence
> Is all I can thinke wealthy, or worth th' enjoying,
> And which once lost, I haue nought to loose beyond it,
> Cannot be taken with these sensuall baites: (III, vii, 205–10.)

If Celia's virtue were not mere parody of virtue, she might have reacted with scorn or anger to the implied comparison with Lollia

Paulina. Instead her reply is charmingly fatuous. One wonders which is more absurd, Celia herself, or Volpone, wooing her with a song from Catullus and a series of references to classical debauchery the like of which Celia has surely never heard. She is, as one critic has observed, the little seamstress in the clutches of a foul ravisher,[2] and if the actor who plays Bonario reads his lines with all the misguided vehemence they deserve, the audience will dissolve with laughter when he frustrates Volpone's attempted rape:

> Forbeare, foule rauisher, libidinous swine,
> Free the forc'd lady, or thou dy'st, impostor.
> But that I am loth to snatch thy punishment
> Out of the hand of iustice, thou shouldst, yet,
> Be made the timely sacrifice of vengeance,
> Before this altar, and this drosse, thy idoll.
> Lady, let's quit the place, it is the den
> Of villany; feare nought, you haue a guard:
> And he, ere long, shall meet his iust reward.
>
> (III, vii, 267–275.)

How many heroes of melodrama have leaped from behind the arras with words almost as silly as these?

As for the horrendous sentences passed against Volpone and Mosca, one might recall—or recognize—that they are part of an elaborate comic pattern in which the judges themselves are presented as being exceedingly dull witted. They believe literally everything they are told, and pass sentences when people stop telling them things. There is, incidentally, no rigorous noncomic justice in this play. Volpone's and Mosca's sentences, in keeping with the obtuseness of the judges, are out of all proportion to their pleasant crimes. This, it seems to me, is part of the comedy, and those readers

[2] H. R. Hayes, "Satire and Identification: An Introduction to Ben Jonson," 267–83. Knights also comments on Celia's and Bonario's fatuousness. *Drama and Society*, 203.

who feel that the play verges on tragedy at the end would do well to remember that Volpone is really no Lear or Othello.

Another point might be made in this connection: if the play has a flaw, it lies in the fact that, unlike most of Jonson's comic figures, Volpone almost becomes a human being. He is vicious enough, to be sure, but his surface is so clever, witty, and engaging that his harsh sentence seems to be inflicted on a *person,* rather than on a comic character. It may be this, rather than the sentence itself, that makes the punishment disturbing.

Jonsonian comedy, as we have seen before, presents, on the social and satiric level, a more or less systematic perversion of those principles commonly felt to be conducive to an ordered and sane society. This is apparent on almost every level in *Volpone,* and is clearly established in *Volpone's* magnificent opening soliloquy. It would be well to recall a few of the details, for Volpone's sublime rhetoric typifies, on a grand scale, the avarice common to almost everyone in the upside-down world of this play. Gold, then, is his saint, its repository his shrine; its sight is more welcome than day to the earth or light over chaos. His treasure is sacred, and takes, in his imagination, the form of sacred relics. The golden age was justly named by the wise poets, because gold is the best of things. It is Venus, a saint, and a dumb god; it is of equal value with souls, and hell with gold is worth heaven without it. It is "vertue, fame,/ Honour, and all things else!" (25–26.) And its possessor will "be noble, valiant, honest, wise." (27.)

Religion and all moral principles are thus inferior to gold, and Volpone's moral principles are completely and systematically perverted. The irony of this brilliant passage is greatly intensified when he points out that he glories more in the cunning purchase of his wealth than in the glad possession. He gains in no common way and therefore considers himself to be morally superior to those who must seemingly be destructive in order to attain wealth:

I vse no trade, no venter;
I wound no earth with plow-shares; fat no beasts
To feede the shambles; haue no mills for yron,
Oyle, corne, or men, to grinde 'hem into poulder;
I blow no subtill glasse; expose no ships
To threatnings of the furrow-faced sea;
I turne no moneys, in the publike banke;
No vsure priuate—(I, i, 33–40.)

And Mosca points out his patron's kind-heartedness:

No, sir, nor deuoure
Soft prodigalls. You shall ha' some will swallow
A melting heire, as glibly, as your *Dutch*
Will pills of butter, and ne're purge for't;
Teare forth the fathers of poore families
Out of their beds, and coffin them, aliue,
In some kind, clasping prison, where their bones
May be forth-comming, when the flesh is rotten:
But, your sweet nature doth abhorre these courses;
You lothe, the widdowes, or the orphans teares
Should wash your pauements; or their pittious cryes
Ring in your roofes; and beate the aire, for vengenace.
(I, i, 40–51.)

Volpone is thus, ironically, innocent of all those wicked things men do in order to get money and of those miserly things they do once they have it. As the first scene ends, the source of his wealth is explained, but in such a way that it seems more like a virtue than a vice—with some reason, since his clients seem substantially worse than he.

At this point appear the dwarf, the eunuch, and the hermaphrodite with the story of the transmigration of the soul of Pythagoras from the great philosopher through a series of descending gradations to Androgyno, the hermaphrodite-fool. The history of this

55

metempsychosis is crucially important for an understanding of the play. The soul came originally from Apollo, and descended through a son of Mercury, a warrior, Pythagoras, a whore, a cynical philosopher, a fool, a Carthusian, a lawyer, a mule, an ass (*i.e.*, a Puritan), to a creature of delight, an hermaphrodite, who insists, however, that the identity of fool is more important than that of hermaphrodite. The soul of Apollo has thus descended in a grand sweep through all the estates, and now resides in a sexually ambiguous fool. But it is specifically identified as a soul which came originally from Apollo, and this establishes the art-theme for the play; it is also specifically identified as a soul whose earthly habitat was Pythagoras, who thus becomes the earthly Apollo, an identity not at all far-fetched in view of Pythagoras' accomplishments in the sciences and arts, particularly mathematics and music. It is relevant here to remember that the poet-figure in Jonson's last play is Compass, the "scholar-mathematic," and that the poet's *impress* centers on the figure of the broken compass.

As the soul of Apollo descends through his earthly manifestation until it resides in the fool, so, for this play, everything that Apollo represents is finally subsumed in the idea of comedy—comedy seen from a very particular point of view. The little entertainment thus becomes a kind of natural history of folly, in which Apollo's soul, which is also the soul of Pythagoras, by virtue of the increasingly debased forms it occupies—concluding with that of the indifferent Androgyno—itself becomes debased and perverted. That it should finally inhabit the body of an hermaphrodite indicates the final blurring of all relevant distinctions, a point raised again in social terms in *Epicoene* in the figures of the silent woman, who is really a man, Captain Otter and his wife, and Lady Centaur.

By implication, then, folly involves the placing of virtues in figures who are unable to sustain them. When they finally reside in the hermaphrodite the very bases of life itself become indistinct and indifferent—totally ambiguous. Presumably the Apollonian soul of Pythagoras speaks in the body of the deformed fool, which suggests the idea, specified in the song that follows the entertainment, that the fool has special license to speak the truth. In the song from Erasmus, the fool is enviable because he is able to speak truth, "free from slaughter." If the fool is to be equated with the idea of comedy, a central aspect of which is folly, then it follows that the entertainment which occupies a large part of I, ii, is an oblique but hardly obscure comment on the freedom of comedy to speak the truth engagingly and with impunity.

To some readers the deformity of Volpone's household has seemed excessively repulsive, although the reasons for the deformity are perfectly clear and a number of critics have explained them. One might point out however that since, according to classical theory, comedy presents the ludicrous, and since the ludicrous is an aspect of the ugly, there is no inherent reason why the household entertainers of the principal figure in a comedy should not be ugly. Their very deformity underlines the perversion of values presented explicitly in the opening scene, and it is not insignificant that Mosca, talking to Corvino, describes them as his patron's children:

> 'Tis the common fable,
> The Dwarfe, the Foole, the Eunuch are all his;
> H'is the true father of his family,
> In all, saue me: (I, v, 46–49.)

Volpone's children thus seem to represent a comment on comedy, since they are ludicrous—that is, ugly and amusing—and this in turn would seem to suggest that Volpone himself, because of the symbolic relationship, is designed to represent a type of morally imperfect comic poet, the symbolic progenitor of a house full of deformed but clever entertainers.

It is interesting and significant that when it is time for Mosca to turn the tables on Volpone, thus preparing the way for bringing the state, in the form of the judges, into the satire, he sends Nano, Castrone, and Androgyno out into the public streets to entertain themselves. Since on the realistic level there is no particular reason for this, it must be symbolic, indicating that the scope of the comic commentary is being expanded. And of course Volpone himself is also out in the world, and his presence there as satirical goad is underlined by the presence of his creatures, as it is in the mountebank scene by the presence of Nano.

If Act I, Scene ii, establishes the tone and significance of the play by localizing and inverting the spirit of Apollo, the mountebank scene (II, ii), as a kind of *parabasis,* introduces the complicating spirit of Dionysus and the figure of the imperfect poet. The ostensible purpose of this scene is to enable Volpone to see the beautiful Celia, but, like a similar scene in *The Alchemist* (II, iii), it has a symbolic function which has escaped notice, even though it is extremely important. The controlling spirit of the play has been established in I, ii, and the conspirators and principal victims have been introduced and some of their essential qualities revealed. Volpone's passion for Celia is to be the most important single complicating factor in the action, for it directly precipitates the court action which will lead ultimately to the downfall of Volpone and Mosca and the further discomfiture of Voltore, Corvino, and Corbaccio; but his passion for Celia will also reveal indirectly the central symbolic function of Volpone.

In this altogether wonderful scene Volpone disguises himself as the famous mountebank Scoto of Mantua, who is ludicrously misunderstood by Sir Politic Would-Be and described with unimaginative accuracy by Peregrine the traveler. In their attitudes toward Scoto, Sir Politic seems to prefigure Sir Epicure Mammon and Peregrine the ironically ironic Pertinax Surly. The mountebank's speech is long—disproportionately long, when we consider that its apparent purpose is merely to allow Volpone a glimpse of the somewhat less than heavenly Celia. And it therefore requires explanation.

The mountebank, as Jonson well knew, was not only a purveyor of patent medicines, he was also a public entertainer, often of a rather deplorable sort. The physic which Scoto would like to purvey is useless, but the claims for it are wonderful, and it anticipates the effects of the philosopher's stone in *The Alchemist,* a point made specific when Sir Politic asks, "Is not his language rare?" and Peregrine replies, "But *Alchimy,*/ I neuer heard the like: or BROVGHTONS bookes." (II, ii, 118–19.)

Now alchemy, in the later play, is among other things a metaphor for comic art, debased in the hands of the fake alchemist, Subtle.

In *Volpone,* a play not quite so well integrated, Scoto's oil has pretty much the same function. Scoto himself speaks contemptuously of his rivals, *"with their mouldy tales out of BOCCACIO, like stale TABARINE, the Fabulist:"* (51–52), *"These turdy-facy-nasty-paty-lousy-farticall rogues* [the epithet is Aristophanic] . . . *want not their fauourers among your shriuel'd, sallad-eating* artizans:" (60–65.) The oil, which will cure everything, including the dreadful disease, "torsion of the small guts," has been prepared by alchemy: Scoto has *"bestow'd great cost in furnaces, stilles, alembeks, continuall fires, and preparation of the ingredients."* (151–52.)

And Scoto is sorry for his incompetent competitors: *Poore wretches! I rather pittie their folly, and indiscretion, then their losse of time, and money; for those may be recouered by industrie: but to bee a foole borne, is a disease incurable. For my selfe, I alwaies from my youth haue indeuour'd to get the rarest secrets, and booke them; either in exchange, or for money: I spared nor cost, nor labour, where any thing was worthy to bee learned. And gentlemen, honourable gentlemen, I will vndertake (by vertue of chymicall art) out of the honourable hat, that couers your head, to extract*

the foure elements; that is to say, the fire, ayre, water, and earth,
and returne you your felt without burne, or staine. For, whil'st
others haue beene at the balloo, *I haue beene at my booke: and*
am now past the craggie pathes of studie, and come to the flowrie
plaines of honour, and reputation. (157–70.)

Surely this bravura passage, with all its wonderful insolence,
suggests that Volpone, as Scoto of Mantua, represents, in addition
to the obvious, a tremendously amusing version of the morally
imperfect poet. The fake universal cure for physical ills is described in terms suggestive of a fake cure for psychic ills: the
healing hands of Scoto brilliantly pervert the function of the poet
as Jonson conceived it and as he described it eloquently in the dedication of this play. And Scoto's rivals are very much like the morally
and artistically inferior poets so scathingly described by the author.

Jonson chose Scoto of Mantua for this passage because the historical Scoto was well known in England. But it seems to me that
there is another quite characteristically Jonsonian reason for choos-
ing this particular mountebank for this particular scene: as Percy
Simpson has pointed out,[3] Scoto of Mantua's real name was Dionisio; characteristically Jonsonian because, although he obviously
knew it himself, he did not choose to be so crude as to remind his
audience of the fact.

The mountebank scene, therefore, is crucial. In the opening scene
of the play, Volpone's apostrophe to his gold effectively perverts
all moral and social standards. Mosca's entertainment establishes,
while perverting, the Apollonian spirit, the realm of knowledge
and art which still retains its identity although now residing in a
ludicrously misshapen and ambiguous form. Now the perversion
of Apollo is again specified, in another interlude which is at the
same time part of the major realistic action of the play, in which

3 Vol. IX, 704.

Volpone becomes Dionysian and thus seriously at odds with the pervasive spirit of Apollo.

A number of things besides the name Dionisio serve to connect Volpone with Dionysus, although we must remember that the connection is a comic one: Dionysus' early association with drama (for Jonson, particularly Aristophanic drama), his reputation for merry and wild debauchery, his association with fertility (Volpone's misplaced passion for Celia), his propensity for changing his shape; and perhaps his wanderings among the proverbially stupid Boeotians will have suggested to the poet something like his own affairs in London. Jonson's use of Dionysus is not anthropological but literary, and the closest parallel comes in *The Frogs,* where the figure of the god is treated with the same irreverence it meets in Jonson's play. Volpone and Mosca resemble, for the time being, Dionysus and Xanthias, with Volpone in disguise—as Dionysus was in disguise—as Scoto, making scathing references to inferior mountebanks just as Dionysus and Xanthias make jokes about the bad jokes in bad plays by Aristophanes' contemporaries. Even Aeacus' beating of the disguised Dionysus has a rough equivalent in Corvino's beating of the disguised Volpone, although the shifting of the disguise which occurs in *The Frogs* has no direct counterpart in *Volpone.*

Volpone as the urbane Dionysus thus represents a perversion of the comic spirit. As a mountebank he entertains the crowd, but there is no moral instruction in his performance—at least not for the crowd watching him in the street by Corvino's house. He is not speaking truth "free from slaughter." Indeed, he is not speaking truth at all. His own real motives have trapped him into a beating by Corvino, who, ironically, suspects Celia's motives to be the same as we know Volpone's to be. Volpone as artist has presented an entertainment, but with an ulterior motive complicating the irony—Celia's seduction. Corvino suspects that Celia is an incipient whore, a ludicrous enough suspicion. Volpone hopes she is; and this is equally ludicrous because the audience, having heard of the indescribably beautiful Celia, and associating the name with the concept, is in no way prepared for the simpering parody of heavenly beauty that is revealed as soon as Celia begins to speak. Thus Volpone, as comic poet *manqué,* wishes to seduce, or if necessary rape—or, as one lady-scholar put it, "court"—Celia. His lust makes him morally obnoxious and hence not capable of what Jonson regarded as the high office of poet. Furthermore, to rape someone named Celia, of all things—or of all names—would seem to intensify the moral fault.

The whole matter resolves itself in an irony which reflects back on the self-deluding qualities of Volpone-as-poet, for the divine Celia turns out to be nothing but a humorless, prim, fatuous girl without a brain in her head and nothing but clichés in her mouth. The fox in the play deludes himself just as effectively as the fox in the fable.

What is revealed about Volpone in this scene should make it possible for us to hear the sentence passed on him with something approaching equanimity, not because it is "just" in any acceptable sense of the word but because it is consistent with his Dionysian nature. Note that although he is first brought into the Scrutineo on a charge of attempted rape, that is not what he is sentenced for:

> And, since the most was gotten by imposture,
> By faining lame, gout, palsey, and such diseases,
> Thou art to lie in prison, crampt with irons,
> Till thou bee'st sicke, and lame indeed. Remoue him.
>
> (V, xii, 121–24.)

This sentence reveals the stupidity of the judges,[4] but it also rep-

---

[4] Knights mentions "Their complete fatuity." *Drama and Society,* 203. See also Ralph Nash, "The Comic Intent of *Volpone." SP,* XLIV (1947), 34.

resents the symbolic flagellation of a god who must at all costs be kept under control. In a sense this is a symbolic sentence, representing the rejection of the comic poet by a society unwilling to accept the implications of his art. Indeed this society is unable to *recognize* its implications because it does not understand itself. The fact that Volpone is the deficient rather than the ideal poet does not alter this point. In the kind of closed and self-contained comedy which Jonson here presents, an ideal poet would have been an artistic flaw. As an aspect of the realistic action the sentence reminds us that in Jonsonian comedy through *Bartholomew Fair* there is hardly such a thing as an identifiable moral norm: Volpone as artist has deluded his victims and must therefore be made to suffer in reality that which he has feigned in art.

It has been said that in the dedication Jonson apologizes for the severity of the sentence, but I don't think this is what he really does:

> But my speciall ayme being to put the snaffle in their mouths, that crie, out we neuer punish vice in our *enterludes, etc. I tooke the more liberty; though not without some lines of example, drawne euen in the ancients themselues, the goings out of whose* comoedies *are not alwaies ioyfull, but oft-times, the bawdes, the seruants, the riuals, yea, and the masters are mulcted: and fitly, it being the office of a* comick-Poet, *to imitate iustice, and instruct to life, as well as puritie of language, or stirre vp gentle affections.* (115–23.)

And he does "put the snaffle in their mouths," the mouths of those who have complained that "we neuer punish vice in our enterludes"; here vice is punished, in a way that should fully satisfy those so uncritical as to demand that in comedy vice should be punished.

The audience, Jonson seems to imply, demands punishment because it doesn't understand comedy; and it will accept these punishments because it doesn't understand life. This is not an apology, it is an ironic explanation. One is reminded again of the wonderful denouement of *The Frogs:* Dionysus chooses Aeschylus, which is right, but for the wrong reasons: his words literally weigh more than those of Euripedes. Dionysus has become a false judge of poetry, and, in effect, so have Volpone's judges.

In a superficial but important sense, Volpone deserves to be sentenced—not for making his victims reveal the depths of their ludicrous folly, but for doing it for a sordid end: "I long to haue possession/ Of my new present." (I, ii, 116–17.) The effect of his avarice is salutary for his victims, but it remains avarice; the judges are part of the society that also includes Volpone, Mosca, Voltore, Corvino, and Corbaccio, and they therefore do not recognize the salutary effect. So far as they are concerned, he has simply imposed on other people, rather like a scurvy satiric poet, whose words they do most powerfully and potently believe, only they hold it not honesty that it should be put thus.

It also seems appropriate that Volpone's victims, who all through the play have been receiving their satirical punishment, should now be punished again by the judges who cannot perceive that fact, and that Celia's and Bonario's stupidity should be rewarded with large sums of money. When the truth is finally revealed, Bonario observes, with implacable fatuousness, "Heauen could not, long, let such grosse crimes be hid." (V, xii, 98.) Heaven had nothing to do with it, so that on all levels the comic spirit is comically perverted.

An amusing commentary on that I have been describing is provided by Sir Politic Would-Be, Lady Would-Be, and Peregrine, the wise traveler. Sir Politic, of course, would be a politician in the Elizabethan sense, a politic man who misunderstands the secret workings of everything from the drama to the secret affairs of state. His comments on the mountebank establish his somewhat limited perceptiveness as a critic and his wonderful observation about Spinola's whale reveals his statecraft. Lady Would-Be is the bluestocking, a type to appear in somewhat more meaningful fashion in *Epicoene*. As such, her main function is to torment Volpone with her marvelous harangue about poets, philosophers, medicine, art, and philosophy.

These two we might describe as ordinary Jonsonian humor characters, as opposed to the rather extraordinary ones who populate this play. Sir Politic ludicrously misgauges Volpone's performance as Scoto, and Lady Would-Be is far too much concerned with her own wild theories to pay more than the slightest attention to Volpone's game. And significantly, unlike Voltore, Corbaccio, and Corvino, she has nothing to offer Volpone. They feed not only his coffers but his talent as a comic artist. She gives him nothing but a knit cap, an act symbolic of her supreme fatuousness.

Peregrine might at first glance be regarded as the reverse of Volpone, as the comic poet in complete control of his art, who manipulates and discovers his characters with perfect assurance and aplomb. But Peregrine in fact seems to represent a comic poet intellectually inferior to the kind represented by Volpone himself. After all, when Mosca, Volpone's *alter ego,* rescues his patron from the tongue of Lady Would-Be by telling her that her husband is in the company of the most cunning courtesan of Venice, she rushes out, finds her husband in the company of Peregrine, whom she assumes to be a courtesan disguised as a young man, quarrels with him, is disabused by Mosca, apologizes, and invites Peregrine to call on her—at which point Peregrine thinks it was arranged this way by Sir Politic and that Sir Pol is therefore a bawd:

> This is rare!
> Sir POLITIQVE WOVLD-BEE? no, sir POLITIQVE bawd!
> To bring me, thus, acquainted with his wife!
> Well, wise sir POL: since you haue practis'd, thus,
> Vpon my freshman-ship, I'le trie your salt-head,
> What proofe it is against a counter-plot. (IV, iii, 19–24.)

Peregrine's motive for unmasking Sir Politic is not the disinterested stripping of folly, but revenge for the one offense Sir Pol has not committed—acting as bawd for his wife. Peregrine is to be equated with the inferior mountebanks and his humiliating of Sir Politic with a stale jest. The action in which he is involved thus represents something inferior to the Dionysian spirit of Volpone's escapades, while in its denouement, with the "unjust" revenge on Sir Pol, it roughly parallels the ironic denouement of the main action.

EPICOENE

Epicoene fully deserves the praise given it by John Dryden. If it seems at first to be intellectually less striking and brilliant than *Volpone,* it is in many ways a better integrated and more engaging play, and it marks another step forward in Jonson's development as a comic writer. Although I dislike the term as pompous, misleading, and irrelevant, I am tempted nevertheless to say that this is the most *successful* play thus far in Jonson's career, because it accomplishes what it sets out to do with an absolute minimum of extraneous material. Its argument is completely self-contained in a play characterized by psychological deftness and brilliance of structure, both linear and thematic.

In discussing the structure of Jonsonian comedy in general and of this play in particular, we may speak of two schools of criticism, the first represented by Dryden's famous comments in *The Essay of Dramatic Poesy,* and the second by Freda Townsend's study of Jonson's baroque technique in *Apology for Bartholmew Fayre,* which has been ably seconded by Ray Heffner[1] and Edward Partridge.[2] Dryden sees an essentially classic structure, with a logical

[1] "Unifying Symbols in the Comedy of Ben Jonson," in *English Stage Comedy,* Ed., W. K. Winsatt, Jr. (English Institute Essays), 74–97.

[2] "The Allusiveness of Epicoene," *ELH,* XXII (1955), 93–107. See also Partridge's very stimulating book, *The Broken Compass.*

66

order, proceeding through a consistently rising action, with the events of each act "greater" than those of the preceding act.

Miss Townsend and Messrs. Heffner and Partridge, on the other hand, are concerned with what might be called a symbolic structure, that is, with a structure predicated on the use of central themes or symbols, rather than line, as the ordering principle. It is interesting to note that, although Miss Townsend and Mr. Heffner seem convinced that their view is correct and Dryden's is not, their views are not really mutually exclusive. There is no reason why there cannot be both a linear and a thematic or symbolic structure, and the only reason we don't look for both in a single play is that few artists have minds like Ben Jonson's.

For *Epicoene,* the comments of Dryden on the one hand and of Miss Townsend and Messrs. Heffner and Partridge on the other, taken together, provide an accurate commentary. There is, it seems to me, the beautifully ordered plot structure which Dryden describes—although I am disposed to agree with one or two of Mr. Heffner's strictures—and there is also the symbolic structure centering on noise and the epicene nature of the society of the play, well described by Heffner and Partridge. This suggests an aspect of Jonsonian comedy which we have already been considering— at least two levels of meaning carried in a single action. In *Epicoene* there is a single action concerned with Dauphine's outwitting Morose; and since this event is in itself symbolic, it engages the participation of many other members of society. It is symbolic because it involves a contest between two moral worlds, the private, inverted, obsessive world of Morose and the gallant, free, open world of Dauphine. In the working out of this single action, there is contained a detailed and elaborate commentary on contemporary society and the by now familiar commentary on the artist's function within this society.

The level of action, because of its order and clarity, does not require comment, but the other levels do. In general, for the following comments I am principally indebted to the studies of Heffner and Partridge, although it will be apparent that here and there one or two observations of my own have crept into the discussion. Even before we move into the play the dramatis personae gives an indication of the nature of the symbolic commentary on society, because Epicoene, Captain Otter and his wife, and Madame Centaur all represent, to put it mildly, blurred distinctions. Epicoene is a young man posing as a young woman. Tom Otter, as his surname implies, is a land and sea captain, but amphibious had a broader meaning in Jonson's day than now, and Otter's amphibiousness is reflected also in his relationship with his wife, who is really the captain in the Otter household. The captain's masculinity is thwarted by a domineering wife, so that he exists on a symbolic level similar to that of Epicoene.

Madame Centaur suggests a deeper disturbance because the name implies a combination of man and animal—seldom woman and animal—not always noted for the most exemplary kind of life. The title *Epicoene* thus refers to something more than the name of a minor character in the play, and even the subtitle, *The Silent Woman,* suggests a comic aberration applied not only to a person but to the aberrant and upside-down society represented in the play. This, I think, is to be regarded as an extension to society at large of the implications of the hermaphrodite-fool in *Volpone*. In that play the aberration relates to the defective comic poet, but in *Epicoene* it indicates the aberrant nature of the society that is the comic poet's concern.

The social satire thus centers in a society where, again, relevant distinctions are blurred, and the chief symbol is an impossible comic ideal—a silent woman. Since this symbol, as such, will not sustain the weight of a play, it is enforced at all points by the ironic representation of a situation that underscores its significance—the existence of a world in which most talk is noise and most language essentially meaningless. The importance of this must not be underestimated: in the *Discoveries* Jonson made a characteristic statement about language:

> *Speech* is the only benefit man hath to expresse his excellencie of mind above other creatures. It is the Instrument of *Society* . . . In all speech, words and sense, are as the body, and the soule. The sense is as the life and soule of Language, without which all words are dead. Sense is wrought out of experience, the knowledge of humane life, and actions, or of the liberall Arts. . . . (H. and S., Vol. VIII, 620–21.)

In this play, Sir Amorous La-Fool's language is inane; Sir John Daw's is entirely consistent with the implications of his nickname, Jack Daw; Morose's is predicated on the idea that "all discourses, but mine owne, afflict mee, they seeme harsh, impertinent, and irksome" (II, i, 4–5); that of the collegiate ladies reflects the unnaturalness of their lives; Mrs. Otter's reflects her ascendancy over her husband; and the hilarious misuse of law-Latin in V, iii, utterly perverts the function of that discipline which should maintain the social order. The principal symbols seem to be epitomized in V, i, when Sir Amorous La-Fool and Jack Daw both claim to have received favors from Mistress Epicoene before her marriage to Morose. As in the other plays, Jonson establishes the idea that the world's disorder is to be controlled by art. And since in this play one of the basic symbols of disorder is meaningless talk—noise—the first act consists of language without action, of what appears to be more or less desultory conversation of which the only purpose is to prepare for the action that follows and to introduce the characters. But the conversation is not really desultory; it just appears to be until we learn what it means. The interesting and characteristic thing about it, though, is that it can pass for mere desultory conversation and still fulfill admirably the expository function of preparing us, in amusing terms, for the faces we are to meet later in the play. As the first scene begins, Clerimont has written a song and asks his boy servant if he has learned it yet. The boy has, but would prefer to sing it only for his master; if he were to sing it in public, it might get Clerimont "the dangerous name of a *Poet* in towne. . . ." (I, i, 6–7.) There is then some talk about the subject of the song, Lady Haughty, her indifference to Clerimont, and her jesting but suggestive attempts to dress the boy like a woman.

Music, the almost universal symbol of order, has thus been unobtrusively introduced, and Clerimont has been likened to a poet, the figure who, according to Jonson, is able to effect that order. The epicene nature of the world outside Clerimont's door has been implied in Lady Haughty's desire to play turn-about with Clerimont's boy. This is followed by some apparently idle chitchat between Clerimont and True-wit. True-wit's first words are important:

> Why, here's the man that can melt away his time, and neuer feeles it! what, betweene his mistris abroad, and his engle at home, high fare, soft lodging, fine clothes, and his fiddle; hee thinkes the houres ha' no wings, or the day no post-horse. Well, sir gallant, were you strooke with the plague this minute, or condemn'd to any capitall punishment to morrow, you would beginne then to thinke, and value euery article o' your time, esteeme it at the true rate, and giue all for't.
>
> (I, i, 23–31.)

True-wit twits Clerimont for his supposed indolence and points the moral:

> See but our common disease! with what iustice can wee complaine, that great men will not looke vpon vs, nor be at leisure to giue our affaires such dispatch, as wee expect, when wee will neuer doe it to our selues: nor heare, nor regard our selues.
>
> (57–61.)

True-wit no doubt has a point, but it does seem significant that

Clerimont, already associated with the poet, is represented as being independent of time and the regard of great men. In fact, rather than dispatching his affairs, Clerimont has been writing a song. The song, one of the best that Jonson ever wrote, is central to the play:

> Still to be neat, still to be drest,
> As, you were going to a feast;
> Still to be pou'dred, still perfum'd:
> Lady, it is to be presum'd,
> Though arts hid causes are not found,
> All is not sweet, all is not sound.
>
> Giue me a looke, giue me a face,
> That makes simplicitie a grace;
> Robes loosely flowing, haire as free:
> Such sweet neglect more taketh me,
> Then all th' adulteries of art.
> They strike mine eyes, but not my heart.

The poem is ostensibly about Lady Haughty, but its argument obviously goes far beyond that subject. The first half is about false art, the second half about true art. The art described in the first six lines is false because it disguises instead of enhancing nature. The perpetual sameness of the lady's external appearance suggests inner corruption—"All is not sweet, all is not sound." In always presenting the same face and appearance to the world, Lady Haughty denies both time and nature. In the last six lines, the ideal of true art appears, an ideal in which art and nature are precisely joined, with art enhancing, not concealing, the nature that lies beneath. The lady's appearance must be natural, but such an appearance is to be achieved through art. The neglect is sweet, not slovenly; simplicity becomes a grace; the loosely flowing robes will presumably be made of appropriate material; and the "free" hair will be neither dirty nor tangled. If Botticelli's Venus were clothed, she would fulfill the ideal admirably; as it is, a good example of the ideal would be one of the attendant graces in "Primavera."

Clerimont has been identified with the poet; in True-wit's comments on time, he has been disassociated from the everyday business of men; and he has written a poem about Lady Haughty, his alleged but certainly not his real mistress. Clerimont's song has a varied function: it offers a comment on Lady Haughty, a significant inhabitant of the world outside Clerimont's house; it offers a comment on the relationship between false art and nature, and between true art and nature; and in suggesting that true art and nature are inseparable, it typifies the tone of the first act of the play, where the easy, graceful, and witty conversation is both natural and artful. In the conversation that follows, True-wit jestingly disagrees. He argues that if the surface appearance is pleasant, nothing more is necessary. Cosmetic arts should be both practised and professed.

CLE. How? publiquely?

TRV. The doing of it, not the manner: that must bee priuate. Many things, that seeme foule, i' the doing, doe please, done. A lady should, indeed, studie her face, when wee thinke shee sleepes: nor, when the dores are shut, should men bee inquiring, all is sacred within, then. Is it for vs to see their perrukes put on, their false teeth, their complexion, their eye-browes, their nailes? you see guilders will not worke, but inclos'd. They must not discouer, how little serues, with the helpe of art, to adorne a great deale. How long did the canuas hang afore *Ald-gate?* were the people suffer'd to see the cities *Loue,* and *Charitie,* while they were rude stone, before they were painted, and burnish'd? No. No more should seruants approch their mistresses, but when they are compleat, and finish'd.

(I, i, 112–26.)

To all this Clermont pleasantly replies, "Well said, my TRVE-WIT." (127.) It is well said, of course, because the metaphorical

72

ground of the argument has shifted slightly but significantly. True-wit's analogies are with art; the spectator is not properly concerned with the labor, but with the finished product. But the artist is concerned with both, and the arguments of the song and its attendant conversation are beautifully illustrated in the ensuing presentation of character. What the author of the play seems to be implying here is that he will consider both the surface and what lies beneath, in all of his characters—including True-wit, who is only approximately a true wit. Thus the characters are described, more or less accurately, in advance—a regular Jonsonian technique—and then appear and act out their roles. For example, Sir John Daw is described as an ass and then appears, pretending to sophistication in the ways of the world but behaving like an ass.

So artfully casual is the conversation in this opening scene that there is some possibility of our missing its significance, particularly since as conversation it is sufficiently entertaining to hold our interest. The subject of Lady Haughty and her art is dropped, and the subject of Dauphine's uncle, Morose, is introduced. He is amusingly described, but apparently not amusingly enough to prevent at least one critic's assuming that he is really a sick man and that the others are little better than sadists for picking on him.[3] Such an idea would never have occurred to anyone in Jonson's day, but his psychology was somewhat tougher minded than ours. In any case, it is clear that the author intends us to regard Morose as ridiculous:

CLE. O, i' the Queenes time, he was wont to goe out of towne euery satterday at ten a clock, or on holy-day-eues. But now, by reason of the sicknesse, the perpetuitie of ringing has made him deuise a roome, with double walls, and treble seelings; the windores close shut, and calk'd: and there he liues by candlelight. He turn'd away a man, last weeke, for hauing a paire of new shooes that creak'd. And this fellow

3 Edmund Wilson, "Morose Ben Jonson," 213 ff.

73

waits on him, now, in tennis-court socks, or slippers sol'd with wooll:
and they talke each to other, in a trunke.

(I, i, 181–90.)

We learn in II, i, that Morose's love of silence is not quite complete: he hates all noise but the sound of his own voice, and *he*
talks a good deal. Surely this is ludicrous, not pathetic, and it is
hard to imagine any circumstances under which such a character
would not be amusing. (It would be different, of course, if he
suffered from migraine and the young men were in the habit of
giving noisy parties to make him miserable.)

An interesting contrast is implicitly established between Clerimont and Morose. Clerimont, indifferent to time, lives in his own
lodging and has a boy servant who sings. Morose lives in *his* own
house, is perpetually busy about nothing, and has a manservant who
is required to be mute. Clerimont's house is open to his friends;
Morose's is closed to almost everyone. Clerimont is obviously prepared to take the world very much on its own terms without becoming obsessively involved with it, while Morose, equally involved with the world but in a different way, attempts to take it
on no terms but his own, always a destructive practice.

As True-wit, Clerimont, and the boy continue their conversation
about Morose, Dauphine enters, and further touches are added
that expand the symbolism of the character and relate the character
to the society. Morose intends to marry, for example, and disinherit
his nephew.

He has imploid a fellow this halfe yeere, all ouer *England,* to harken
him out a dumbe woman; bee shee of any forme, or any qualitie, so
shee bee able to beare children: her silence is dowrie enough, he saies.

(I, ii, 23–26.)

This in answer to True-wit's question, "Can he endure no noise,
and will venter on a wife?" (20–21.)

74

The comic paradox leads to a symbolic statement. Someone's having been employed to *harken* out a dumb woman anticipates the wonderful passage (III, iv, 27) in which Epicoene suddenly begins talking, ironic enough in itself, for the suddenly loquacious Epicoene is really male, an irony which is complicated by Morose's outraged comment, "O immodestie! a manifest woman!" (III, iv, 42.) The dumb woman, as is indicated often in the play, is a prodigy, a gross comic violation of nature. The one thing that Morose insists on is impossible. The significance of the impossibility is intensified by the fact that she may be of any form or quality so long as she be able to bear children. If she is a dumb woman she will, for all practical purposes, be no woman at all; hence, of whatever form or quality she is, she will *not* be able to bear children. The violation of nature, therefore, is not represented by Epicoene, but by Morose's prodigious desire for something not to be found in nature or society.

Morose has an agent in his quest, Cutbeard the barber, a fact which oppresses True-wit with wonder: "A woman, and a barber, and loue no noise!" (I, ii, 35–36.) This increases the absurdity of Morose's search, and it also serves to involve at least part of society in the comic sphere. Cutbeard has been employed this half year all over England, harkening after, rather than looking for, a silent woman. The barber, with his reputation for aimless talk, can serve well as a representative of the society satirized in this play as is shown later in the play (V, iii) when he is metamorphosed to a canon lawyer turning a peculiarly social jargon back on the tormented Morose.

To make matters worse, Mistress Epicoene lives in the same house occupied by Sir John Daw, next door to the barber's. "The onely talking sir i' th' towne! IACK DAW! And he teach her not to speake—" (I, ii, 66–67). So says True-wit as he leaves on his ill-advised errand of mercy. Jack Daw represents the very antithesis of rational discourse. He is, as True-wit says, "a fellow that pretends onely to learning, buyes titles, and nothing else of bookes in him." (75–77.) Daw's identity as talker and pretender to learning becomes more specific and significant when, in II, iii, he is presented as poetaster, with his "madrigal of modesty," and criticaster, with his comments on the dullness of all the poets and critics.

> DAW. There's ARISTOTLE, a mere common-place fellow; PLATO, a discourser; THVCIDIDES, and LIVIE, tedious and drie; TACI-TVS, an entire knot: sometimes worth the vntying, very seldome.
>
> CLE. What doe you think of the *Poets,* sir IOHN?
>
> DAW. Not worthy to be nam'd for authors. HOMER, an old tedious prolixe asse, talkes of curriers, and chines of beefe. VIRGIL, of dunging of land, and bees. HORACE, of I know not what.
>
> (II, iii, 57–65.)

When Dauphine asks him what authors he prefers, the answer is revealing: *"Syntagma Iuris ciuilis, Corpus Iuris ciuilis, Corpus Iuris canonici,* the King of *Spaines* bible." (81–82.) And it reveals more than Sir John's ignorance, for it implies that the civil and canon law are somehow preferable to Aristotle, Plato, Homer, Virgil, and Horace, an idea which explodes into verbal riot when Otter and Cutbeard appear, as divine and canon lawyer, to torment Morose with the legal language which will *not* extricate him from the situation into which his hatred of all discourse save his own has led him. The way has been prepared for this splendid revelation of Sir John Daw when, in I, iii, Dauphine describes the *"decameron* of sport fallen out" last night at Mistress Epicoene's:

> DAW do's nothing but court her; and the wrong way. Hee would lie with her, and praises her modestie; desires that shee would talke, and bee free, and commends her silence in verses: which hee reades, and sweares, are the best that euer man made. Then railes at his

fortunes, stamps, and mutines, why he is not made a counsellor, and
call'd to affaires of state.

(14–20.)

Daw, as one of the principal figures symbolic of the inverted society of the play, is here and elsewhere represented as absurdly
misunderstanding everything with which he is confronted.

As the expository, symbolic, wonderfully conceived first act progresses, more and more of this strange society is brought into the
play, directly or through the conversation of the gallants and some
of the gulls themselves. In I, iv, Sir Amorous La-Fool appears to
invite Clerimont to the little dinner at Tom Otter's house, a dinner
at which a large segment of this chaotic society will be chaotically
presented.

With La-Fool's account of his genealogy, the *protasis* is complete. Sir Amorous is related to Mistress Otter—"she is my kins-
woman, a LA-FOOLE by the mother side"—and the fact that the
comic symposium begins in her house—nominally, but only nominally, her husband's—and then moves to Morose's house, indicates,
like Mosca's entertainment, the universality of fools and folly. A
preliminary and delightful statement of this universality by La-
Fool prepares us for the main action of the play:

> They all come out of our house, the LA-FOOLES o' the north, the
> LA-FOOLES of the west, the LA-FOOLES of the east, and south—
> we are as ancient a family, as any is in *Europe*—but I my selfe am
> descended lineally of the *french* LA-FOOLES—and, wee doe beare
> for our coate *Yellow,* or *Or,* checker'd *Azure,* and *Gules,* and some
> three or foure colours more, which is a very noted coate, and has,
> some-times, beene solemnely worne by diuers nobilitie of our house—
> but let that goe, antiquitie is not respected now—I had a brace of
> fat Does sent me, gentlemen, & halfe a dosen of phesants, a dosen
> or two of godwits, and some other fowle, which I would haue eaten,

77

while they are good, and in good company—there will be a great lady, or two, my lady HAVGHTY, my lady CENTAVRE, mistris DOL MAVIS—and they come a' purpose, to see the silent gentle-woman, mistris EPICOENE, that honest sir IOHN DAW has promis'd to bring thether—and then, mistris TRVSTY, my ladies woman, will be there too, and this honorable Knight, sir DAV-PHINE, with your selfe, master CLERIMONT—and we'll bee very merry, and haue fidlers, and daunce—I haue beene a mad wag, in my time, and haue spent some crownes since I was a page in court, to my lord LOFTY, and after, my ladies gentleman-vsher, who got mee knighted in *Ireland,* since it pleas'd my elder brother to die— I had as faire a gold ierkin on that day, as any was worne in the *Iland*-voyage, or at *Caliz,* none disprais'd, and I came ouer in it hither, show'd my selfe to my friends, in court, and after went downe to my tenants, in the countrey, and suruai'd my lands, let new leases, tooke their money, spent it in the eye o' the land here, vpon ladies—and now I can take vp at my pleasure.

DAVP. Can you take vp ladies, sir?

CLE. O, let him breath, he has not recouer'd.

DAVP. Would I were your halfe, in that commoditie—

LA-F. No, sir, excuse mee: I meant money, which can take vp any thing. I haue another guest, or two, to inuite, and say as much to, gentlemen. I'll take my leaue abruptly, in hope you will not faile— Your seruant.   (I, iv, 37–75.)

This speech—busy, funny, and symbolic—is spoken, as the punc-tuation and Clerimont's observation indicate, in a torrent, a breath-less rush of words; it precisely anticipates the satiric range of the action which is to follow. It comes just before the end of the first act, and as the act ends, Dauphine and Clerimont move out of Cleri-mont's lodging and into the main action of the play. (When the second act begins, we will meet Morose, the principal figure in that world of folly whose symbolic spirit is Sir Amorous La-Fool.)

La-Fool's oration is therefore of some significance, and its allusive qualities should be recognized. It establishes the following points, all of which have continuing relevance throughout the play: Fools are everywhere, and they always have been; they occupy even the upper reaches of society, and they are of an ancient line (37–46); Sir Amorous would have his meats eaten while they are good— and in good company.

This suggests a kind of *festa stultorum,* which, because of the implied nature of the guests, will be a mockery of a sane society (46–49); *everyone* will be there, from the knight to my lady's woman, including, significantly, Dauphine and Clerimont. They are less fools, by far, but they *are* deceived: Dauphine admires the wrong ladies, and Clerimont doesn't know Epicoene is a boy (49–56); the feast will represent a perversion of the universal order, the two great symbols—fiddlers and dancing—put to a perverted use (56–57); La-Fool is the universal fool. He values spurious titles and false social distinctions. The chief virtue of the soldier lies in the clothes he wears, of the knight in the money he gets, how he gets it, and how he spends it; and money will get anything (57–73); with just a few more guests the feast of fools will be complete (73–75).

The feast does take place, and Sir Amorous La-Fool is a most appropriate host, but surely it is not stretching a point to suggest that the whole play is itself a kind of feast of fools, quite secular to be sure, in which a social order that Jonson felt to be out of balance anyhow is, most amusingly, turned completely upside down. Sir Amorous' speech, therefore, sums up the first act and symbolically anticipates the play.

If, in describing the rich implications of the first act, one has not precisely described the play, one has, to a large extent, explained what the play is about. In inviting Clerimont and Truewit to his dinner, La-Fool has in effect invited the audience to a feast of fools. The feast for the audience begins with the introduction of Morose at the beginning of the second act, and La-Fool's dinner party has its preliminaries at the beginning of the third act. Everything that happens from III, i, to the end of the play has some connection with La-Fool's entertainment, since the gallants conspire with Sir John Daw to move the party from Captain Otter's house to Morose's, ostensibly to celebrate the nuptials and to allow Sir John to get revenge on Sir Amorous for a purely imaginary affront.

The last three acts occur in Morose's house, and everyone in the house, except Morose, Epicoene, and Cutbeard, is a guest of La-Fool. The pattern of folly suggested so well in the first act is intensified in II, ii, when Truewit appears to attempt to dissuade Morose from marrying. In a scene of elaborate social satire, he describes the disadvantages of marriage, quoting Juvenal rather freely. Unchastity in wives, he says, is only to be expected in times like these: "Alas, sir, doe you euer thinke to find a chaste wife, in these times? now? when there are so many masques, plaies, puritane preachings, mad-folkes, and other strange sights to be seene daily, priuate and publique?" (II, ii, 32–36.)

The basis of Morose's folly has already been mentioned, but in view of the charges of something like sadism on Jonson's part in representing his anguish so graphically, it would be well to remember not only that Morose is represented in genuinely ridiculous terms, but also that society's revenge on him is no more outrageous than his social views deserve. As the monologue of II, i, indicates, Morose is antisocial in every conceivable sense of the term. There is nothing in the least satirical about his attitude: he will have nothing to do with the world and takes the most absurd measures to see that it will never impinge on his isolation. Jonson has chosen an extremely important way of specifying the nature of the isolation. All discourse save his own is tedious to Morose, so that language, the instrument of society, as Jonson called it, theoretically makes no impression on this character.

There is a splendid irony here. Morose's discourse is as tedious and absurd as anyone's, so that it would seem altogether appropriate that the society he so passionately wants to exclude from his life suddenly bursts into his house, not only with its own noise but with the additional din of the musicians who have followed La-Fool's feast through the streets from Otter's house. If it seems that Dauphine speaks to his uncle with unnecessary harshness at the end of the play, this also has a reasonable enough explanation.

> Now you may goe in and rest, be as priuate as you will, sir. I'll not trouble you, till you trouble me with your funerall, which I care not how soone it come.   (V, iv. 214–16.)

If we view Morose simply as an old man with delicate ears, we are likely to find Dauphine shockingly brutal. But if we view him as a comic symbol of the absolute negation of what holds society together—of the negation of rational discourse, indeed, *any* discourse—then the denouement is understandable. Anyhow, after learning that his new wife is apparently unchaste but that he cannot get a divorce, Morose has achieved immortality with one of the funniest lines Jonson ever wrote: "Marry a whore! and so much noise!" (V, iv, 150.)

Before the party moves to Morose's house, the theme of the inverted soceity is very concretely re-established in the first three scenes of Act III, particularly in the first scene, which begins with Captain Otter and his Amazonian wife arguing over the subject of his bear and his bull. It is neatly done:

> . . . vnder correction, sweete Princesse, gi' me leaue—these things I am knowne to the courtiers by. It is reported to them for my humor, and they receiue it so, and doe expect it. TOM OTTERS bull, beare, and horse is knowne all ouer *England,* in *rerum natura.*

MRS. OT. Fore me, I will *na-ture* 'hem ouer to *Paris*-garden, and *na-ture* you thether too, if you pronounce 'hem againe. Is a beare a fit beast, or a bull, to mixe in society with great ladies? thinke i' your discretion, in any good politie.

OTT. The horse then, good Princesse.

MRS. OT. Well, I am contented for the horse: they loue to bee well hors'd, I know. I loue it my selfe.

OTT. And it is a delicate fine horse this. *Poetarum Pegasus*. Vnder correction, Princesse, IVPITER did turne himselfe into a—*Taurus, or Bull*, vnder correction, good Princesse.

(III, i, 10–27.)

The good princess goes on to remind Poor Tom that according to the instrument of their marriage ". . . I would bee Princesse, and raigne in mine owne house: and you would be my subiect, and obay me?" (33–35.)

This entertaining nonsense, with women implicitly coupled with animals, with Tom Otter's unreal and unnatural animals accepted as being *"in rerum natura,"* and with the wife reigning in her own house over her husband, prepares us for the inspired nonsense to follow, in which Morose, who has his own way of negating the very basis of harmonious society, is himself victimized to the fullest extent by that society, a central symbol of which is a silent woman who turns out to be a noisy man, the comic unnaturalness of which has already been prefigured in Sir John Daw's atrocious poem on his silent mistress:

> *Silence in woman, is like speech in man,*
> *Deny't who can.*
> . . .
> *Nor, is't a tale,*
> *That female vice should be a vertue male,*
> *Or masculine vice, a female vertue be:*

You shall it see
Prou'd with increase,
I know to speake, and shee to hold her peace.
(II, iii, 123–31.)

As is customary in Jonson, none of the characters in *Epicoene* is completely right. Instead, there are gradations, in the arrangement of which the three gallants came closest to the elusive moral and intellectual norm without quite achieving it. True-wit, as one might expect, is verbally the most clever of the three, but, as is indicated when he attempts to dissuade Morose from marriage, his wit is a trifle too spontaneous, and his first-act conversation with Clerimont indicates that he is slightly superficial. Dauphine, the cleverest manipulator of the three, must still be educated himself because of his unfortunate desire to have the ladies—any ladies— fall in love with him. Clerimont is the least imperfect of the three; apparently his only failing is his inability to perceive Dauphine's plot until it is explained to him—and this is hardly a real failing at all.

If there is a poet-figure in the play, he is Clerimont, who, more than his two friends, is the observer and commentator, a role implied in his conversation with True-Wit in the opening scene. Since the three gallants are the best of friends without ever quite completely understanding each other, we infer that in the kind of inverted world presented in this play, in a society in which the customary standards are reversed, even three talented wits will have some difficulty in establishing perfect communication, which brings us back to the idea of faulty language—language as noise—as a basic symbol of this masterfully bad world.

A glance at Percy Simpson's commentary for *Epicoene* will reveal the tremendous wealth of sources, classical and otherwise, for many of Jonson's ideas in this play. And I have suggested that the old tradition of the *festa stultorum* is also involved. There may be an Aristophanic parallel as well, particularly and specifically in the figures of Mistress Otter and the collegiate ladies, who represent such a dreadful threat to the traditional rule of men. Certainly it would not be far-fetched to suggest that there is something of the marvelous satire of *The Ecclesiazusae* in the society of ladies living apart from their husbands, domineering over them, and attempting to legislate for the world of men. Even the compulsive Morose may have something in common with poor Blepyrus in Aristophanes' play, and perhaps, too, he may be associated with the figure of the woman-hating Euripides in *The Thesmophoriazusae,* a play more clearly associated with *Bartholomew Fair*. The figurative emasculating of Morose in the marriage with Epicoene may have some reference to the unfortunate means of disguising Mnesilochus in *The Thesmophoriazusae*. In any case, Jonson's presentation of the monstrous regiment of women seems to have more in common with Aristophanes than with John Knox, and the phrase "collegiate ladies" would, without stretching a point, be translated into Greek as *Ecclesiazusae*.

THE ALCHEMIST

Unquestionably *The Alchemist* is one of the great triumphs of comic art. It is wonderfully amusing, formidably intellectual, and, if its symbolic structure is rightly understood, almost universal. It is, moreover, a deeply moving play, not in itself but as an illustration of the comprehending, analyzing, and organizing powers of the mind of its maker. It is superior to *Volpone* in construction, to *Epicoene* in conception; indeed, there is nothing quite like it.

Certain elements in *The Alchemist* are familiar, although, as I shall try to show, what finally emerges is new. Again there is a world turned upside down, a society motivated by folly. Again there is a lack of a clearly-defined moral norm. (Viewing Surly in this role is palpably absurd unless a cardsharp can really constitute a moral norm.) Again there is a marvelous array of characters representing almost every degree of folly and gullibility. Again there is an implied commentary on comic art, couched, as usual, in terms different from those in which it appeared in preceding plays. And finally, there is a welding together of theme and structure in a seamless fabric. Though *The Alchemist* has, indeed, been cut, there is no way to do it without artistic damage. It will still be a good play, but not the masterpiece it was.

The world of *The Alchemist* is a world turned upside down, a world in which the motivating forces are folly and avarice. Jonson has created a microcosm, complete in itself, not so much a reflection of the world of ordinary experience, as one in which a single aspect of the experiential world, folly, acts as the prime mover for all that occurs. This seems a duplication of the Aristophanic method, which eschews factual verisimilitude but presents a clearly understandable symbolic reality in which the world is turned topsy-turvy by a logical extension of its shortcomings in order to comment didactically on the real world of experience.

The play begins portentously: in I, i, we are introduced to Subtle, Face, and Dol Common, who are quarreling, surprisingly, in the language of alchemy. This scene, where we get our first glimpse of the central characters, also prepares us for the final breakup of the partnership; it engages the social and political spheres through the references to the venter tripartite and the body politic (Dol's reference in "Haue yet, some care of me, o' your *republique*—"(110), thus extending the implications of the actions in the room far beyond the confines of that room; and it seems to indicate that the language of alchemy is to be used to comment on the action as well as to play a part in it.

We are confronted, therefore, with a trio of sharpers. The quarrel between Face and Subtle suggests the explosive nature of their relationship and the not very stabilizing influence of Dol Common, who in order to stop their quarreling simply out-quarrels them. We learn that Subtle is a confidence man who until very recently has been down on his luck, to put it mildly; and that Face is actually a butler whose master's house serves as their base of operations. We get the distinct impression that these three constitute a kind of independent body politic engaged in perpetual warfare with the society that exists outside the confines of Lovewit's house. The language of Dol's plea, before she stops the fight, is typical of Jonson's verbal technique in the play. She wants them to have some care of their "republic," a word ordinarily glossed as a fraternity of thieves, which is quite correct as far as it goes.

But Jonson's language is nothing if not allusive and flexible. They are a fraternity of thieves, to be sure, yet they are much more than that: they are like an independent republic surrounded by another larger one—the world outside. It is their function to be at odds with the other republics or, at worst, to live parasitically at its expense, as though this were the most natural arrangement in the world. In this respect the word suggests both a body politic and an ironically inverted ideal state, ruled now not by philosopher-kings, but by the philosophical Subtle, the alchemist of the piece. And finally, considering the word in strictly etymological terms, it reflects directly on the nature of the lovely lady who applies it to herself; because Dol is indeed, in the realistic action, a *res publica*.

The next two scenes introduce us to the incomparably stupid and avaricious Dapper and Drugger, and here we see Face and Subtle at work and begin to get a clear idea of how they operate. Dapper wants a familiar, a fly, to enable him to win his bets on the horses. Instead of letting him off with an inexpensive charm, they play on his avarice until he admits he would like a familiar for all games. As careful testing reveals the extent of his gullibility, they become more and more confident of their ability to convince him that he is allied to the queen of fairy—an outlandish idea, but it represents a confidence game actually worked in Jonson's London. Drugger is equally avaricious, with some nice distinctions; Dapper would appear as a spruce young man about town:

> I had a sciruy *writ,* or two, to make,
> And I had lent my watch last night, to one
> That dines, to day, at the shrieffs: and so was rob'd
> Of my passe-time. Is this the cunning-man? (I, ii, 5–8.)

And his wondrous denial that he is a *Chiause* is beyond description. Drugger, on the other hand, is more characteristically and cringingly middle-class. He wants to learn by necromancy, he says, implying a problem in definition, how to lay out his shop so that it will be most profitable. His stupidity requires less testing, and like Dapper he is put on the send, to use the confidence man's term.

Since we are concerned at the moment with the realistic action, it might be well to observe that Face and Subtle behave like real professionals. Note Face's good-fellow handling of Dapper and his method of allowing him to think himself sufficiently worldly to handle any legal difficulties that may arise; and the stern and serious manner of Subtle's greeting to Drugger before Face reappears, boisterously confident that the doctor will do anything for him: "He shall doe any thing. Doctor, doe you heare? / This is my friend, ABEL, an honest fellow." (I, iii, 21–22.)

In these opening scenes, there is a hint of a deeper moral disturbance than we have yet considered. An epidemic of the plague has not completely run its course, and Dapper's request for a familiar and Drugger's for necromantic knowledge seem to imply a sick society whose condition is the devil's work. Familiars and necromancy are associated with black magic.

Another aspect of this highly allusive commentary suggests itself later in the play. Face, with his revealing name and multiple identity, may be regarded, on the symbolic level, as the comic spirit itself, rather like Tranio in Plautus' *Mostellaria,* or, in quite different terms, like the always changing and challenging chorus of clouds in Aristophanes' play. But his real name is Jeremy, an identity in which he appears first and most significantly to his master, Lovewit, who, again on the symbolic level, represents the bad audience, as his taste in entertainment shows. If the play were not so exceedingly amusing, if it were not a comedy, Jeremy could easily be prophesying the doom of the wicked city.

But far bigger things are in store: a broad social range is represented by the victims who come trooping into Lovewit's house to deal with the cunning man and the apocryphal captain, and our first indication of this range comes when we are introduced to that superbly conceived comic character, Sir Epicure Mammon. Jonson's technique, familiar by now, is to precede the entrance of an important character with some description. Subtle's comments on Mammon prepare us for the flood of oratory that begins Act II, and also begins to suggest a little more clearly the significance of alchemy in the play:

> This is the day, I am to perfect for him
> The *magisterium,* our *great worke,* the *stone;*
> And yeeld it, made, into his hands: of which,
> He has, this month, talk'd, as he were possess'd.
> And, now, hee's dealing peeces on't, away.
> Me thinkes, I see him, entring ordinaries,
> Dispensing for the poxe; and plaguy-houses,
> Reaching his dose; walking *more-fields* for lepers;
> And offring citizens-wiues pomander-bracelets,
> As his preseruatiue, made of the *elixir;*
> Searching the spittle, to make old bawdes yong;
> And the high-waies, for beggars, to make rich:
> I see no end of his labours. He will make
> Nature asham'd, of her long sleepe: when art,
> Who's but a step-dame, shall doe more, then shee,

In her best loue to man-kind, euer could.
If his dreame last, hee'll turne the age, to gold.
(I, iv, 13–29.)

This brilliantly prepares the way for the first revelation of Sir Epicure's grandiose ambitions, his fantastic gullibility, and his altogether tropical imagination. And it also suggests the very interesting thematic use to which alchemy will be put as the play progresses. And then he appears. As Charles Lamb put it, "The judgment is perfectly overwhelmed by the torrent of images, words and book-knowledge with which Mammon confounds and stuns his incredulous hearer."[1] A statement which, however, will hardly mitigate his stunning assertion that "It is just such a swaggerer as contemporaries have described old Ben to be."[2]

Dapper and Drugger have modest ambitions. With the appearance of Mammon and Surly at the beginning of Act II, we meet two far more ambitious gulls. That Mammon particularly is far bigger game in more ways than one is indicated by a typically revealing statement. Mammon has just been casually cozened out of another ten pounds for fresh materials, and Subtle observes,

For two
Of our inferiour workes, are at *fixation*.
A third is in *ascension*. (II, iii, 96–98.)

In the context there is no doubt that the inferior works are the gulling of Dapper and Drugger, while the third and greater one is the cheating of Sir Epicure himself. Fixation is the fixing of a volatile spirit in permanent bodily form, and ascension means distillation or evaporation. Though more is still to be done with Dapper and Drugger, they have already assumed their essential artistic forms, while much more is yet to be revealed of the nature of Sir Epicure Mammon.

[1] Quoted in Herford and Simpson, Vol. X, 67.
[2] *Ibid.*, 68.

Mammon is quickly, and in detail, characterized as the avaricious sensualist that he is; and Surly, in the same act, is exposed as equally dishonest in a different way:

> You shall no more deale with the hollow die,
> Or the fraile card. No more be at charge of keeping
> The liuery-punke, for the yong heire, that must
> Seale, at all houres, in his shirt. No more,
> If he denie, ha' him beaten to't, as he is
> That brings him the commoditie. (II, i, 9–14.)

Surly is a gambler who uses loaded dice and marked cards; he is also involved in the commodity racket and is apparently a pimp in his spare time. So much for the suggestion that he is really the honest man and Jonson's spokesman in a play which is itself Jonson's spokesman.

On the symbolic level, also, Surly is put in the same class, although on a lower plane, with the confidence man. Face has described Subtle's unfortunate condition before he was taken into Lovewit's house. Face found him

> at *pie-corner,*
> Taking your meale of steeme in, from cookes stalls,
> Where, like the father of hunger, you did walke
> Piteously costiue, with your pinch'd-horne-nose. . .
> (I, i, 25–28.)

Surly, who will soon be playing his own abortive confidence game in an attempt to unmask Face and Subtle, confesses to Subtle that he is "somewhat caustiue of beliefe/ Toward your *stone*: would not be gull'd." (II, iii, 26–27.) The confidence man is necessarily costive of belief, while Sir Epicure Mammon suffers from verbal diarrhea.

Mammon, as I have said, is bigger game and is more important than Dapper and Drugger. He gets very special treatment, entertainingly connected with the gulling of the Puritans, Ananias and

Tribulation Wholesome. Unlike the other gulls, Mammon and Tribulation are first presented to us not inside Lovewit's house but in the street outside, and for the same reason in both cases. Mammon is a knight of the realm and should, in accordance with Jonson's social morality, be exemplary in his conduct; Tribulation Wholesome is a comically perverted clergyman whose material interests should ideally remain somewhat submerged. But Mammon's conduct is not exemplary and Tribulation is a complete materialist. We get very revealing views of these two while they are still in their native habitat, the streets of London, before they enter the special world of the alchemist, a world in which several things will happen to them, not precisely envisaged in their bargains with Subtle but implicit in the idea of alchemy, a point to be considered in detail later.

In addition to Sir Epicure's avarice and sensuality, we are given, early in II, i, some examples of his gullibility, which has been heightened by the other qualities. He will change all the metals in his house to gold, then buy up all the tin and lead in town and transmute that too, and finally, as his imagination breaks completely from the bounds of sanity, he will purchase Devonshire and Cornwall—to turn the tin mines into gold mines. "You admire now?" (II, i, 36.) To which Surly replies, with Jonson's masterful ambiguity, "No faith." (37.) Several important points are joined in Mammon's enthusiastic reply:

> But when you see th' effects of the great med'cine!
> Of which one part proiected on a hundred
> Of *Mercurie,* or *Venus,* or the *Moone,*
> Shall turne it, to as many of the *Sunne;*
> Nay, to a thousand, so *ad infinitum:*
> You will beleeue me. (II, i, 37–42.)

Mammon's enthusiasm carries the speech, even if the audience is not familiar with the symbolism. In alchemy Mercury is quicksilver, Venus copper, the moon silver, the sun gold. In the familiar Renaissance symbolism Mercury is wit, Venus of course love, the moon chastity and purity, and the sun the epitome of the virtues. When we consider these alternate values, we are confronted not only with Sir Epicure's guillibility, enthusiasm, and alchemical learning, but also with a symbolic statement relative to the inverted social values presented throughout the play. This becomes particularly clear when we read gold as the over-riding symbol of avarice as well as the symbol of virtue implicit in the idea of the golden age—"hee'll turne the age, to gold."

Wit, love, and purity will all be set aside in the fool's quest for gold, a theme already familiar in Jonson and one to be emphasized even more strongly in some of the later plays as Jonson becomes more and more aware of the effects of the establishment of capitalism as a way of life and almost as a religion.

Surly, before he is himself deflated, has a way of deflating his learned friend—or at least of trying to; the wholly unsuccessful results of these attempts recall the fact that anyone firmly in the grip of an able confidence man is virtually in a state of hypnosis; nothing can shake his belief, and nothing does here.[3] If Surly can't change his friend's mind, however, he is certainly able to bring the audience rather violently back to earth. His reply to Sir Epicure's speech just quoted has this function:

> Yes, when I see't, I will.
> But, if my eyes doe cossen me so (and I
> Giuing 'hem no occasion) sure, I'll haue
> A whore, shall pisse 'hem out, next day. (II, 1, 42–45.)

---

[3] An expert account of the workings of confidence men is given in David W. Maurer's *The Big Con*. My comments in this chapter on Jonson's knowledge of all details of confidence games are based on Mr. Maurer's fascinating book, which, incidentally, bears out the common belief that before Jonson dealt with any subject, he first learned all he possibly could about it.

There is in this passage a certain lack of innuendo that will no doubt appear less than elevating to groveling, vulgar minds, but which is at least consistent with Aristotle's observation that the Old Comedy is characterized by obscenity rather than innuendo; in fact it seems to echo a passage in *The Ecclesiazusae,* where one citizen replying to another's account of the wonderful effects wrought by the new women's government, observes, "Whom, by Posidon, I will never allow to piss on my nose."[4] In its relationship to Aristophanes *The Alchemist* is of course on extension of *Plutus,* not *The Ecclesiazusae.*

In Mammon and Surly, then, we have the willing victim and the jealous rival. Surly is dishonest, but is outraged that Face and Subtle should be dishonest too, and this feeling of outrage leads to his attempt to unmask them, with disastrous results for himself. This is a fairly complicated matter: Surly is one of those ironic commentators who would be effective if he were moral. Since, unlike Clerimont, Surly is never even implicitly associated with the poet-figure as such, but is completely a part of the consistent, realistic comic fabric, this is a new departure for Jonson.

But if for a moment we use, for convenience, the poet metaphor, Surly is a character who cannot be a good poet because he is not a good man. He is quite able to unmask Subtle's and Face's impostures, but on the realistic level the other victims are so avaricious, and have been so fully convinced by the confidence men, that nothing Surly can say will change their minds; and on the symbolic level they are works of art now alchemically at fixation and are thus inviolable in their stupidity.

The second act is the thematic center of the play. Two of the lesser gulls and their inspired tormentors have already been introduced, and now Mammon the great is on the stage. Socially he is

---

[4] Quoted from Oates and O'Neill, *The Complete Greek Drama,* Vol. II, 1039.

the most exalted figure in the play, and he is plainly designed to be a regular compendium of all the social vices. Furthermore, since he is the first of the gulls to be concerned with alchemy as such, the alchemical language becomes much more densely distributed. And since we are now concerned with Subtle specifically as alchemist and with Face as the alchemist's assistant, their identities expand and become more significant. The lesser gulls are all aspects of Mammon in the sense that their vices and follies seem all to be subsumed in his.

The old world of the clever plot, the conspiracy, the confidence game now becomes a new world in which all of these things are important but in which their importance is given a new significance. Mammon, standing in the street with Surly, invites him to enter the alchemist's house: "Come on, sir. Now, you set your foot on shore/ In *nouo orbe*." (II, 1, 1–2.) This new world is metaphorically the rich Peru; it is also a new world for Mammon and Surly, and a new comic world, complete, self-contained, and perfect, within the four walls of the alchemist's room in Lovewit's house, a world which, as we have seen, is perpetually at odds with the other world out of which Sir Epicure and Surly are about to step.

That other world, the "real" world, as it were, is the kind of world in which a man like Pertinax Surly is a familiar fixture, a fairly clever cheat who doesn't care for cheats more clever than himself. People step out of that real world into this alchemical world, and, as one would expect, surprising things happen to them, because the alchemist's world is the world of comic art, and an altogether wonderful world at that. This world, like the world of the confidence man, is in a state of warfare with the other world, the world of reality, or the world of organized human society. Its function is to disorganize that world, to reduce it—to use the alchemical term—to its quintessence.

The presiding genius of this world is, like Aristophanes' Plutus, a character who has been wandering around in the streets dressed in rags. (The parallel is very close here.) In *Plutus,* Chremylus learns the beggar's identity and Cario the slave reveals it to the populace, with the pleasant news that they will all become Midases, provided they grow asses' ears. To the gulls the alchemist Subtle is like Plutus, god of wealth, and as such he brings out the worst in them, so that his identity doubles and he becomes also the comic poet, the center of a world of art in the confines of which is effected the perfect fusion of art and nature: the gulls enter resembling social animals, but those qualities that make them human in social terms are immediately separated from their essential natures.

Thus Dapper, who would no doubt function quite adequately as a lawyer's clerk in the world outside, becomes the perfect ass as soon as he enters Face and Subtle's world of comic art. The moment he enters the scene we see him as he would like to be seen—the spruce young man about town—and also as he really is, a young man whose avarice agitates his gullibility to the point where he is willing to believe he is the nephew of the queen of fairy. And, as Mammon tells Surly, in this new world Surly can shuck off his old identity: "You shall no more deale with the hollow die,/ Or the fraile card."

Indeed, the whole city will be transmuted—even Devonshire and Cornwall. And the virtues will be transmuted, too, according to Sir Epicure's understanding of Subtle's art. Mammon's language indicates the total perversion of social and moral values, engaging the social and moral world in both the comic action and the symbolic commentary; and the great agent in effecting this perversion will be the philosopher's stone, Sir Epicure's great obsession, which, as he enters the alchemist's world, will effectively replace everything properly held to be of value in the world outside, the world which

he is now leaving under the hypnotic spell of Subtle. The stone
will bring back the golden age in more ways than one: it will effect
the kingdom of heaven on earth, although in a new way:

> Restore his yeeres, renew him, like an eagle,
> To the fifth age; make him get sonnes, and daughters,
> Yong giants; as our *Philosophers* haue done
> (The antient *Patriarkes* afore the floud)
> But taking, once a weeke, on a kniues point,
> The quantitie of a graine of mustard, of it:
> Become stout MARSES, and beget yong CVPIDS.
>
> (II, i, 55–61.)

The wealth of allusion is staggering, but even more staggering
is the way in which the allusions are confused; so that the grain
of mustard unto which, in another context, is likened the kingdom
of heaven, will make us like the patriarchs afore the flood, that
like stout Marses we can beget young Cupids. In Mammon's frantic obsession the stone does everything and is everything and will,
for him, pervert everything, a fact of which we are reminded when
stone itself becomes a pun:

> SVR. And do you thinke to haue the *stone,* with this?
> MAM. No, I doe thinke, t'haue all this, with the *stone.*
>
> (II, ii, 95–96.)

The perverted religious symbolism and the sublime lust are con-
veyed even in the alchemical language: "And, lastly/ Thou hast
descryed the *flower,* the *sanguis agni?*" (II, ii, 27–28), and "Th'art
sure, thou saw'st it *bloud?* FAC. Both *bloud,* and *spirit,* sir." (40.)
He will have an art gallery hung with pornographic pictures (the
imaginative vigor here is tremendous); he will seduce sublimed
pure wives, using fathers and mothers as bawds; he will be flat-
tered by the gravest of divines; he will entertain poets who have

written so subtly of the fart—a symbolic comment on his own somewhat less than divine afflatus.

To all of this, Surly poses a reasonable objection:

> Why, I haue heard, he [who has the stone] must be *homo frugi,*
> A pious, holy, and religious man,
> One free from mortall sinne, a very virgin.

To which Sir Epicure, with supreme fatuousness, replies,

> That makes it, sir, he is so. But I buy it.
> My venter brings it me. He, honest wretch,
> A notable superstitious, good soule,
> Has worne his knees bare, and his slippers bald,
> With prayer, and fasting for it: and, sir, let him
> Do it alone, for me, still. (II, ii, 97–105.)

This gets us back to the heart of the social commentary, a society so moved by avarice that all moral standards are abandoned. His venture—his capital, that is—replaces virtue. If one is rich, one need not be good.

But now we meet Subtle again, and he has undergone a change. He is now "father" and calls Mammon "Gentle son," and he has, according to Mammon, been praying and fasting. The stone is, in his words, "So great, and catholique a blisse." (II, iii, 21.) Thus Subtle, who will lead Mammon to the kingdom of heaven, is now Sir Epicure's confessor, and threatens that if he abuses his possession of the stone "A curse will follow, yea, and ouertake/ Your subtle, and most secret wayes." (22–23.) Mammon's subtle ways have been imposed by Subtle. Subtle becomes, for Mammon and implicitly for the other gulls, the director of their spiritual lives, while Face, who is now Lungs, Zephyrus, and Ulen Spiegel, becomes the legendary jester and the harbinger of spring and source of life, Zephyrus the west wind. This in iself may represent a learned jest indeed. If it contemplates Paracelsus' interest in the *zibeta occi-dentalis* it anticipates Swift and reminds us again of the poetical fart, an altogether appropriate allusion which makes one wonder whether Subtle's first speech in the play is possibly directed at the audience as well as at Face.

I have said that Act II is the thematic center of the play, but so far we have been concerned only with peripheral aspects of this. The crucial passage is the great alchemical dialogue between Subtle and Surly, the form and function of which are essentially the same as they are in the Aristophanic *agon*. In so far as the dialogue de-scribes the symbolic argument of the play it may also have some-thing in common with the *parabasis,* but since it is actually a con-test between two verbal disputants it is an *agon,* and, as in Aristoph-anes, the first speaker, Subtle, is wrong, at least with respect to the realistic action.

Subtle is explaining the principles of alchemy to Pertinax Surly, the heretic, as Mammon calls him in a word closely relevant to the pattern of symbolically perverted religion. Surly's comic heresy has already been revealed by the man himself: "Faith, I haue a humor,/ I would not willingly be gull'd." (II, 1, 77–78.) Surly has told Subtle that it is improbable "That you should hatch gold in a fornace, sir,/ As they doe egges, in *Egypt!"* Subtle regards the transmutation of eggs into chickens as being the greater miracle, and the contest is under way.

SVR. . . . The egg's ordain'd by nature, to that end:
And is a chicken in *potentia*.

SVB. The same we say of lead, and other mettalls,
Which would be gold, if they had time.

MAM. And that
Our art doth furder.

SVB. I, for 'twere absurd
To thinke that nature, in the earth, bred gold

Perfect, i'the instant. Something went before.
There must be remote matter.

SVR. I, what is that?

SVB. Mary, we say—

MAM. I, now it heats: stand Father.
Pound him to dust—

SVB. It is, of the one part,
A humide exhalation, which we call
Materia liquida, or the *vnctuous water;*
On th' other part, a certaine crasse, and viscous
Portion of earth; both which, concorporate,
Doe make the elementarie matter of gold:
Which is not, yet, *propria materia,*
But commune to all mettalls, and all stones.
For, where it is forsaken of that moysture,
And hath more drynesse, it becomes a stone;
Where it retaines more of the humid fatnesse,
It turnes to *sulphur,* or to *quick-siluer:*
Who are the parents of all other mettalls.
Nor can this remote matter, sodainly,
Progresse so from extreme, vnto extreme,
As to grow gold, and leape ore all the meanes.
Nature doth, first, beget th' imperfect; then
Proceeds shee to the perfect. Of that ayrie,
And oily water, *mercury* is engendered;
Sulphure o' the fat, and earthy part: the one
(Which is the last) supplying the place of male,
The other of the female, in all mettalls.
Some doe beleeue *hermaphrodeitie,*
That both doe act, and suffer. But, these two
Make the rest ductile, malleable, extensiue.
And, euen in gold, they are; for we doe find
Seedes of them, by our fire, and gold in them:

And can produce the *species* of each mettall
More perfect thence, then nature doth in earth.
Beside, who doth not see, in daily practice,
Art can beget bees, hornets, beetles, waspes,
Out of the carcasses, and dung of creatures;
Yea, scorpions, of an herbe, being ritely plac'd:
And these are liuing creatures, far more perfect,
And excellent, then mettalls.

MAM. Well said, father!
Nay, if he take you in hand, sir, with an argument,
Hee'll bray you in a morter.

SVR. 'Pray you, sir, stay.
Rather, then I'll be brai'd, sir, I'll beleeue,
That *Alchemie* is a pretty kind of game,
Somewhat like tricks o' the cards, to cheat a man,
With charming.

SVB. Sir?

SVR. What else are all your termes,
Whereon no one o' your writers grees with other?
Of your *elixir*, your *lac virginis*,
Your *stone*, your *med'cine*, and your *chrysosperme*,
Your *sal*, your *sulphur*, and your *mercurie*,
Your *oyle* of *height*, your *tree of life*, your *bloud*,
Your *marchesite*, your *tutie*, your *magnesia*,
Your *toade*, your *crow*, your *dragon*, and your *panthar*,
Your *sunne*, your *moone*, your *firmament*, your *adrop*,
Your *lato*, *azoch*, *zernich*, *chibrit*, *heautarit*,
And then, your *red man*, and your *white woman*,
Of pisse, and egg-shells, womens termes, mans bloud,
Haire o' the head, burnt clouts, chalke, merds, and clay,
Poulder of bones, scalings of iron, glasse,

> And worlds of other strange *ingredients,*
> Would burst a man to name? (II, iii, 133–98.)

The frantic rush of words here is the *pnigos* which characteristically closes the Aristophanic *agon.*

We should always pay particular attention to long speeches in plays. To some critics they are no doubt tiresome and should have been expunged; but here Jonson is doing more than parading the knowledge of which he was justifiably proud. Subtle's long speech gives an accurate scientific-philosophical rationale for alchemy, and Surly gives the sceptic's reaction. It is reasonable to assume that if, after Dapper, Drugger, and Sir Epicure Mammon are introduced on the scene, Subtle can say "two of our inferior works are at fixation. A third is in ascension," then the explanation of alchemy is also an explanation of comic art. The idea is re-enforced by Subtle's questions in reply to Surly's objections:

> Was not all the knowledge
> Of the *Egyptians* writ in mystick *symboles?*
> Speake not the *Scriptures,* oft, in *parables?*
> Are not the choisest *fables* of the *Poets,*
> That were the fountaines, and first springs of wisedome,
> Wrapt in perplexed *allegories?*[5]
>
> (II, iii, 202–207.)

These are significant analogies, but the major point has been made in the long speech: Alchemy—"our art"—brings nature to its final perfection:

> ... But, these two [mercury and sulphur]
> Make the rest ductile, malleable, extensiue.
> And, euen in gold, they are; for we doe find
> Seedes of them, by our fire, and gold in them:

[5] Paracelsus advocated secrecy with respect to the philosopher's stone, and claimed that the ancients "used parables to keep unworthy persons from knowing and misusing it." Henry M. Pachter, *Paracelsus: Magic into Science,* 188.

And can produce the *species* of each mettall
More perfect thence, then nature doth in earth.

If alchemy furthers and perfects the intentions of nature, if Dapper and Drugger are at fixation, if the "perplexed *allegories*" of the poets offer an amusing analogy to the alchemist's jargon, then, symbolically, alchemy is art, and *The Alchemist* is a play not only about vice, London confidence games, and an upside-down society but also about the relationship between art and nature, a relationship specified metaphorically in Subtle's speech. This speech tells us on the symbolic level what the play is about, and it is very strategically placed: gulls (Dapper, Drugger and Mammon) have been balanced off against rogues (Dol, Face, and Subtle); the general pattern of cheater and cheated has been introduced; and alchemy as the general means of cheating and reforming has been established.

Now, in Subtle's long speech about alchemy, in his quip about the inferior works, and in his analogy of the choicest fables of the poets, alchemy has been made a metaphor for art. Without this transfer the title of the play presents certain difficulties. Subtle is, of course, an alchemist of sorts, but fake alchemy is only one of the trio's methods of fleecing the victims, for they practice most of the confidence games known to the mind of man. But if we regard Subtle as the symbolic comic alchemist, who brings to perfection the intentions of nature, who strips nature of its superfluities and impurities and reduces it, in Paracelsian terms, to its quintessence, all within the context of the purest comedy, then the alchemist of the title is not Subtle alone, but the comic play, and, by implication, the *other* artist-alchemist, Ben Jonson.[6]

The theme of alchemy-as-art introduced in Subtle's long speech is, quite properly, unrecognized by Surly, who, as a professional—

[6] This is not, of course, to equate Subtle with Jonson, any more than Macilente is to be equated with Jonson.

and crooked—gambler, has no ear for philosophical moralizing and who not only does not care about philosophy but also sees through Subtle. The irony of the entire passage, Subtle's and Surly's speeches together, is that they are both right on one level and both wrong on another. Subtle's account is accurate, but it is not the basis for his own actions. Surly's is an accurate appraisal of Subtle's alchemy, but it is not an accurate appraisal of alchemy as science-philosophy nor as metaphor.

The theme of alchemy-as-art is followed out very carefully for the rest of the play. From now on we watch Subtle's—and Jonson's —alchemy in action as the various gulls, those who have been introduced already and those who appear later—Ananias, Tribulation Wholesome, Kastril, Dame Pliant, even Lovewit himself—are allowed, as it were, to bake in the lent heat of Athanor, and are reduced to their quintessence in such a way that, although they themselves do not change, we are clearly aware of the difference between their quintessence and their social impurities.

This virtuoso passage redirects our attention. We will still watch with astonishment the unfolding of the realistic action, but from now on, while Subtle retains his identity as confidence man and fake alchemist, he is also a new version of our old acquaintance, the bad poet, and Face, his ever changing assistant and finally his betrayer, is the comic spirit. Alchemy is still a racket, but it has a thoroughly respectable if not, by modern terms, a completely valid basis, and in perverting this Subtle is perverting his art, or perhaps he is making deliberate use of an art already perverted.

The realistic action continues with increasing complexity through a series of crises to the most serious crisis of all, the return of Lovewit. The first three scenes of the last act, on the street outside Lovewit's house, thus suggesting the relationship between the outer world and the secret world of art within, are adapted from the scene in *The Mostellaria* of Plautus, where Tranio the slave, apparently representing something like the comic spirit, attempts to hold off his old master, Theopropides, just returned from a three-year journey, while his young master and a friend, with their girls, are trying to make their getaway, an attempt complicated by the fact that the friend is drunk.

At the end of the second scene, Face, now Jeremy once more, seems to have succeeded in convincing Lovewit that the neighbors are all mad or addled, when Surly and Mammon appear, obviously bent on revenge. Face's "Nothing's more wretched, then a guiltie conscience" (V, ii, 47) is a direct echo of Tranio. In quick succession Kastril, Ananias, and Tribulation Wholesome appear, all having finally believed Surly. Face is valiant and almost successful in his attempts to convince Lovewit that they are all mad or imposters, until Dapper, forgotten by everyone but the author, suddenly howls in anguish from Fortune's privy lodging, where he had been reposing since late in the third act.

The unexpected outcry again is from *The Mostellaria,* and again it looks as though Face is finally defeated. But inspiration does not forsake him: it is still possible to gull Lovewit, an idea which had apparently not occurred to him before. In fact, however, Lovewit has betrayed himself in V, i.

> What deuice should he bring forth now!
> I loue a teeming wit, as I loue my nourishment.
> 'Pray god he ha' not kept such open house,
> That he hath sold my hangings, and my bedding:
> I left him nothing else. If he haue eate 'hem,
> A plague o' the moath, say I. Sure he has got
> Some bawdy pictures, to call all this ging;
> The Frier and the Nun; or the new *Motion*
> Of the Knights courser, coouering the Parsons mare;
> The Boy of sixe yeere old, with the great thing:

Or't may be, he has the Fleas that runne at tilt,
Vpon a table, or some Dog to daunce?

(V, i, 15–26.)

If these enlightening forms of entertainment are examples of
what Lovewit regards as a teeming wit, he is perhaps to be equated
with the untutored audience about which Jonson had made so
many exasperated observations, and his taste would reveal the lack
of sophistication that makes it possible for Face to gull him. If
Lovewit himself is not entertained by bawdy pictures and phe-
nomenal boys, he has at least grossly underestimated the kind of
entertainment which has called all this ging, and he himself symbolically becomes part of this ging at the end of V, iii:

> FAC. Sir, you were wont to affect mirth, and wit:
> (But here's no place to talke on't i' the street.)
> Giue me but leaue, to make the best of my fortune,
> And onely pardon me th' abuse of your house:
> It's all I begge. I'll helpe you to a widdow,
> In recompence, that you shall gi' me thankes for,
> Will make you seuen yeeres yonger, and a rich one.
> 'Tis but your putting on a *Spanish* cloake,
> I haue her within. You need not feare the house,
> It was not visited.
>
> LOV. But by me, who came
> Sooner then you expected.
>
> FAC. It is true, sir.
> 'Pray you forgiue me.
>
> LOV. Well: let's see your widdow. (V, iii, 80–91.)

Lovewit's gulling, like Mosca's entertainment, suggests the universality of folly. Lovewit is obviously a person of more intelligence,

even of wit, than any of the other victims, and when the victims return he takes the greatest pleasure in adding to their torments, because he is now firmly allied with Face. Yet the fact remains that he has donned the Spanish cloak and married Dame Pliant, both acts by now clearly associated with folly. And since he has done this directly under the influence of Face, the implication seems to be that no one, not even the nominal lover of wit, is really immune to the universal disease of folly.

All that remains is to apply the finishing touches to poor Dapper and for Face to get rid of Subtle and Dol. It seems altogether Jonsonian that it is the comic artist, not the comic spirit, who is defeated. As comic artist, Subtle has had a grossly ulterior motive— his art has had a purely commercial end. But his final defeat may have another significance as well, as though the author, "betrayed" himself on occasion by scurvy receptions of his plays, and to be so betrayed again, were saying that, in spite of the manifest imperfection of the artist, the comic spirit is universal and will survive, by the very elusiveness of its nature. This elusiveness is important. After all, Face's offer of the widow to Lovewit was a desperate gamble, and surely no one was more surprised than he to learn that Lovewit had actually returned. Yet after informing Subtle and Dol that he has told Lovewit the house is haunted (*The Mostellaria* again) to keep him out for a while, he calmly tells them (V, iv, 129) that he had in fact sent for Lovewit. He hadn't, of course, but one might say that symbolically he had, for the lover of wit will be attracted by comedy, and Lovewit is now his, as is clearly indicated in the last scene, when Lovewit has the pleasure of dealing once more with all of the gulls except Dapper, who, after the queen of fairy scene, is immortal.

Lovewit now reigns triumphant except for one thing: he is delighted with his new wife. Face's triumph as the spirit of comedy is established in his epilogue:

My part a little fell in this last *Scene,*
Yet 'twas *decorum.* And though I am cleane
Got off, from SVBTLE, SVRLY, MAMMON, DOL,
Hot ANANIAS, DAPPER, DRVGGER, all
With whom I traded; yet I put my selfe
On you, that are my countrey: and this pelfe,
Which I haue got, if you doe quit me, rests,
To feast you often, and inuite new ghests.

(V, v, 158–65.)

In summarizing so extensively the action of this play, I have attempted to show the close alliance between linear structure and symbolic argument, but to show this sort of thing precisely in a play so full of complications as *The Alchemist* would require a commentary substantially longer than the play itself. I would like, therefore, to recall the discussion of alchemy and to discuss its relationship to a specific aspect of the structure.

The *agon* clearly established that alchemy is to be read as a metaphor for comic art while simultaneously retaining its identity as the efficient confidence game which gulls Sir Epicure Mammon and the Puritans. Thus it constitutes a kind of symbolic structure on which hangs an important part of the symbolic argument of the play. But another structural principle, seldom thought of as symbolic in any sense, is closely associated with it. Jonson's phenomenally successful use of the unities of time, action, and place has been commented on often enough. It undoubtedly provided part of the basis of Coleridge's judgment that *The Alchemist* has one of the three finest plots in all literature.

Jonson follows almost to the letter Castelvetro's curious pronouncement that the time represented must be no longer than the time required for the acting. He does this, not because Castelvetro said it had to be done, but because following the unity of time necessitates the consistent speeding up of the action as the sharpers try to keep their victims apart. Unity of time is observed here because of its great comic potentiality. Unity of action is self-evident. One's only regret is that Aristotle had no opportunity to comment on its manifestation in this play.

The most important point here is the way in which Jonson has observed the unity of place and his reason for doing so. Virtually all the action occurs in a single room of Lovewit's house, a fact of the greatest significance, and closely related to the alchemy theme as established in the *agon*. The house is located in the Blackfriars district, as was the Blackfriars Theater, where the play was performed. It is no accident on Jonson's part that when the audience walks out of the Blackfriars into the theater, it finds itself once more, in effect, in the Blackfriars. For the significance of this fact, consider the prologue:

> Our *Scene* is *London,* 'cause we would make knowne,
>> No countries mirth is better then our owne.
> No clime breeds better matter, for your whore,
>> Bawd, squire, impostor, many persons more,
> Whose manners, now call'd humors, feed the stage:
>> And which haue still beene subiect, for the rage
> Or spleene of *comick*-writers. Though this pen
>> Did neuer aime to grieue, but better men;
> How e'er the age, he liues in, doth endure
>> The vices that shee breeds, aboue their cure.
> But, when the wholsome remedies are sweet,
>> And, in their working, gaine, and profit meet,
> He hopes to find no spirit so much diseas'd,
>> But will, with such faire correctiues, be pleas'd.
>> (5–18.)

This is a characteristic statement of the Jonsonian (and Horatian) moral bent. The playwright here instructs and delights, and in doing so effects a theoretical transformation in his audience; that is, if the audience is properly instructed by the delectable matter on the stage, it will have been improved. Hence a kind of alchemy will have been practiced on the audience in the theatre as well as on the gulls of the play. The audience will see recognizable human folly on the stage—not its own perhaps but something very familiar. It will see people as they want to be seen, their manners (now called humors), and simultaneously it will see them as they really are, when the comic alchemist as confidence man extracts their quintessence and thus exposes the society which supports them.

And, gazing into the steel glass of satire, it will see, in the ironic reversed image, the source of its own salvation. Comedy, as one great critic observed, presents on the stage actions which ought never to be imitated in life—one might add, actions like those which often *occur* in life. The moral point is made with great precision: the fair correctives of the play will please even the most diseased spirit. The action occurs in the Blackfriars, and the theater is in the Blackfriars. From the district, from London at large, from every shire's end (Kastril, for example), even from across the channel (Ananias and Tribulation Wholesome), the gulls come to Subtle's room in Lovewit's house where the ancient and wonderfully comic alchemist will work his magic on them. So from the district, from London, from England at large, and, as contemporary documents show, from the continent, the audience comes to the theater, where, as the author implies in his prologue, wholesome remedies and fair correctives for the vices and follies of the time are dispensed by the *other* alchemist, Ben Jonson the poet.

Subtle's alchemy is thus directly related to the alchemy of art. Representatives of the major social classes of Jacobean England appear in the play, to be reshaped by ancient Subtle, and they also appear in the theatre, to be reshaped by the archalchemist, Ben Jonson. So theme and structure are inseparably joined to present the symbolic argument of *The Alchemist*.

The alchemical references in *Volpone* show that Jonson had been aware for perhaps five years before the first performance of *The Alchemist* of the tremendous metaphorical possibilities of alchemy. In this play he seems to have realized almost all of them. Like all medieval sciences, alchemy was part science, part philosophy, and as such it could effectively cover a huge area of human experience, particularly since metamorphosis is its very essence. Alchemy is a metamorphosis of nature effected by the alchemist, and the metamorphosis is designed to make the imperfect perfect.

In comedy also the imperfect is made perfect, but in a different way: folly is idealized, presented in a form it never achieves in nature. To use the appropriate alchemical language, it is reduced to its quintessence. In the conception of character those qualities not essential to the presentation of folly are stripped away, which means, in language familiar to the student of Jonson, that the humor, the psychologically oversimplified quintessence, is revealed. This is in effect an alchemical change because the impurities are removed—those qualities which make the character an efficient social being. What is left is the humor, the quintessence, the motivation.

The same process is observed in the artistic selectivity which determines the action, which is predicated partly on the nature of the characters, partly on a sense of what is appropriate to the revelation of folly. And the process also occurs in the metamorphosis of standards. Sex, religion, science, virtue, morality, learning, literature, mythology, everything is seen as alchemy, so that alchemy itself becomes a kind of universal humor.

Alchemy thus reduces itself to its own quintessence and becomes the ultimate sublime impossibility, the universal panacea. When alchemy is seen as comic art, the implication seems to be that while comedy is certainly an admirable cure for the diseases of society, it is far from being the universal cure, an idea perhaps underlined by Face's own mistakes—desiring Dame Pliant, forgetting about Dapper. And comic alchemy was very far from being the only weapon of Jonson the moralist. By the time he wrote *The Alchemist* his career as poet was well established, and his career as masque writer had been brilliantly inaugurated. Understandably, one is apt to forget these points when contemplating the unsurpassed excellence of the comedies.

Chapter Four

Interlude: The Tragedies

||||||||||||||||||||||||||||||||||||||||||||||||||||||||||||||||||||||||||||||||||||||||||||||||||||||||||||||||||||||||||||||||||||||||||||||||||||||||||||||||||

Sejanus AND *Catiline* are, it seems to me, rather better than most critics would allow, and *Sejanus* perhaps not quite so good as one critic has asserted. I am not sure, for example, that it is "a purer work than the English stage deserves";[1] but high praise is salutary in view of the consensus that these plays, too early to be dotages, are nevertheless failures.

I think that they failed on the contemporary stage mainly for one reason: they both have a great many long speeches, and an audience not schooled to long speeches did not like them. For the failure of *Sejanus* I suspect that there may have been other artistically irrelevant reasons—a hostility, for example, toward the author of *Poetaster,* who had very publicly turned to tragedy because he found comedy so ominous; or bewilderment at Jonson's extraordinarily careful representation of the Roman scene in both plays. The Rome of Shakespeare's Roman plays is Rome universalized, Rome only incidentally, a popularized Rome familiar through

[1] John J. Enck, *Jonson and the Comic Truth,* 109.

North's Plutarch, populated by towering figures working out their destinies in epic battles with the universe. Jonson's Rome, on the other hand, is the Rome of Tacitus, Sallust, Dio, Juvenal, and Suetonius. Its culture, topography, customs, religion, psychology, politics are all as authentic as the poet could make them. To Jonson's audience, and to many modern readers, it seems foreign, and at first almost incomprehensible.

Another point to which some weight perhaps should be given is that as tragedies these plays are almost unique. The tragic protagonists, Sejanus and Catiline, do not evoke a trace of sympathy from the audience, except possibly in the comments made on their deaths. Although there is pity in *Sejanus,* it is not pity for the protagonist but for his innocent children and his abandoned wife. And at the end of *Catiline* there may be a trace of regret, a mild sense of loss and waste at the reflection that Catiline might have been better than in fact he was:

> A braue bad death.
> Had this beene honest now, and for his countrey,
> As 'twas against it, who had ere fallen greater?
> (V, 688–90.)

But these are minor points, and the principal figures in the two tragedies engage our sympathies no more than do the principal figures in most of the comedies through the middle period. As tragic figures, Sejanus and Catiline are largely responsible for bringing about their own downfall, but not in such a way as to give us any real cause for regret about the two men themselves.

The tragic world of these plays has much in common with the comic world of Jonson's other plays, with obvious differences. But the comparison is important, for with Jonson the body politic provides the background for both tragedy and comedy. Most tragic protagonists engage our sympathies strongly because they are en-

113

gaged in a battle that we can, with some justification, call our own; they are locked in a struggle with a hostile or indifferent universe which we recognize as imposing intolerable burdens. They live in different regions of a universe that we also inhabit.

Shakespeare's and Webster's tragedies are primarily ontological in their arguments, while Jonson's tragedies are hardly ontological at all. The goddess Fortuna averts her face from Sejanus' sacrifice and thus in effect engages the universe, but Sejanus is brought down by Tiberius through Macro and is never represented as being engaged in any kind of cosmic or universal struggle. And Catiline is brought down not by the gods or fate but by the political supergenius of Cicero. *Catiline* is not a play about an essentially virtuous man being led through some moral flaw to his own doom, but a play about how the state can be saved if its chief ministers are incorruptible and extremely intelligent. It might, then, be called not *Catiline his Conspiracy* but *Cicero his Triumph*.

Jonson as tragic poet has clearly not felt free to depart radically from his sources. The annotations for *Sejanus* are famous or, in some circles, notorious. And in *Catiline* also he has attempted to be historically accurate. His procedure is different in this respect from that of the greatest tragic poets of his age. Jonson has allowed his historical sources to interpret history; Shakespeare and Webster interpret it themselves, whether it is Roman, Italian, or English. It is perfectly clear, therefore, that Jonson's conception of tragic drama is quite different from that of Shakespeare and most of the other tragic writers of the age.

Two differences we have specifically noticed: the battleground in Jonsonian tragedy is the state, not the universe; and history is the guiding and shaping force. For Jonson the tragic muse is really the muse of history, and the tragic poet becomes the poet of history. Shakespeare's and Webster's major tragedies would have been great tragedies even if the history on which they are based had really been fiction; but if Tiberius, Sejanus, Cicero, and Catiline had never actually lived Jonson would simply not have written his plays, which are specifically designed to recreate on the tragic stage certain events whose significance lies precisely in the fact that they did occur, one signifying a period of social decay, the other suggesting the temporary salvation of society.

One can learn a good deal about certain periods in Roman history by reading *Sejanus* and *Catiline*. One can learn a great deal that is immensely revealing about Shakespeare's special views of history by reading his historically based plays. The situations are quite different, and this is a difference not only between Jonson and Shakespeare but between Jonson and almost all other tragic writers. Much more often than not, tragic writers have used real or legendary history as a basis for tragic drama, but, so far as I know, Jonson is the only one who seems to use history for its own sake or for the ethical instruction true history will provide. For him, a tragic drama based on history had to represent history as it was to be found in reputable historians. In a very similar way, comedy had to be based on the life of the times, with deeds and language such as men do use. With tragedy, it was deeds and language such as men *did* use.

For Jonson, then, the tragic struggle is not between a protagonist and a universe dramatically embodied in characters in the play, such as Claudius, Augustus Caesar, Iago, Goneril and Regan, Socinius and Junius and Aufidius. Even in *Coriolanus,* perhaps the most masterful and certainly the most overtly political of Shakespeare's Roman plays, the implications are cosmic. In *Sejanus* and *Catiline* the struggle is social and political, and the moral argument is seen specifically in those terms.

These plays represent the reverse of the coin whose obverse we have seen in the comedies. The tragic villains are, on the political scale, the rogues and cheaters we have laughed at in the comedies.

The gulls are now the unprincipled senators living in deadly fear of both Sejanus and Tiberius. In the comedies the dangers that vices and follies present to the body politic are not overtly specified as dangers. The world is turned upside down so that the vices and follies seemed normal. The image in the mirror of the stage is reversed.

But in the tragedies the image is not reversed. The purity of *Sejanus* which Mr. Enck has described so well,[2] the total lack of anything at all comic, derives from the fact that the events represented in that play really did happen, and in the kind of society in which such things happen the time is too late for laughter.

Volpone and Mosca, in their marvelous ways so similar to Tiberius and Sejanus, are after all private citizens. If Volpone had been a doge of Venice rather than a magnifico, he would have been in a position to indulge all of his ambitions, and then he would not have been comic. In the tragedies we see the significance of Jonson's view that comedy should sport with human follies, not with crimes. In the tragedies Jonson is concerned with real crimes, incredible—but true—vices. Another distinction, then, between Jonsonian comedy and Jonsonian tragedy is that comedy deals with vices and follies in the body politic in general, while Jonsonian tragedy deals with vices and follies in high places; and, because they occur in high places, they become crimes. There is much leeway for the foolish citizen in comedy, none at all for the foolish or vicious governor in tragedy. The body politic can absorb Volpone's vices, but not those of Tiberius or Catiline.

When we come to *Sejanus* and *Catiline* after a careful consideration of the comedies, it is as though Volpone's and Mosca's struggle for the money of Corvino, Voltore, and Corbaccio is now to be seen in a new light, as Tiberius' and Sejanus' struggle for Rome and the world; or as though Sir Epicure Mammon has arisen as

2 Enck, *op. cit.*, 89–109.

the ghost of Sulla; as though Captain Bobadill has become Cethegus; Lady Haughty, Sempronia; Subtle, Cicero; Surly, Catiline. Jonson's comedy is social, and its soul is laughter; in the tragedies he represents the social scene with all cause for laughter removed, including the language which often evokes it.

It is idle to complain, as many critics have done, that Jonson's tragedies do not move us as *Hamlet, Lear,* or *The Duchess of Malfi* do. They are not intended to move us as those plays do. As Jonsonian comedy is essentially a unique rendering of Old Comedy, so Jonsonian tragedy is a unique rendering, in tragic-historical terms, of the themes of Old Comedy seen in the serious context of political morality and the state. And it would be idle to say that this cannot be moving. It is just that, as Jonsonian comedy often requires thought before it evokes laughter, so Jonsonian tragedy often requires thought before it evokes pity or sorrow.

In the closing scene of *Hamlet* Fortinbras enters while the stage is littered with corpses, and asks, "Where is this sight?" To which Horatio replies, "What is it you would see?/ If aught of woe or wonder, cease your search." The words "woe or wonder" sum up the essential tragic emotion. Surely one should feel a similar emotion at the end of *Sejanus,* when Arruntius and Lepidus, almost the only decent people left alive, hear the dreadful account of the deaths of Sejanus and his children and of the grief of their mother, so remarkably similar in details and in emotional effect to that of Hecuba in the player's speech. And the reaction must be pure horror when, earlier in Act V, Sejanus is led off to prison and the senators shout their approval of Macro, "who hath saved Rome." To a modern audience particularly, its implications should be shattering. No one at all familiar with the internal politics of a modern totalitarian state can fail to get the point, nor can anyone who has read *Animal Farm* or *1984.*

With *Catiline* the situation is different, because that play ends in victory, a fact only partly mitigated by the reflection that in a few years Caesar will come to power. Indeed, one might say that in making the central figure not only sympathetic but victorious, Jonson is anticipating his practice in the later comedies, the practice of introducing sympathetic if slightly defective characters into a kind of comedy which had hitherto generally eschewed them.

But the real parallel, as with *Sejanus,* is with a specific comedy. The first tragedy had been followed by a comedy which in effect transmuted the two principal tragic figures into comic figures. The ghastliness of *Sejanus* is dissipated in the laughter so frequently evoked in *Volpone*. *Volpone* springs from a tragedy, *Catiline* from a comedy. The figure of Cicero, historically accurate, at least according to Jonson's sources, represents, it seems to me, a serious version of Subtle, with the great difference that now all the deviousness and cleverness, the ability to see into men's motives, the subtlety of mind, and the talent for controlling the actions of other people are devoted to a good end rather than an amusingly bad one. Cicero and his friends are balanced off against Catiline and his followers, in a manner remarkably similar to the way in which Subtle, Face, and Dol are balanced off against the gulls.

The difference in genre is crucial, but it is hard to imagine that *Catiline* was not written directly under the influence of *The Alchemist,* with Subtle transmuted into the alchemical statesman. Since *The Alchemist* uses a basic technique of old comedy, Subtle is only a relatively sympathetic character—we approve of his manipulation of the gulls without absolutely approving of *him*. Cicero is designed to be a genuinely sympathetic character and a model statesman as well. As historical figure and statesman-alchemist, he seems also to be based on the figure of Bacon, solicitor general in 1611 and greatly admired by Jonson. As Subtle embodies in comic terms the qualities necessary for the chastising of the vices and follies of society, Cicero embodies in serious terms the qualities of the ideal statesman, a figure who does not appear at all in *Sejanus.*

The two tragedies, it seems to me, are to be seen in the light of the comedies that preceded and followed each. *Sejanus* creates on the tragic stage the image of a real society fallen into decay, a world turned upside down, but this time a real world. Here characters who in comedy would be rigidly circumscribed by the comic condition, have absolute control over the lives and fortunes of people and the state itself. *Catiline* presents on the tragic stage the image of society being righted, again a real society, saved by an ideal statesman who, as it happens, was also a real statesman.

Sejanus, produced in 1603, comes midway between *Poetaster* and *Volpone,* and the pattern is hardly accidental. The parallels between *Sejanus* and *Volpone* are too obvious to require further comment, but what about *Poetaster?* In the epilogue to that play Jonson announced that his next work would be a tragedy, and he strongly implied that he had settled on a subject. There can be no question that Poetaster suggested the scene and hence the subject of *Sejanus.* The scene of *Poetaster* was the Rome of Augustus Caesar, whom Jonson greatly admired and was to see reincarnated in James. But the Rome of Augustus had also its Tucca, Crispinus, Demetrius, and Asinius Lupus, the unscrupulously opportunistic consul. In *Poetaster* it was clear that Jonson knew the Rome of the first century intimately, even though he did not choose to represent it with complete accuracy.

This Rome was blessed, as Jonson saw it, with a moral, wise, and munificent prince, zealous for the welfare of the state, eager and understanding in his patronage of artists—Jonson's ideal prince, whose characteristics are quite consistent with those presented in his notes on statecraft in the *Discoveries.* Jonson had presented a comedy in which the prince was instrumental in resolving the various moral, social, and intellectual abuses. And just as the historical Augustus was followed by his politically adapted son Tiberius, so Jonson's *Poetaster* was followed by *Sejanus*.

We know the poet had turned to tragedy because comedy had proved "ominous" to him, because the popular audience had not grasped the implications of the early comedies. This will explain his turning—or returning³—to tragedy, but the reason for his choice of this particular subject appears to be that his studies of the history of the age of Augustus had carried over to a consideration of the nightmarish era to follow; a tragic theme lay ready to hand for the author of *Every Man Out* and *Poetaster,* for the author who saw both comedy and tragedy pre-eminently as vehicles for social analysis and criticism. After the glorious reign of Augustus, when the poetasters, fools, and opportunists all received their due, the reign of Tiberius, which followed directly, would naturally provide a tragic theme.

It is difficult to escape the conclusion that the choice of Sejanus as central figure for a tragedy was influenced by the poor reception of *Poetaster,* as though Jonson were suggesting that a society that refuses to be instructed by comedy is in danger of tragic corruption. If it is unable to laugh at its follies and correct them, it will soon be past either laughter or correction. At the end of the play Sejanus is dead, but Tiberius and Macro are not, and perhaps Jonson counted on his audience's knowing that in a few years even Arruntius would be accused and would commit suicide. And he certainly counted on their remembering that the nightmare reign of Tiberius was to be followed by the unspeakable reign of Caligula, which began when that amiable young man helped murder the old gentleman. The tragic effect of *Sejanus* is intensified by the historical context.

The relative failure of *Poetaster* drove Jonson to write *Sejanus,*

³ Assuming some accuracy in Meres' mentioning him as a tragic writer in 1598.

with its bitter attack on the unthinking, uncritical mob. The complete failure of *Sejanus* drove him back to comedy, to *Volpone,* where Tiberius and Sejanus undergo remarkable metamorphoses and emerge as Volpone and Mosca. What makes *Sejanus* effectively tragic, in Jonsonian terms, is that the rogues are no longer victimizing gulls who richly deserve it; they are now victimizing the whole body politic. In comedy we laugh as we recognize the disparity between the character's pretensions and his true nature. It is the disparity, representing folly, that makes the character only an implicit threat to the body politic. With Sejanus, there is no disparity; the pretension has become the real thing, and he cannot be exposed, only destroyed.

Sejanus, as we have seen, is as different from other tragedies as it is from Jonson's comedies, although both are grounded in the criticism of society. Just as there is no comic disparity between the pretension and the reality, so there is really no tragic disguise either, at least in the customary sense. There is, for Sejanus, no moment of recognition, no *anagnorisis*. He is not deceived about himself, only about Tiberius, and that is understandable. With practically all other Elizabethan and Jacobean tragic protagonists, indeed with almost all tragic protagonists, we can assume on their part some basic and fatal misunderstanding of themselves and of their universe.

What makes *Sejanus* such an awesome tragedy is that the universe is social and that the protagonist really does understand its general operation. What he does not understand until it is too late is that Tiberius is far more clever than Sejanus thinks he is, and that Macro has tricked him. These normally comic devices are here put at the service of a peculiarly effective tragedy.

The universe of this play is not a mysterious abstraction, as in Shakespeare and Webster, for example; it is the body politic, and there really have been, as there really still are, people like Tiberius,

Sejanus, Caligula, Eudemus, Livia, Satrius, Natta, Afer, and Macro. In *The Duchess of Malfi* Bosola kills Antonio by mistake and observes, "We are merely the stars' tennis balls,/ Struck and bandied which way please them." In *The Devil is an Ass* Jonson was to imply that if we worry about the devil without and ignore the devil within, we are the asses. In *Sejanus* the evil omens are effective ornamental symbols. When the goddess Fortuna averts her face it is symbolic, not deterministic. She averts her face not because she has determined Sejanus' downfall, but because Tiberius and Macro have done so. If Jonson had commented specifically on this situation, he might have said that we must resign ourselves to fate but not to our own vices and stupidity. The tragedy of Sejanus, which was really the tragedy of the Roman state, could have been averted, a conclusion warranted by *Catiline*. The tragedies of Hamlet or King Lear could not because the universe as well as society was engaged.

A number of critics have admired *Sejanus,* although usually with reservations. It certainly makes absorbing, as well as instructive, reading, whether or not it could ever be played successfully on the stage. And it is certainly a monument to the practical morality of its author at this stage of his career. *Catiline* has found almost no admirers, with or without reservations. I must confess this puzzles me, because I do not understand how anyone can genuinely admire *Sejanus* without being able to generate some enthusiasm for *Catiline* also. I suppose one reason is that few people can really believe that there were such people as Catiline or Sulla, whose ghost opens the proceedings.

For the record, it is worth remembering that there *were* such people and that the imaginative embroidery added by Jonson is not at all inconsistent with the generally accepted facts about the two men.

Lucius Cornelius Sulla, who became consul in 80 B.C., was particularly infamous for having instituted the proscription. The proscription was a list, published in the Forum, of enemies of the consul who were to be killed. They automatically became outlaws who could be killed with impunity by anyone, and their property was subject to confiscation by the state and sale at auction. On subsequent lists Sulla included enemies of his personal friends, or people who had property his friends wanted. They could then purchase it for nominal prices at public auction, or Sulla could give it to them outright.

Lucius Sergius Catiline was the descendant of an impoverished patrician family. The use of Sulla's ghost as prologue to introduce Catiline is designed to show Catiline as a worthy follower of the monster. As a very young man Catiline was a real follower of Sulla, participated in the proscription, and named and killed his own brother-in-law, Quintus Caecelius. He was reputed also to have committed incest and to have murdered his wife. The play's horrifying details of his plot against the city are historically accurate. His own plan, from 64–62 B.C., included burning the city, slaughtering anyone who got in the way, canceling all debts, proscribing the wealthy, and distributing all offices to his fellow conspirators. Like Sulla, he was not a nice man.

The careers and ambitions of Sulla and Catiline, and those of many other historical brutes down to the present time, are really almost too dreadful to contemplate. But they are unfortunately real. One's reaction to them may be almost like Cicero's reaction to Fulvia's account of Catiline's plot:

> Sit downe, good lady; CICERO is lost
> In this your fable: for, to thinke it true
> Tempteth my reason. It so farre exceedes
> All insolent fictions of the tragick *scene!*
> (III, 256–59.)

Precisely. And for Jonson its significance lies in its reality.

The figures of Sulla and Catiline introduce the play. The effect, as with the comedies, is to show a world turned upside down—but, as in *Sejanus,* a real world representing verifiable history—and particularly to show a mad, irrational, and almost overwhelming evil. Throughout the first two expository acts we are concerned only with the state, the body politic, on the verge of complete destruction. The spirit of Sulla has become the spirit of an important aspect of the Roman state, intent on slaughter and destruction. Catiline is not the central dramatic figure of the play, but his conspiracy evokes the political genius of Cicero.

The first two acts are relatively short, simply presenting Catiline and his fellow conspirators and showing the madness, danger, folly, and complete seriousness of their designs. Significant commentary comes in the figures of Fulvia, Sempronia, and Curius, who turn out to be either foolish or basely opportunistic. Comic motives again are effectively introduced into a very austere kind of tragedy. For the two women, participating in the plot seems the fashionable thing to do, and Fulvia deserts out of jealousy of Sempronia. When she betrays Curius to Cicero, he has no choice but to go along with the consul rather than with the conspirators.

These characters exhibit a new dimension in Jonson's technique as a writer of tragedy, and their significance lies in the nature of their relationship to Cicero and the particular way in which he uses such thoroughly base characters for what is ultimately an exemplary end. The successful politician must deal with things as they are, not with things as he would like them to be. One gets the impression that Jonson is here experimenting with the artist-theme in a strictly political context.

The business, as Jonson calls it, begins in Act III, with the introduction of an entirely new set of characters, headed by Cicero. With the entrance of Cicero, Jonson's ideal statesman, we begin to see more clearly the point of the extended introduction of the conspirators in the first two acts. The art of statecraft will be most fully brought into play when the state itself is in the greatest danger. The last three acts of *Catiline* represent an illustrated lecture on statecraft and political morality against the tragic background of the conspiracies of Catiline. The point is established in III, 61–74:

> The voice of *Rome* is the consent of heauen!
> And that hath plac'd thee, CICERO, at the helme,
> Where thou must render, now, thy selfe a man,
> And master of thy art. Each petty hand
> Can steere a ship becalm'd; but he that will
> Gouerne, and carry her to her ends, must know
> His tides, his currents; how to shift his sailes;
> What shee will beare in foule, what in faire weathers;
> Where her springs are, her leakes; and how to stop 'hem;
> What sands, what shelues, what rocks doe threaten her;
> The forces, and the natures of all winds,
> Gusts, stormes, and tempests; when her keele ploughs hell,
> And deck knocks heauen: then, to manage her
> Becomes the name, and office of a pilot.

Cato's speech describes the attributes of the ideal statesman who is finally to thwart the conspiracies of Catiline. It suggests the method of a Subtle turned serious, and the speech prepares us for the devious skill that Cicero will use. The qualities here attributed to the statesman are similar to those attributed earlier to the poet in the dedication to *Volpone*. Cicero is really the encompassing figure, the statesman who uses the skill and perceptiveness of an artist. The precepts that Cato introduces in the speech are put into play by Cicero, and the speech must be remembered if we are to understand why Cicero does not hesitate to get his hands dirty when the situation seems to require it. Thus he must resist his moral antipathy when Fulvia betrays Catiline's plot to him and Curius' role is revealed, must not hesitate to call Fulvia "good lady" even though he knows perfectly well what she is. His method of bringing Curius around is little better than blackmail, although it is put in much more polite terms; but it is politically necessary, it is directed to a good end, and it enables Cicero to unravel Catiline's further plots.

Many modern readers, no doubt, have thought Cicero far too devious and subtle to be a really virtuous political leader. But Cicero's aim is the salvation of the state and the protection of Catiline's potential victims, and Jonson was not a sentimental liberal. His system is based on the theory that the state must be under the direction of men who are not only just and virtuous, but who also have the ability to manipulate other men for the achievement of the ends of justice and virtue.

The significance of Cicero the statesman is pointed up by the figure of Caesar, who is the unprincipled Machiavel. He has Cicero's brains and deviousness—almost—without his overriding sense of high principle. This is particularly illustrated in his secret meeting with Catiline in Act III. Here Jonson has apparently departed from all historical sources, with the deliberate intention of illustrating his point. Caesar is the skilled politician without principle, the immoral counterpart of Cicero.

By the end of the play, Cicero has become a kind of political Compass, with Cato as his Ironside, as it were. Jonson's view is certainly that, in a confused and chaotic age, the statesman must be a kind of political virtuoso, using every stratagem known to statecraft, while at the same time he is governed by the highest moral principles consistent with the welfare of the state. To object to the use of the Allobroges to trap Lentulus, Cethegus, and the others is to miss the desperateness of the political situation. The tragedy is Catiline's, but there is no point in looking for a Shakespearean or Websterian ontology in this play or in *Sejanus*. Jonson is not concerned with the abstract meaning of existence. This play, instead, is in the tradition of political tragedies, the plays of Sackville and Norton, Sir William Alexander, and Fulke Greville. A tragedy is essentially a play in which one or more of the principal figures meet death in such a way as to provide a significant moral conclusion. The conclusion here is that a Cicero can save the body politic from the depredations of a Catiline.

Always we get back to the identity of Cicero as the virtuoso politician who is also virtuous. Although Jonson would never have admitted it, in view of some of the comments in the *Discoveries* (1158–1196) it seems to me that Cicero has a great deal in common with Machiavelli (the true Machiavelli, not the mythological one), who would do almost anything to preserve the pristine virtue and strength of the body politic. In presenting the figure of the perfect statesman Jonson is here functioning as a political theorist, and I must say that for one modern reader at least his tough-mindedness is appalling.

Chapter Five

Bartholomew Fair
and the Later Comedies

||||||||||||||||||||||||||||||||||||||||||||||||||||||||||||||||||||||||||||||||||||||||||||||||||||||||||||||||||||||||||||||||||||||||||||||||||||||||||||||

Bartholomew Fair is the summing up of Jonson's career to 1614 as a comic writer, and prepares us for the interesting changes to occur, beginning in 1616. The play was acted in 1614 but not included in the Folio of 1616. The generally accepted reason for this is that the author had not had time to prepare it accurately for the press, something he had done with great care for the other plays. This may well be true, but perhaps it was omitted for another reason: in the four years since *The Alchemist,* Jonson had begun to move into a new comic world, or at least a very greatly elaborated old one, and *Bartholomew Fair* may have been omitted because its implications go far beyond those of the earlier plays.

There are clear points of resemblance between this and the earlier plays; but the clearest, the presentation of a social world turned upside down, is intensified and the terms of its presentation engage new worlds of experience hardly admitted earlier. And though the play provokes laughter at almost every point, there comes a time toward the end when one smiles instead of laughing; this is certainly something new.

The most important and the most complex problem which *Bartholomew Fair* presents is that of the actual nature and identity of the comic world in which the action occurs. Important aspects of this have been discussed by Ray Heffner,[1] who points out that the thematic center of the play is Troubleall's perpetual question: Do you have Justice Overdo's warrant for what you say and what you do? The question, as Heffner says, touches on epistemology and ethics, but I think it would be well to insist that the madman is not asking for any warrant, but specifically for Justice Overdo's warrant, a point inseparable from an important aspect of the symbolic argument.

All comedy asks epistemological and ethical questions—why do you think you know this? why do you do that?—and ordinarily it asks these questions from a point of view, author's or character's. In *Bartholomew Fair* the question is asked by a former clerk who has been dismissed from his post by Adam Overdo and has run mad upon the conceit. This is closely related to the question of the nature of the comic world of *Bartholomew Fair* because Justice Overdo is caught up in that world and, beaten for his pains, emerges triumphant in good-natured humility. He is, as Quarlous says, Adam flesh and blood, and this truth is brought home to him in the Fair. In defining the world of the play, therefore, one must define the Fair itself, its inhabitants, and its activities.

The nature of the historical Fair is of some importance here because it is a partly religious, partly secular institution. By 1614 it had been observed, apparently without interruption, for 494 years. Like many fairs it was originally associated with a religious house, in this instance the Priory of St. Bartholomew, and in 1154, thirty-

[1] "Unifying Symbols in the Comedy of Ben Jonson."

four years after its inception, the Fair was given the royal privilege by Henry II. Bartholomew Fair is thus ancient, religious, secular, and almost universal in its appeal, established by an ecclesiastic and sanctioned by a temporal ruler. As the scene for the play it provides an almost universal panorama. And since it is stinking and dirty and is populated by rogues and cheaters, it provides a typically realistic locale.

In addition to being a fair at Smithfield, which gives London citizens an admirable opportunity to be separated from their money, not to say their wits, it provides a symbolic locale, because the Induction seems to suggest that the world of the Fair is to be equated simultaneously with two things—with human life seen in broad symbolic terms, and with the world of the comic drama. In the Induction the emphasis is on the latter, although the Stage-Keeper's remarks at the beginning suggest broad ramifications of the social and political world. The articles of agreement relate the Fair to the drama:

> It is further couenanted, concluded and agreed, that how great soeuer the expectation bee, no person here, is to expect more then hee knowes, or better ware then a *Fayre* will affoord: neyther to looke backe to the sword and bucklerage of *Smithfield*, but content himselfe with the present. In stead of a little *Dauy*, to take toll o' the Bawds, the *Author* doth promise a strutting *Horse-courser*, with a *leere*-Drunkard, two or three to attend him, in as good *Equipage* as you would wish. And then for *Kinde-heart*, the Tooth-drawer, a fine oyly *Pig-woman* with her *Tapster*, to bid you welcome, and a consort of *Roarers* for musique. A wise *Iustice* of *Peace meditant*, in stead of a *Iugler*, with an *Ape*. A ciuill *Cutpurse searchant*, A sweete *Singer* of new Ballads *allurant*: and as fresh an *Hypocrite*, as euer was broach'd, *rampant*. If there bee neuer a *Seruant-monster* i' the *Fayre;* who can help it? he sayes; nor a nest of *Antiques?* Hee is loth to make Nature afraid in his *Playes*, like those that beget *Tales, Tempests,* and such like *Drolleries*, to mixe his head with other

mens heeles, let the concupisence of *Iigges* and *Dances,* raigne as strong as it will amongst you: yet if the *Puppets* will please any body, they shall be entreated to come in. (113–34.)

The inhabitants of the Fair are described as though they were the characters of a play, and in the closing lines of the passage the Fair itself seems to be equated with a play superior to other plays. The author will substitute certain characters of his own conceiving for those normally associated with a fair, and the substitutions are significant. He specifies a horse-courser, a pig-woman with a consort of roarers, a wise justice, a cutpurse, and a sweet singer. Now there seems no inherent reason why these particular figures should not be associated with a fair, and yet the author seems to say that they represent something new in the way of attractions; this implies that they must have special significance, and they do.

Dan Jordan Knockem, Ursula the pigwoman, Adam Overdo, Edgeworth, and Nightingale are singled out in the Induction. In their different ways they are, except for Overdo, the "deities" presiding over Bartholomew Fair. Others, inferior in station but quite important, appear later in the play itself. The people to whom we are introduced in the first act, in Littlewit's house, come to participate, for different reasons, in the annual festival presided over by these figures. On the realistic level none of them presents any particular problem, for they are all either rogues or gulls, part of an ancient comic pattern. After Act I all the action occurs in the Fair, and at the end the victims leave, to have dinner with Justice Overdo.

The first figure met in the Fair is Adam Overdo, disguised as a fool—that is, a madman. This is amplified and made more specific at the end of II, ii:

I shall by the benefit of this, discouer enough, and more: and yet get off with the reputation of what I would be. A certaine midling thing, betweene a foole and a madman. (142–45.)

He is, at first glance, the first presiding genius of the Fair, a wise justice of the peace who would appear as a middling thing between fool and madman, and he is disguised in order to uncover and punish the enormities he knows the Fair will produce; as the action progresses it becomes apparent that Adam Overdo is not a part of the inner life of the Fair, that he, like the other "outsiders," is an interloper, and that he, like them, must be educated and corrected through his experiences in the Fair.

After this scene the action will move freely about the Fair, but the realistic and thematic centers of action will be Ursula's booth and the puppet tent. In more ways than one, Ursula's booth is *the* thematic center of the play. Virtually all the rogues and gulls, once they have entered the Fair at Smithfield, converge in her booth before they appear anywhere else. It is headquarters for Edgeworth the cutpurse and Whit and his associate pimps. It also contains the only ladies' room the Fair has to offer, a fact worth noting on more than humanitarian grounds. Furthermore, it is the object of Win-the-Fight Littlewit's desires. She longs for roast pig as an excuse to see the Fair, and the rationale is her pregnancy. Even Zeal-of-the-Land Busy longs for roast pig, although he won't admit it.

Ursula's booth is characterized by large congregations of people, bawdry and thievery, huge consumption of pigs and ale, vapors, enormity, justice, folly, pissing, pregnancy, and the burning of the pig-woman. Realistically the action here is all of a piece, and symbolically it is too, but with almost infinite scope. The major action of the play moves from Littlewit's house to the Fair, from Ursula's booth to the puppet tent, and from the puppet tent, we are told, back to Justice Overdo's house, with the pig-booth apparently the focal point.

From the points already suggested, and from others which will be presented shortly, it seems certain that Ursula is the vital center of this play. As she is described, and as she describes herself, she seems to be earth itself, the great Mother, Demeter, and Eve, a great goddess with all her shapes combined in one vast unshape—Ursa Major, the great bear which is also a wagon, appropriate enough to her function as bawd. As Demeter, the great mother of fertility, she wears the aspect of Sow Goddess; but as she presides over the sacrifice of that beast of the waning year she is in danger of trans-mutation:

> . . . I shall e'en melt away to the first woman, a ribbe againe, I am afraid. I doe water the ground in knots, as I goe, like a great Garden-pot, you may follow me by the S.S.s. I make. (II, ii, 50–53.)

In the expansive comic view of this play it is hard to imagine a more appropriate presiding goddess than Ursula who presides over a world of fools as mother, nurse, bawd, priestess, and verbal chas-tiser.[2] As the universal mother she has a rather peculiar brood, whose identity has been signified first by Bartholomew Cokes's in-sistence on the Fair's being *his,* since he is the archetypical fool. He is the figure most perfectly at home in the Fair, the only fool whose folly is purely disinterested and who is made spiritually perfect by the deliberate and systematic stripping away of all ma-terial excess—money, clothes, and, ironically enough, Grace Well-born, evidence of the thoroughness of the comic purgation in this play, because in being denied "grace" he achieves comic perfection.

One may associate *Bartholomew Fair* with Aristophanes' *The Thesmophoriazusae,* the comic occasion for which was the annual festival of Demeter, although that play is one of Aristophanes' lighter works, while this is one of Jonson's weightiest. Ursula as bawd reflects some of the scandalous accusations made by the dis-guised Mnesilochus, whose role is taken here, in very different terms, by Quarlous, in the splendid quarrel which takes place in

---

[2] Joan Trash partly shares this identity: at II, v, 11, she is referred to as Ceres.

II, v. There is also more than a suggestion of secret rites in Ursula's booth. The pigs and ale are comically sacramental, with Mooncalf assisting as an attendant eunuch priest; and the relief which Ursula provides for the exigencies of Win and Mistress Overdo may suggest a comic ritual purification of a very secret kind about which the men have imperfect notions—Whit, for example, is not sure about the kind of sacred vessel used.

If Ursula is a kind of comic Demeter, her attendants have parallel identities. Dan Jordan Knockem, horse-courser and ranger o' Turnbull (*i.e.,* pimp), will be comic Poseidon. (The mythological Poseidon kept a splendid herd of white horses, and his association with the jordan had been implied by Aristophanes in *The Ecclesiazusae.*) When Winwife describes him as "the roaring horse-courser," Quarlous replies, "S'lud, I'le see him, and roare with him, too, and hee roar'd as loud as *Neptune,* pray thee goe with me." (II, v, 25–28.) The sea is here circumscribed in a chamber pot. Edgeworth and his friend Nightingale will represent a characteristically Jonsonian fragmented version of the dual nature of Hermes as thief and musician, with a possible suggestion of Orpheus.

But the most amusing of all these metamorphoses occurs in the figure of Lantern Leatherhead, the puppet-master, who as the puppet schoolmaster Dionysius finally confutes Zeal-of-the-Land Busy. As puppetmaster, Leatherhead performs Littlewit's outrageously funny play, which combines the stories of Hero and Leander, and Damon and Pythias. The tyrant Dionysius of the Damon and Pythias story becomes the schoolmaster Dionysius who instructs Busy. And as the schoolmaster Dionysius he is both an instructor and, like Ursula, another fertility figure, the god Dionysus, the guiding spirit of the drama. Before the puppet-play begins, he also becomes Apollo, bringer of light, so that the two figures deliberately kept separate in *Volpone* are here comically united. The

Apollonian identity is implicit in his first name, Lantern; "Master *Lanterne*," as Littlewit says, "that giues light to the businesse." (V, iii, 54.)[3]

With some of these points suggested, it is possible to consider the relationship between the Fair and the world outside, represented by Littlewit's house. The relationship is about the same as that between the Induction and the first act. In the Induction the audience at the Hope was invited to view a play, after making an agreement with the playwright to exercise no more than its proper prerogative to censure the proceedings on the stage. After the first act Littlewit's ménage also enters the Fair, where, as with the gulls in *The Alchemist,* their inner natures are revealed. The relationship is analogous to that between the real world and the theater, with the Fair serving as a kind of *theatrum mundi.* Littlewit is thus a new version of the poet, whose production is presented under the aegis of Demeter, Dionysus, and Apollo, and his play is really a play within the play within the play—the apparent remoteness from reality paradoxically gets us back very close to reality—ending almost coincidentally with the play itself.

John Littlewit must go to the Fair to see his play performed, but before he can conduct his business he must receive the "sacrament" of the pig in Ursula's booth. Thus purified, he is able to go about his affairs. The audience at early performances of *The Alchemist,* entering the Blackfriars Theatre, found itself once again in the Blackfriars district. The audience on the Bankside, entering the Hope, finds itself in Smithfield—so does the audience at court, for that matter. The process is comparable but the scope is greater. Lovewit's house was the world of comic art; Bartholomew Fair is the world which engenders comic art, and generation is an important theme in the play.

The Alchemist, funny as it is, is intellectually austere. One

---

[3] He is also ironically associated with Orpheus, by Quarlous, at II, v, 8.

is always aware that the masterpiece he is reading—or, if he is extremely lucky, seeing—is just that, consciously, as well as genuinely, a masterpiece. *Bartholomew Fair* is formidably intellectual and literary, yet seems so only when one is trying to explain it. But one is always aware of getting the fullest account of human experience which comedy can afford without becoming something else.

The recently fashionable idea of comedy as an outgrowth of ancient ritual has for some reason not been seriously applied to *Bartholomew Fair*. This play, like a number of others, is not an outgrowth of ritual as such, though it embodies in its action strong suggestions of those rituals closest to the engendering of life itself —the worship of Demeter and Dionysus.

Different characters have different reasons for wanting to go to the Fair, but there is some connection between them. Bartholomew Cokes wants to go because he is a fool, and the Fair is, in addition to the other things we have seen, a *festa stultorum*—and he would like to buy some fairings for Mistress Grace. Littlewit wants to attend to his puppet show. The device to justify the two Littlewits' going, in the eyes of Win's mother, Dame Purecraft, is that Win, being pregnant, can legitimately long for roast pig, a fact Rabbi Busy can accept as long as he is sure that her longing is of the essence—they can scent after the pig, but must not be led to it by idols.

Not to render the argument absurd by bald oversimplification, Win, teeming with life herself, is the symbolic—I almost said real —daughter not of Dame Purecraft but of Ursula-Demeter, returning from the world of Rabbi Busy to commune with her mother— a justifiable enough reading when we remember that she herself really wants to see the Fair, in addition to providing a plausible excuse to take her husband there. The analogy with Demeter's daughter Persephone is not at all far-fetched: Winwife describes her as "A wife heere with a *Strawbery*-breath, *Chery*-lips, *Apricot-*

cheekes, and a soft veluet head, like a *Melicotton*." (I, ii, 15–16.) She is very like nature itself, which Littlewit's wit is too little to comprehend, although she will bear his child: he is enamored not so much of her as of her new cap, which is so charming he would like to kiss it. (I, i, 23–26.) This is not fetishism but stupidity.

The first act, in Littlewit's house, presents the raw implications of ideas that will be enlarged on in the Fair. Proctor John Littlewit has found a pretty conceit, one of many fine ones. He has a marriage license for Bartholomew Cokes and Grace Wellborn. When the significance of the Fair begins to sink in, one remembers several details from Littlewit's opening speech.

The presiding deities of the Fair are fertility figures, but as we first look at the world outside we see fertility implicitly denied or inverted: Littlewit spins conceits out of himself like a silkworm; Cokes, the epitome of folly, intends to marry Grace Wellborn, something like biological miscegenation; Bartholomew upon Bartholomew is a "leapfrogge chance," the obscene pun again contravening fertility; Win appears and Littlewit begins kissing her hat, with which he has fallen in love. He is so taken with his quiblins and carwhitchets that he would like to be a Justice of Wit "and giue the law to all the *Poets,* and *Poet-suckers* 'i Towne." (I, i, 38–40.) Thus he is presented as an amusing comic paradox: the antithesis of fertility and a wit superior to the poets.

When Winwife enters, Littlewit invites him to kiss Win, which he apparently does, commenting on the strawberry breath, cherry lips, etc., but observing that he prefers fruit of a later kind, the sober matron Dame Purecraft. This, although one would prefer to give it no more specific emphasis than Jonson does, is another denial of fertility, the alternative to which seems to be madness. Win tells Winwife that the cunning men have cast her mother's water and told her that if she would be happy she must marry a madman, and within a week. It behooves Winwife to be a little

mad if he wants Dame Purecraft, for the lady is studying another
suitor who appears entirely mad:

> [She is] studying an old Elder, come from *Banbury,* a Suitor that puts
> in heere at meale-tyde, to praise the painefull brethren, or pray that
> the sweet singers may be restor'd; Sayes a grace as long as his breath
> lasts him! Some time the spirit is so strong with him, it gets quite
> out of him, and then my mother, or *Win,* are faine to fetch it
> againe with Malmesey, or *Aqua coelestis.* (I, ii, 64–70.)

Again, of course, a denial of life and fertility. He is not only an
elder, but an *old* elder; he comes at meal-*tide,* not meal-time, a
ludicrous mockery of the genuine pleasures of the belly; he prays
for the painful brethren—for those who deny the free and innocent
pleasures of life; he says grace until the spirit is quite out of him
so that he must be revived by wine and *aqua coelestis,* an alchemical
drink—a "rectified wine"—the naming of which prepares us for
the very amusing metamorphosis which occurs in Busy's character
when the puppet Dionysius confutes him in the Fair.

Quarlous' long discourse on the folly of Winwife's suit to Dame
Purecraft is again a comment on infertility, presented ironically,
since Quarlous is a suitor himself. But the ironic commentator may
speak truth, even if he does so for self-serving reasons. It is Quarlous who finally gets the lady by feigning to be mad in truth, so
that, ironically, he comes around to precisely where he belongs, in
a situation roughly equivalent to that of Lovewit, but more broadly
exemplary.

The trouble with Winwife, according to Quarlous, is that he goes
nosing after old women, a procedure comparable to Busy's impure
scenting after the sacrificial roast pig, the comic symbol of renewed
life and fertility, whose sustaining virtues the rabbi explicitly denies. The honest instrument of procreation has not dwelt in Winwife's women for forty years, and Winwife wastes the brand of

life in such a course, "raking himselfe a fortune in an old womans embers." (I, iii, 78–79.) And if he should marry Dame Purecraft, he will be beset by Puritans; even his son-in-law, Littlewit, might drone out a dry grace until all the meat on the board is cold, while the good laborers and painful eaters noise about a question in predestination.

After Quarlous' harangue on infertility and its folly, attention is redirected to Zeal-of-the-Land Busy, who is the antithesis of fertility. He had been a baker once, but he gave up the trade,

> out of a scruple hee tooke, that (in spic'd conscience) those Cakes hee made, were seru'd to *Bridales, May-poles, Morrisses,* and such prophane feasts and meetings; his Christen-name is *Zeale-of-the-land.* (I, iii, 121–24.)

This kind of zeal is the opposite of life, and Zeal-of-the-Land will not have his cakes served to profane feasts and meetings, particularly if one of them has the very symbol of Dionysus standing at its center. Furthermore, he

> derides all *Antiquity;* defies any other *Learning,* then *Inspiration;* and what discretion soeuer, yeeres should afford him, it is all preuented in his *Originall ignorance.* (I, iii, 143–46.)

Denial of the value of antiquity and learning seems to be associated with infertility, and in this context original ignorance becomes a kind of original sin. Rabbi Busy's love of ignorance anticipates Humphrey Wasp's scorn of books, reading, and learning, which reaches its apotheosis in the game of vapors, the negation of everything. Wasp comes for his charge's license, and Littlewit offers to read it to him, a favor Wasp rejects:

> That's well, nay, neuer open, or read it to me, it's labour in vaine, you know. I am no Clearke, I scorne to be sau'd by my booke, i' faith I'll hang first. (I, iv, 6–8.)

When Wasp asks the price, Littlewit asserts that he knows it already:

> I know? I know nothing, I, what tell you mee of knowing? (now I am in hast) Sir, I do not know, and I will not know, and I scorne to know, and yet, (now I think on't) I will, and do know, as well as another; you must haue a *Marke* for your thing here, and *eight pence* for the boxe; I could ha' sau'd *two pence* i' that, an' I had brought it my selfe, but heere's *fourteene shillings* for you. Good Lord! how long your little wife staies! pray God, *Salomon,* your Clerke, be not looking i' the wrong boxe, Mr. *Proctor.* (I, iv, 19–28.)

Lack of knowledge, associated with infertility in Littlewit and Busy, is wilful and hence sinful.

As soon as Wasp remembers, after his attack of wilful ignorance —anticipating Troubleall's epistemological question—that he really does know the price, the fertility theme reappears, appropriately— for Wasp—in the form of a scurrilously obscene jest. But Wasp, who insists on hating everything and knowing nothing, is one of the archetypes of barrenness: his favorite abusive phrase, to put it too solemnly, substitutes excrement for sustenance. When the idea of fertility appears in Wasp's language, it does so in a curiously perverted form—images of copulation without generation. Thus Wasp speaks of his exasperating charge:

> If he goe to the *Fayre,* he will buy euery thing, to a Baby there; and houshold-stuffe for that too. If a legge or an arme on him did not grow on, hee would lose it i' the presse. Pray heauen I bring him off with one stone! And then he is such a Rauener after fruite! you will not beleeue what a coyle I had, t'other day, to compound a businesse betweene a *Katerne*-peare-woman, and him, about snatching! 'tis intolerable, Gentlemen. (I, v, 113–20.)

Bartholomew's marriage has been seen by Wasp almost strictly in terms of the price of the license and the box (with, no doubt, an obscene *double-entendre*); Cokes will buy a baby (a doll, but the equivocal word is significant); and his almost non-existent sexuality, implicit in the physical description Wasp gives, is implied again in the business about snatching symbolic pears, an event acted out in the Fair when Cokes is systematically stripped of all his external trappings by Edgeworth and Nightingale—as Hermes, on the symbolic level, takes first his money, then his clothes, in the process of extracting his perfect quintessence. When he finally appears as chorus in Littlewit's puppet-play, he has been stripped of money, clothes, and Grace and is thus the most perfect commentator on the most sublimely imperfect of plays.

Quarlous also, once he is inside the Fair, is presented as almost the antithesis of fertility, when Ursula delivers the paralyzing insult: "You were engendred on a she-begger, in a barne, when the bald Thrasher, your Sire, was scarce warme." (II, v, 136–37.) The bald thrasher, scarce warm, is a perfect inversion of the fertility theme.

The Puritans would like to go to the Fair, but their compulsive rejection of life requires the invention of a convincing rationale, part of which has already been supplied by Win, with her "naturall disease of women; call'd A longing to eate Pigge." (I, vi, 41–42.) This supplies Dame Purecraft's acceptable rationale for what she pretended to take originally as the work of the wicked tempter. Zeal-of-the-Land has been called away from his cold turkey pie, white loaf, and glass of Malmsey, and being still hungry, justifies the expedition. Pig may be eaten with a reformed mouth, in sobriety, and humbleness; and, now that he thinks of it, it might be a good way of showing, by the public eating of swine's flesh, the brethren's hatred and loathing of Judaism. On this enlightening note they leave for the Fair.

Bartholomew Fair has an extended *protasis,* which makes up the first two acts. The first exhibits the citizens who will go to the Fair; the second exhibits the denizens of the Fair itself and shows the first engagements of the outsiders with the insiders, of the unbelievers with their destined gods. At the beginning of the third act the first violation of the shrine has occurred, but Whit, Haggis, and Bristle are too late to apprehend the desecraters, although Justice Overdo has received his first salutary chastisement.

The Fair as play is identified when Quarlous laments having missed the prologue of the purse but consoles himself with the thought that they will have five acts of Cokes ere night. (III, ii, 1–3.) The ritual nature of the Fair is again suggested when Busy urges his party not to look at the idols:

> Look not toward them, harken not: the place is *Smithfield,* or the field of Smiths, the Groue of Hobbi-horses and trinkets, the wares are the wares of diuels. And the whole *Fayre* is the shop of *Satan!* They are hooks, and baites, very baites, that are hung out on euery side, to catch you, and to hold you as it were, by the gills; and by the nostrills, as the Fisher doth: therefore, you must not looke, nor turne toward them—The Heathen man could stop his eares with wax, against the harlot o' the sea: Doe you the like, with your fingers, against the bells of the Beast. (III, ii, 39–48.)

The religious and mythological elements are expanded. The place is called, quite incorrectly, the field of smiths, appropriate enough as the designation for the world where Captain Whit the pimp is a comic Ares and Punk Alice a degenerate Aphrodite. In fact, the name Smithfield is a corruption of smooth-field. Busy's ignorance of this leads him away from the green pastoral world of Demeter, Dionysus, fertility, and art, to a field of smiths. The trinkets become degenerate icons, hooks in the hands of a spurious Fisher who is no longer a King but an object in deliberately debased comic pastoral. Odysseus has become merely the heathen man, and the siren the harlot of the sea. On every level, Zeal-of-the-Land Busy calls attention to the point by missing it.

The Fair has been identified as ritual and as drama. The existence of the ritual and the vastness of its peculiar scope are emphasized again and again, several times in the scene with which we are here concerned. Knockem invites the travelers to stop: "Take a sweet delicate Booth, with boughs, here, i' the way, and coole your selues i' the shade: you and your friends." (57–59.) This is Ursula's wayside shrine for the pilgrim, and it suggests the smooth field which has become a field of smiths. Win's glass will be washed with the water of Dame Annis Clare (66), the well so named from the rich widow who married the riotous courtier and, when he had consumed her wealth and deserted her, drowned herself in the stream which then became a well or spring.[4] This is an unparalleled example of the way Jonson has joined the realistic, legendary, and mythological elements in this beautiful play. Whit pronounces the name Cleare, suggesting a further metaphorical extension. Win's chalice will be appropriately purified in water sacred to the citizen-saint who is further linked with Arethusa and/ or Echo, although the water of Dame Annis Clare may also suggest something more realistic. And Whit has specified a delicate sow-pig, "with shweet sauce, and crackling, like de bay-leafe i' de fire, la!" (III, ii, 63–64.) The assumption of ritual implications again seems justified when Knockem calls Ursula's sign "The Oracle of the Pigs head." (71.)

Ursula, however, has no confidence that the newcomers are qualified to participate in her sacred rites. Knockem asks "what aile they *Vrs?*" and she replies

> Aile they? They are all sippers, sippers o' the City, they looke as they would not drinke off two penn-'orth of bottle-ale amongst 'hem. (III, ii, 110–13.)

Adam Overdo is more than a confused onlooker searching for enormities. In overdoing his function as Justice he is also overlooking his own nature, Adam flesh and blood. He reflects, in III, iii, on the cause of his beating:

---

[4] Herford and Simpson, Vol. VIII, 196.

To see what bad euents may peepe out o' the taile of good purposes!
the care I had of that ciuil yong man, I tooke a fancy to this morning, (and haue not left it yet) drew me to that exhortation, which
drew the company, indeede, which drew the cut-purse; which drew
the money; which drew my brother *Cokes* his losse; which drew on
Wasp's anger; which drew on my beating: a pretty gradation!
(13–20.)

In view of the extreme good nature displayed by this latter and
enormously enlarged version of Justice Clement, it is important
to recognize that he does not see Edgeworth-Hermes as a cutpurse, and that he disapproves of the singing of Nightingale-Her-
mes. The composite figure, if we may view him as such, is a civil
young man addicted to the bad habit of singing. With the best
intentions in the world, Adam Overdo draws the wrong conclusions from almost everything he sees, a fact directly related to his
fondness for quoting the poets for their moral maxims while at
the same time professing something like an abhorrence of poetry.
It seems singularly appropriate that as a wise justice of the peace
he should be under the influence of Hermes, here god of a very
special kind of thieves, a unique cutpurse whose special function
is to be instrumental in the laying bare of Coke's folly.

It is interesting that Hermes, god of thieves and inventor of the
lyre, should be influential in the stripping of Cokes and the enlightening of Overdo, particularly if, as seems possible, Overdo,
with his amusing strictures against tobacco, glances jestingly at
James, and Cokes glances not so jestingly at the Chief Justice of
the King's Bench, James's mortal enemy who, two years after the
play was written, was to be removed from his post. The scope of
the play seems quite large enough to admit this peripheral reading
as a possibility. Other aspects of Overdo's character, not entirely
germane to the present discussion, may also point to a necessarily
limited identification of Overdo with James—his conscious but en-

tertainingly misguided morality, his sententiousness, his rather ambiguous love of learning. If such an identification is to be made, it is naturally of secondary importance, but it is probably there.

In III, v, Quarlous and Winwife, already impressed by the apparent dignity and reserve of Grace Wellborn, begin their attempt to separate her from her foolish fiancé. In view of the outcome of this attempt—her marriage to Winwife as the lover Palemon, on the say-so of Troubleall the madman—one should remember Quarlous' observations about Winwife's wife-seeking and consider Grace's relationship to the Fair as symbol. She hadn't wanted to go there in the first place—she absolutely, not hypocritically, had not wanted to go there—because "there's none goes thither of any quality or fashion." (I, v, 131–32.) Busy at least had *wanted* to go there, even if he had to find a plausible excuse in view of the brethren's strictures.

But Grace Wellborn is authentically hostile to everything she sees in the Fair, and in order to escape an intolerable legal restriction is quite willing to accept the whim of a madman as the infallible guide in the choice of a husband. Her relationship to her guardian is quite technical: she is his ward as the result of an old and no doubt unjust law. Since she is not his daughter, she is not part of Adam's flesh and blood and not susceptible of instruction, change, or reformation in the Fair. She is part of the half-foolish, half-mad world eternally at odds with everything the Fair represents, and as such she is joined in marriage with someone who has been castigated for nosing after old women and wasting the brand of life raking for a fortune in their embers.

As the *epitasis* reaches its height, Busy is zealously tearing down idols, with the result that he will be martyred in the stocks, the standard punishment for those who desecrate idols or violate shrines in Bartholomew Fair.

I was mou'd in spirit, to bee here, this day, in this *Faire,* this wicked, and foule *Faire;* and fitter may it be called a foule, then a *Faire*: To protest against the abuses of it, the foule abuses of it, in regard of the afflicted Saints, that are troubled, very much troubled, exceedingly troubled, with the opening of the merchandize of *Babylon* againe, & the peeping of *Popery* vpon the stals, here, here, in the high places. See you not *Goldylocks,* the purple strumpet, there? in her yellow gowne, and greene sleeues? the prophane pipes, the tinckling timbrells? A shop of reliques! (III, vi, 86–96.)

Greensleeves and Goldilocks, Babylon and Popery, music and relics—in more ways than one an abhorrent combination in the Puritan mind. If green was a color affected by whores, it is also the color of spring, of fertility; Goldilocks appears gorgeously arrayed; Greensleeves was a lovely popular tune of the age; the Whore of Babylon was perhaps not quite so wicked as Busy thought; and music and relics are not necessarily inconsistent with piety. Busy's piety is thus directed against everything that the Fair metamorphorically represents, although by the end of the play he approves of one important aspect of the Fair, imported from outside.

The Fair as worship of Demeter is vividly recalled almost immediately. As Leatherhead-Dionysus has the officers drag Busy off to the stocks for his supererogatory busyness, Win must re-enact the secret rites before continuing her exploration of the Fair: "I haue very great, what sha'call'um, *Iohn.*" (III, vi, 125–26.) John himself implies Win's connection with the Fair as ritual:

O! Is that all, Win? wee'll goe backe to Captaine *Iordan;* to the pigwomans, *Win,* hee'll helpe vs, or she with a dripping pan, or an old kettle, or something. The poore greasie soul loues you, *Win,* and after we'll visit the *Fayre* all ouer, *Win,* and see my Puppet play, *Win,* you know it's a fine matter, *Win.* (III, vi, 127–32.)

Many of the comic symbolic implications of the third act will be presented in what might be called the metaphorical-realistic action and language of the fourth act. It is apparent that this is not a bilevel, but a multilevel play. The first act is, on the whole, realistic comedy, with a number of details preparing us for the elaborate ritual of symbolism introduced in Act II. Acts II and III carry a realistic action, at every point reinforced by an extraordinarily rich symbolism relating the fair and its inhabitants to the engendering and sustaining of life.

Once these matters have been established, Act IV poses the epistemological question, and it is asked not by a metaphorical madman like Adam Overdo, but a real one, Troubleall. Naturally enough, his name is symbolic, because he asks the question that comedy asks: what warrant (*i.e.,* what reason) do you have for what you're doing? The fact that Troubleall the madman asks the question, a crucially important one, provides an excellent example of the intellectual and artistic complexity of *Bartholomew Fair*. Act IV, therefore, is not so much a return to the realistic as an extension, in terms of comic social reality, of the symbolic implications of Acts II and III, and it is introduced by Troubleall's question.

Troubleall is the dominant thematic figure of Act IV. He challenges Bristle and Haggis, Dame Purecraft, Edgeworth and Nightingale, Quarlous and Winwife, and finally Knockem. A comprehensive pattern of folly has been established in the first three acts, and it is now time to ask the questions, always in the name of Justice Overdo; for Troubleall the only satisfactory answer comes from Knockem, one of the symbolic figures of the Fair, who simply writes Justice Overdo's name on a warrant and gives it to the madman, thus satisfying him. This may indicate that Troubleall will be satisfied with a mere name; or it may suggest that, in spite of his search for enormities, the Fair, in effect, has Justice Overdo's warrant after all. If he is finally Adam flesh and blood, he will become reconciled with the Fair in which he receives his education. In this case, the epistemological question will become also an ethical one and very nearly a religious one: "Do you have Adam's warrant?"

Troubleall is revealingly introduced in an elaborately amusing scene. Justice Overdo has been put in the stocks and the madman is demanding the officers' warrant for their action. And while Overdo is confined, Bristle explains Troubleall's identity to Haggis, while the Justice listens with amazement and remorse, unaware of the irony of his own situation or of the watch's—who have put him in the stocks without Justice Overdo's warrant.

In the upside-down comic world it is proper enough that the important question is asked by a madman, but the perspective in *Bartholomew Fair* is not that simple. As Justice Overdo says, Troubleall is ". . . out of his wits! where there is no roome left for dissembling." (IV, i, 65–66.) Justice Overdo, disguised as mad Arthur of Bradley, is deficient in his wits, not out of them—in comic terms he is a fool. But Troubleall is quite out of his, can no longer dissemble, and can thus ask, with no verbal ornament whatever, why are you doing that? His name indicates not only his nuisance value to the people he accosts but also the troublesome nature of the epistemological question, which forces men to examine their motives, something that most men, for good reasons, would rather not do.

There is nothing sentimental about Troubleall—he is not the tragic or the tragicomic madman who is symbolically sane; he is mad, his madness is explained, and its manifestation is comically consistent with its cause. This seems to imply that the question should not be considered too curiously, certainly not in the play itself. The more specific the answer, the less comic the play. Troubleall flits about the Fair asking a question which, since he is mad, no one feels obligated to answer. The question hovers over the Fair, but the responsibility for answering it lies not with the characters but with the audience. Strictly speaking, the question is idle in the purely realistic context, and therefore properly asked by a madman.

No one, after all, needs a judge's warrant for *everything* he does.

Yet the question, otiose in its realistic comic context, has relevance for an audience because the audience at a comedy must ultimately share the point of view of the author, not that of characters in the play. In addition to asking the comic question, Troubleall comes startlingly close to giving a non-comic answer, and I think it would have been noncomic and intrusive in the two preceding comedies.

But *Bartholomew Fair* is something new, and Troubleall tells Dame Purecraft that if she doesn't have the warrant, she must keep her work and he'll keep his. "Quit yee, and multiply yee." (IV, i, 111–13.) She has a warrant out of the word, but his word is Justice Overdo's warrant. And a few lines later he tells Edgeworth "an' you haue no warrant, blesse you, I'le pray for you, that's all I can doe." (IV, ii, 5–6.) Later in the same scene he tells Cokes that "Iustice *Ouerdo's* warrant, a man may get, and lose with, I'le stand to't." (IV, ii 90–91.) When Quarlous and Winwife write their literary names in the notebook, Troubleall immediately appears and asks "Haue you any warrant for this, Gentlemen?" (IV, iii, 71.) When he chooses a name, he tells Grace it is "to saue your longing, (and multiply him)." (IV, iii, 95.) And it is Troubleall who is finally responsible for releasing Overdo and Busy from the stocks, because Haggis and Bristle had no warrant for confining them there in the first place.

The implications of all this seem to be that one ought to have a warrant, in the general intellectual sense, but that if he doesn't he should be forgiven anyhow and allowed to multiply his kind. But Jonson is hardly a sentimentalist, and while he recognizes the impossibility of actually reforming mankind—or at least the improbability of effecting such reforms via the comic stage—he is not going to ignore the importance of showing the deplorable results of lacking a warrant. Therefore, after Troubleall has made his point, the scene moves back to Ursula's booth and the game of vapors, for which there is only a madman's warrant.

Vapors, according to the author, is the epitome of nothing—nonsense, every man to oppose the last man that spoke, whether it concerned him or no. The only warrant anyone has in the game of vapors is the warrant of his own insensible will. Whit observes that Wasp must like nothing upon reason, and Wasp makes the appropriate retort:

> I haue no reason, nor I will heare of no reason, nor I will looke for no reason, and he is an Asse, that either knowes any, or lookes for't from me. (IV, iv, 42–44.)

Vapors epitomizes the comic society satirized in the play, and as the chief vaporizer, as it were, Humphrey Wasp is committed to the stocks, an event that leads directly to his comic reform. If an ass looks for reason in Humphrey Wasp, he will ultimately find it, however ironically presented.

Vapors is a nebulous term. Its meaning is specific enough as applied to the game, where Jonson has defined it. But it is also one of Knockem's favorite expressions. When the game is over, Dame Overdo is initiated by the bawd Whit into the sacred mysteries, with the result that she is beaten by Punk Alice, who regards the lady as a professional rival. Knockem then persuades Win to take up the career of a lady of pleasure. "Hide, and be hidden; ride, and be ridden, sayes the vapour of experience." (IV, v. 102–103.) "By what warrant do's it say so?" asks Troubleall (IV, vi, 1), implying that a vapor is an error demanding an answer, although, being an error, it is baseless. A vapor thus becomes symbolic of the multiplicity of error inherent in the Fair, and may possibly have its origin in Aristophanes' *The Clouds,* where the choric clouds seem to represent the always changing, ever challenging comic spirit.

It is characteristic of Jonson, and important to the symbolic argument of the play, that the tempting of Alice Overdo and Win-the-Fight Littlewit by Whit and Knockem at the instigation of Ursula should be effected without a leer. Restoration comedy prided itself on its refinement of manners, and with Congreve, whom the age finally rejected, it did so with considerable justice. But how would even such a great writer as John Dryden have handled this sort of scene? (Shadwell or Aphra Behn we should not even think about.)

Before being prepared for her part in the fertility rites, Mistress Overdo must retire to Ursula's bower, where she is immediately set upon by Alice the whore, which shows, of course, that the two ladies are very different from each other. Whit and the others get her drunk, again part of Ursula's communion, which now becomes almost Dionysian. Knockem prepares for the introduction of Win into the very heart of the life of the Fair with one of the most remarkable and amusing speeches in the play:

> I conceiue thee, *Vrs!* goe thy waies, doest thou heare, *Whit?* is't not pitty, my delicate darke chestnut here, with the fine leane head, large fore-head, round eyes, euen mouth, sharpe eares, long necke, thinne crest, close withers, plaine backe, deepe sides, short fillets, and full flankes: with a round belly, a plumpe buttocke, large thighes, knit knees, streight legges, short pasternes, smooth hoofes, and short heeles; should lead a dull honest womans life, that might liue the life of a Lady? (IV, v, 20–28.)

It is indeed. Win is in danger of being engulfed in the Fair, something desirable on the Fair's terms, but immoral on society's. Win's prostitution will be a kind of debased fertility ritual which is prevented only when she is unmasked by Adam Overdo as he sets out to expose enormities. This statement is a gross oversimplification of something merely implicit in the situation. And Win is not setting out confidently and wickedly to become a whore:

Knockem's vapors of experience have convinced her, and she admits that in her past virtuous life she has been a fool.

Everyone indeed has been a fool except the inhabitants of the Fair, and they have all been rogues. But, as I have tried to show, the fools and rogues are all of rather special kinds, the symbolic overtones of which have been imposed by the nature of the Fair itself. As the action moves to Leatherhead's puppet tent, there is a hint of a return to reality, although it is still a reality shaped by the nature of the Fair.

Wasp enters the tent looking for his charge and finds him in doublet and hose, the rest of his clothing having been stolen. He asks Cokes if he is employed by the puppet company, to which Cokes replies, "Hold your peace, *Numpes;* you ha' beene i' the Stocks, I heare." Wasp is shattered:

> Do's he know that? nay, then the date of my *Authority* is out; I must thinke no longer to raigne, my gouernment is at an end. He that will correct another, must want fault in himselfe. (V, iv, 95–100.)

Wasp's reaction here anticipates that of Overdo in the closing scene, but in view of Wasp's character as it has been presented throughout the play, it would be a mistake to regard this descent into sententiousness as a real return to normality. His statement is true enough, but coming from him it is absurd.

The irony of his situation is revealed almost immediately as Cokes invites him to sit down and offers to interpret the puppet play for him. (109–10.) Cokes, having lost his money, his clothes, and Mistress Grace, has been reduced symbolically to a state of comic innocence, and now the same thing happens to his testy governor. In a different context this would be a tragicomic resolution, but these are authentically ridiculous comic characters sitting down to watch a highly unusual puppet show which does in the Fair what the play does in the Hope—reduces a classical theme to ludicrous absurdity.

The nature of the show and part of its function have been suggested in the preceding scene. The story of Hero and Leander, to be acted by puppets that Cokes regards as simply small actors, will be made palatable and understandable to the multitude: "What doe they know what *Hellespont* is? Guilty of true loues blood? or what *Abidos* is? or the other *Sestos* hight?" "Th'art i' the right," Cokes replies, "I do not know my selfe." (V, iii, 110–14.) As the play is about to begin, the ladies enter escorted by their would-be bawds, Mistress Overdo very drunk and sick.

The puppet show represents Jonson's commentary on popular taste. The fertility and infertility themes appear once more, now in the most excruciatingly obscene forms, and Cokes, as chorus, comments brilliantly. As the puppets Damon and Pythias quite improperly enter the scene and misbehave scandalously, the ghost of the tyrant Dionysius rises from his grave, having discovered the enormity, and, appearing as a schoolmaster, chides Damon and Pythias for calling amorous Leander whore-master knave. As Busy appears to destroy more idols, Dionysius quickly becomes Leatherhead's spokesman.

The scene in the puppet-tent is a superb example of Jonson's skill as well as of his energy. The Hero and Leander story, with its theme of illicit love, glances at a particular symbolic function of the Fair, and the intrusion of Damon and Pythias is suggestive of the roles of Winwife and Quarlous. Dionysius reflects a diminutive version of Justice Overdo. And the scene imagined for the show is appropriate to the scene of the Fair—the Thames, Puddle-wharf, the Bankside, etc., near the location of the Hope theater. As Demeter becomes an overweight bawd in the pig-booth, so Dionysius, now Dionysus, becomes an irate puppet in Leatherhead's tent, successfully defending his domain of the drama against the attack of an unbeliever.

It is tempting to regard the confuting of Busy by the puppet

Dionysius as a rather bitter comment on Jonson's part: the drama has sunk to this low state and its most violent critics are confuted by people no more learned or intelligent than they. I am inclined to think, however, that he is simply reducing the controversy to the purest absurdity—the puppet's proof that the males do not wear female clothes and vice versa is certainly one of the funniest details in the play. Furthermore, if this were simply a bitter comment on the state of the drama, it would be inconsistent with the tone of the rest of the play, and would hardly allow for the significant reduction of Adam Overdo to Adam flesh and blood, which also occurs in the puppet tent.

Throughout the closing scenes the situation is fraught with artistic danger which the poet overcomes with customary brilliance. In this connection C. H. Herford made a very perceptive statement. "The art which conceals art was a difficult gospel for the most masterful and self-conscious of artists to practise; but for once he approaches it."[5] It is only when the student of Jonson attempts to unravel the complexity of the closing scenes that he realizes that the situation is hovering on the verge of sentimental comedy or tragicomedy. There is nothing wrong with tragicomedy, except that here it would be imposing itself on a comic play.

Yet, as I have long suspected, Jonson knew what he was doing. Justice Overdo, Adam flesh and blood, must be brought back to reality and reconciled with his wife, now an incipient whore. The discoverer and chastiser of enormities must be brought to a realization that what he calls enormities are what other people call life and that Adam overdoes his responsibilities if, like Pertinax Surly or Humphrey Wasp or Volpone, he sets out to do what is really beyond his purview. But in *Bartholomew Fair* the argument is far more humane. Though all four of these characters are guilty of self-deception, to be sure, Adam Overdo would really like to do

[5] Herford and Simpson, Vol. II, 137.

the right thing, which cannot be said for Volpone or Surly. Volpone had argued that *"to bee a foole borne, is a disease incurable."* (II, ii, 159.) There is no reason to think that at the time Jonson disagreed with this view.

But here the argument seems to be that folly is not necessarily an incurable disease, that when Adam recognizes his wife and is told the truth about Edgeworth the more egregious aspects of his folly may be corrected. Rather surprisingly, patience is the quality which seems to imply the possibility of redemption, although Overdo is hardly to be compared with Dekker's patient Candido.

How does Jonson avoid sentimentality while still suggesting the potential redemption of Justice Overdo? First, he has Adam set himself up as a "Mirror of Magistrates," a "scourge of enormity," a Hercules, Columbus, or Magellan, discovering outrage, a Drake, the terror of Smithfield, the wonder of London.

> Now, to my enormities: looke vpon mee, O *London!* and see mee, O *Smithfield;* The *example of Iustice,* and *Mirror of Magistrates*: the true top of formality, and scourge of enormity. Harken vnto my *labours,* and but obserue my *discoueries;* and compare *Hercules* with me, if thou dar'st, of old; or *Columbus; Magellan;* or our countrey man *Drake* of later times: stand forth, you weedes of enormity, and spread. (V, vi, 33–40.)

The technique is familiar, but Jonson had never used it so successfully: the more the balloon is inflated, the more resounding will be the explosion. Suddenly Mrs. Overdo calls simultaneously for a basin and her Adam. No more earthy way of bringing Adam back to earth is conceivable. Tending a drunken and sick wife is a very convincing way of getting back to reality, but Jonson tops this off with a stunningly effective piece of equivocal bathos: "Will not my *Adam* come at mee? shall I see him no more then?" (71–72.) Adam can only say, "How?"—an exclamation echoed by Wasp when his attention is called to the missing license. Most significantly, the final thrusts are delivered by Quarlous, perhaps the least moral person in the play, since he has cheated Grace and Dame Purecraft both, and both for money. But it is Quarlous who delivers the final verbal chastisement:

> . . . nay, Sir, stand not you fixt here, like a stake in *Finsbury* to be shot at, or the whipping post i' the *Fayre,* but get your wife out o' the ayre, it wil make her worse else; and remember you are but *Adam,* Flesh, and blood! you haue your frailty, forget your other name of *Ouerdoo,* and inuite vs all to supper. There you and I will compare our *discoueries;* and drowne the memory of all enormity in your bigg'st bowle at home. (V, vi, 93–100.)

It is almost as though Surly had finally emerged triumphant, not only over Face and Subtle, but over Lovewit as well. Yet Quarlous is clearly the right choice as the agent of correction for Adam Overdo, because Quarlous, in his rude and ironic way, welcomes Adam and his frailty back to the human race, which, after all, comprehends all the characters in *Bartholomew Fair.*

The richness and humanity of Jonson's argument becomes most clear at the very end of the play: Adam has, it seems, not been completely deflated. He begins to swell slightly but ominously.

> I inuite you home, with mee to my house, to supper: I will haue none feare to go along, for my intents are *Ad correctionem, non ad destructionem; Ad aedificandum, non ad diruendum*: so lead on.
>
> (110–13.)

But Cokes is ready: "Yes, and bring the *Actors* along, wee'll ha' the rest o' the *Play* at home." In case Overdo forgets the lessons of the day, the puppets will be present to remind him of where and how he once learned humility and rejoined the human race.

THE DEVIL IS AN ASS

The last four comedies, beginning with *The Devil is an Ass,* may be regarded as Jonson's dotages, as they have been by most critics, if a man forty-three years old can properly be said to be on the verge of senility. Dryden apparently used the term first, although whether he intended it to include this play is at least debatable, and whether he had carefully read any of the later comedies is even more debatable. Other critics *have* read them, however, and most of them seem to agree that dotages is what they are. Mrs. Townsend attempted to resurrect them;[1] John Palmer had some equivocal praise;[2] Knights has great praise for the present play and for *The Staple of News,* but not much for the other two in the group;[3] Enck agrees with a vengeance that dotage is the word;[4] while Partridge has quite sensibly gone ahead and examined the plays without undue concern for the almost universal strictures.[5] How radical a departure this is from the customary procedure will be apparent to anyone reasonably familiar with Jonson criticism; how valid an approach it is will be apparent to everyone who has read Mr. Partridge's admirable book.[6]

In some of the earlier plays it has been possible to discern two groups of characters—those whose realistic presentation carries a symbolic value, and those whom we might describe as more or less purely realistic. Thus Volpone and Mosca as opposed to Voltore, Corvino, and Corbaccio; Face and Subtle as opposed to their victims; Dauphine, Truewit, and Clerimont in contrast to the gulls; and earlier, and on various levels, the controlling figures of Brainworm, Asper, Macilente, Carlo Buffone. That is to say, there has

---

[1] *Apologie for Bartholmew Fayre,* 87–88.

[2] *Ben Jonson,* 279 ff.

[3] *Drama and Society,* 210 ff.

[4] *Jonson and the Comic Truth,* 209 ff.

[5] *The Broken Compass,* 178 ff.

[6] R. J. Kaufmann does not deal with *The Devil is an Ass* but rejects the term "dotage" for *The Staple of News* and *The Magnetic Lady.* (*Richard Brome, Caroline Playwright,* 44.)

been one group of characters that we might describe as poet-figures, set up in opposition to another group of characters whose quintessence they expose.

In reviewing this particular point, I wish to insist that the poet-figures are also realistic figures and that their symbolic identity does not "make" any particular play but enriches the satirical comedy in which they appear. For example, I am not aware that any previous critic has insisted that Subtle must be regarded as a symbolic figure for the comic artist or that alchemy represents comic art. That Subtle is such a figure and that alchemy does have such a significance seems to me undeniable. Virtually all critics have agreed that *The Alchemist* is a thoroughly masterful play, even without recognizing just how masterful it actually is.

The symbolic argument, therefore, while it is not precisely essential to a lively appreciation of the play, is there, and once understood, it adds immeasurably to one's appreciation of Jonson's art. *Bartholomew Fair* is another case in point. Almost everyone agrees it is a masterpiece, but certainly one's apprehension of this fact is enhanced greatly by the recognition of the tremendously humane attitude toward human life and human nature which results from a consideration of the symbolic and metaphorical values of the Fair and its inhabitants and of the experiences of Adam Overdo.

The point I wish to make here is that in the plays just mentioned the realistic and symbolic qualities of the symbolic characters must be separated by the critic: the qualities have been perfectly joined by the artist. It seems to me altogether desirable that the critic should recognize these facts while at the same time he understands that the characters are coherent and unified, not artistically schizophrenic figures who represent now one thing, now another.

In the two years intervening between *Bartholomew Fair* and *The Devil is an Ass* Jonson altered his technique, probably through the influence of his own career as a writer of masques and through the influence of his extensive reading in English drama, including the morality play. I have suggested, in connection with *Bartholomew Fair,* that Jonson deliberately put himself in danger of producing a sentimental denouement and that he avoided the danger by forcing Justice Overdo to retain his ridiculous as well as his reformed qualities. In *The Devil is an Ass* he goes even further and produces one character, Mistress Fitzdottrell, who is only equivocally a comic character, although I can not see that she is out of place in what is obviously a comic play.

Wittipoll and Manly also have distinctly noncomic aspects, but again they are subsumed in a comic context, and again they are made to behave with just sufficient absurdity not to break the comic tone. Wittipoll's genuine reform occurs when, like Pertinax Surly, he is wearing a Spanish costume—an even more ludicrous one than Surly's, since Wittipoll is disguised as a lady, "The Infanta of the giants." And Wittipoll's reform leads to the exposing of the folly of Fitzdottrell and Sir Paul Eitherside, who though deflated are scarcely redeemed. In effecting, within the comic context, the regeneration of Wittipoll, Jonson has undertaken an artistic problem of the very greatest difficulty—moral change without tragicomedy. Again, tragicomedy is all very well, except when it is imposed on a comic action.

There are other significant differences between the patterning of characters in the later plays and the process as it occurs in the earlier ones. One generalization particularly should be made here: in the later plays the experiences of the symbolic characters offer an ideal of order and sanity which is lacking in the experiences of the other characters. When the symbolic characters are set on their true and proper courses, the social chaos implicit in the other characters can be brought ideally under control.

When Wittipoll abandons his courtly-adulterous pursuit of Mistress Fitzdottrell, the rogues and gulls can be at least implicitly corrected; the reform of Penniboy Junior in *The Staple of News* implies the reform of a money-mad society; in *The New Inn,* the perceptions gained by Lovell and Lady Frampul imply the reform of the fake Platonism and hence of the corruption of the court of Charles and Henrietta Maria and of the society of which the head is represented for Jonson by the court; and in the two marriages at the end of *The Magnetic Lady* the ethical function of comedy is implied, with the great Aristophanic and Jonsonian ideal that comedy is pre-eminently qualified to reform society at large.

In *The Devil is an Ass* the purely comic characters—Merecraft, Traines, Ambler, Guilthead, Plutarchus, Sir Paul Eitherside, Lady Tailbush, etc.—are, as usual, reflections in the steel glass of satire, while the symbolic characters are more complex. The chief of them, Wittipoll, is also a comic character, but he finally achieves the status, very unusual in Jonson until now, of something like a sane moral norm. The comic characters represent the society which Jonson customarily satirizes; the symbolic characters represent the idealistic answer to the follies and excesses of that society, while at the same time they remain members of that society.

The groundwork for this pattern, it seems to me, had already been laid when Jonson devised the antimasque, which for the masque is what the satirical passages are for the last plays. The masque-antimasque pattern now reappears in a new form in those plays which involve comic satire and elaborate symbolism. The solutions he offers for the follies, vices, and chaos of the world are thoroughly idealistic. In the earlier plays he trenchantly satirized contemporary society. Now he shows how to make society, and hence life, better, by following out the careers of certain characters to an idealized resolution.

The Devil is an Ass was first performed in 1616 and was written perhaps a year or two earlier. The play ostensibly concerns the adventures of a minor devil, Pug, during a day's sojourn on earth, his purpose being to introduce new corruption into the affairs of men and thus gain new and greater triumphs for hell, as well as glory for himself. His "chief" has serious reservations about Pug's ability to perform his self-appointed task and fulfil his ambitions, reservations borne out by the fact that Pug turns out to be some-what less perceptive than Dapper, although more engaging and equally amusing. Indeed, the speech in which Pug attempts to seduces Mistress Fitzdottrell is one of the funniest in the play:

> Deare delicate Mistresse, I am your slaue,
> Your little *worme*, that loues you: your fine *Monkey;*
> Your *Dogge*, your *Iacke*, your *Pug*, that longs to be
> Still'd, o' your pleasures. (II, ii, 126–29.)

Note, in "Your little worme," the wonderful comic parody of the temptation. His wooing is so inept that his mistress can only assume that he has been put up to it by her husband. Predictably, Pug is defeated at every turn, and finds that hell has nothing to compare with the iniquities which he finds on earth. Observing the malicious, scandal-mongering collegiate ladies, he makes his anguished observation: "You talke of a *Vniuersity!* why, *Hell* is/ A Grammar-schoole to this!" (IV, iv, 170–71.) Toward the end of the play, Pug, languishing in jail for theft, is carried off to hell again by the great devil and Iniquity, leaving a terrifying stench of brimstone in the jail, a fact that brings the idiotic Fitzdottrell partly back to his senses.

Since Jonson could have made a perfectly acceptable, if some-what different, play without the devil-plot, its significance should be examined. In the parody of the morality play at the opening, Jonson seems to be bringing the genre up to date and suggesting that its morality was scarcely satisfactory or ethically sufficient in a society whose members include Merecraft, Trains, Everill, Fitz-dottrell, and Lady Tailbush. Pug's adventures on earth provide a kind of frame for the major action, a manageable point of reference and a constant implied commentary, so that Pug is a morality play devil, who very amusingly and appropriately becomes Master De Vile in Lady Tailbush's house, hopelessly defeated by the evils rampant in the world of men. With marvelous irony he is arrested for stealing Ambler's clothes while Ambler was committing more or less public fornication with a wench, under a conduit near Tyburn, just before the execution of the cutpurse whose body Pug is now inhabiting.

Pug, whose misadventures on earth provide the comic perspective through which the play is to be viewed, is a kind of comic Everyman—an Everydevil who, terrified by an earthly hell, is redeemed to *his* hellish heaven. This is expertly handled in terms of his constant mistaking of the motives of the virtuous Mistress Fitzdottrell and his constant inability to cope with the rogues and even with the fools of the play. Pug's experiences, seen in relationship to those of Fitzdottrell, suggest that if society worries about the devil without and ignores the devil within it is begging the moral question. Fitzdottrell *has* to see the devil—even if only by going to the theater to see the new play—and consequently ignores the implications of his own life.

Pug becomes quite superfluous on earth, as his chief had predicted, precisely because men have become their own devils without knowing it. The absurdity of Fitzdottrell's desire to have a devil conjured up is underlined by his unwillingness to miss the new play, *The Devil is an Ass,* in which, if he hadn't been in the habit of going to the theatre merely to be seen, he might have learned how ludicrously supererogatory is Pug's desire to introduce new vices into a world which makes hell look like a grammar school.

The major action of the play has two aspects. There is on the one hand the elaborate gulling of Fitzdottrell by Merecraft and his train and on the other the incipiently illicit love affair between Mistress Fitzdottrell and Wittipoll. On the whole, the first aspect presents the more or less conventional Jonsonian comic characters, a presentation concerned much more incisively than ever before with exploring gullible avarice strictly in terms of the new capitalism, satirized here in the granting of monopolies.

The second aspect presents the new group,[7] what might be called the separable comic-symbolic figures. Wittipoll is effectively brought into the satiric plot of the play through his casual acquaintance with Engine while remaining in a sense separate from it through his identity as the courtly and incipiently Platonic lover. As conspirator he is involved in the realistic action, but he cannot effectively alter the course of that action until he himself undergoes a change. He can only throw an occasional wrench in the works in his realistic function of ironic commentator, as when he appears in Lady Tailbush's house in his Spanish lady's disguise to discourse on Spanish fucuses and other loathsome devices and customs. His easy involvement in the main action is the result of his love for Mistress Fitzdottrell, wife of the principal gull. The pivotal point of this relationship, and therefore of the realistic action as well, is the fact that Wittipoll's courtly and adulterous love for Mistress Fitzdottrell turns, at a crucial point, to virtuous friendship, which in turn becomes the instrument for the theoretical reform of Fitzdottrell.

At the beginning Wittipoll is very much the courtly lover. He is intelligent, witty, eloquent, humble,—and intent on adultery. As he had done with Ovid in *Poetaster,* Jonson here make Wittipoll's love very real, very serious, very sympathetic, and very immoral. Thus far the parallel holds, but beyond that it does not, because of the very different nature of the plot of *Poetaster*. At that stage in his career Jonson had to make his moral point about the

[7] New, at least, since *Poetaster*.

poet who is deficient because he is deficient as a man, in what amounts almost to a second plot. In *Volpone* it is perfectly integrated into an imperfectly integrated play. Here the poet-figure is perfectly integrated in what certainly appears to be a perfectly integrated play.

The problem has been handled with great skill: Wittipoll, if the play is to succeed, must be both highly attractive and morally deficient. And the moral deficiency must be corrected in such a way that when it succumbs to a higher ethical sense that sense must seem to arise from the already attractive aspects of the character. These already attractive aspects of Wittipoll consist of wit, audacity, and eloquence. And yet they are first presented in a context that makes them seem almost ludicrous, since the wit and the eloquence, for all their attractiveness, are being used to pervert what Jonson himself certainly regarded as their highest ethical function.

Jonson was perfectly familiar with Quintilian, and he completely agreed with the rhetorician that the function of language is moral; yet here the function of language is not moral. Its aim is to seduce Mistress Fitzdottrell, an aim which gets a specious comic justifiation from the fact that her husband is listening and that he is an ass. To put it crudely, Fitzdottrell gets what is coming to him, but Wittipoll has a thoroughly defective notion of what his own role should be in bringing this about. In the language which makes the lover, however, he is very effective:

> On the first sight, I lou'd you: since which time,
> Though I haue trauell'd, I haue beene in trauell
> More for this second blessing of your eyes
> Which now I 'haue purchas'd, then for all aymes else.
> Thinke of it, Lady, be your minde as actiue,
> As is your beauty: view your object well.
> Examine both my fashion, and my yeeres.
> Things, that are like, are soone familiar:

And Nature ioyes, still, in equality.
Let not the signe o' the husband fright you, Lady.
But ere your spring be gone, inioy it. Flowers,
Though faire, are oft but of one morning. Thinke,
All beauty doth not last vntill the *autumne*.
You grow old, while I tell you this. And such,
As cannot vse the present, are not wise.
If Loue and Fortune will take care of vs,
Why should our will be wanting? (I, vi, 118–34.)

Wittipoll's attractiveness as he speaks this telling expression of *carpe diem* is emphasized by the contrast with Fitzdottrell, who has oafishly allowed himself to be bribed by Wittipoll with a new cloak. One of his most characteristic affectations is his foppish love of new and gorgeous clothing. Like Penniboy Junior and Nick Stuff, he has implicit faith in the transforming powers of grand clothes. And the clothes he affects become the price as well as the symbol of folly:

With your leaue, Gentlemen.
Which of you is it, is so meere Idolater
To my wiues beauty, and so very prodigall
Vnto my patience, that, for the short parlee
Of one swift houres quarter, with my wife,
He will depart with (let mee see) this cloake here,
The price of folly? (I, iv, 53–59.)

After Fitzdottrell dons the cloak, and as Wittipoll is about to begin his verbal assault, Fitzdottrell repeats the terms of the agreement—as though Jonson were making sure that one does not miss the significance of the cloak. Fitzdottrell thus dons the cloak of folly, while Wittipoll the wit has removed it; and by removing it he has placed himself in a position to achieve wisdom, something he does when he becomes the virtuous friend instead of the successful courtly lover. Still, though, he is a wit only in comparison with

Fitzdottrell, and when his symbolic regeneration finally occurs, he himself is outlandishly garbed.

The process by which Wittipoll's adulterous love gives way to virtuous friendship is Platonic, although still symbolized by a basic comic device, the disguise. Wittipoll has been won at first by Mistress Fitzdottrell's beauty. When he talks to her in the cloak scene she does not reply, in obedience to her husband's orders, and in the second wooing scene (II, vi), when he becomes very eloquent and *very* familiar in his courtship, he misunderstands her, thinking she had deliberately arranged an assignation, when she had merely arranged a meeting. This passage, like the first wooing scene, represents an important aspect of Jonson's new comic technique, and it is masterful. He has again combined the genuinely appealing with the ludicrous, a fact not immediately apparent to the reader unless he visualizes the scene, which is acted, as the author's stage direction says, "at two windo's, as out of two contiguous buildings." (II, vi.)

Wittipoll's love-making, the language of which suggests a defectively Platonic and courtly Volpone or a sensitive Sir Epicure Mammon, is thus conducted under ridiculously unpropitious circumstances, like a tableau of amorous frustration whose desired end is impossible of realization. The fact that the scene ends with one of Jonson's best-known lyrics intensifies the irony: as Wittipoll swells with amorous rhetoric he is suddenly and appropriately deflated by Fitzdottrell, who immediately loses all he has gained, first by striking his wife and then by dissolving in an ecstasy of self-pity:

> O, Bird!
> Could you do this? 'gainst me? and at this time, now?
> When I was so imploy'd, wholly for you,
> Drown'd i' my care (more, then the land, I sweare,
> I 'haue hope to win) to make you peere-lesse? studying,

For footmen for you, fine-pac'd huishers, pages,
To serue you o' the knee; with what Knights wife,
To beare your traine, and sit with your foure women
In councell, and receiue intelligences,
From forraigne parts, to dresse you at all pieces!
Y'haue (a'most) turn'd my good affection, to you;
Sowr'd my sweet thoughts; all my pure purposes:
I could now finde (i' my very heart) to make
Another, *Lady Dutchesse;* and depose you. (II, vii, 28–41.)

Only when she explains her motives to Wittipoll, in IV, vi, and
thus displays to him the virtue that Jonson has been careful to con-
vey to the audience already, does he make his Platonic progression
from love of beauty to love of virtue, a virtue that in the Platonic
context is implicit in the beauty.

Again the problem is to present a serious moral argument in specific terms but in such a way as not to break the comic thread,
and again Jonson has done so by presenting the comic and the
serious simultaneously. Wittipoll has come to Lady Tailbush's
house disguised as a Spanish lady, ostensibly to do Engine a favor,
but actually to see Mistress Fitzdottrell. In IV, vi, they are alone
together, and if a seduction were going to occur, this would be
the time.

And now we have a very serious conversation between a beautiful
young woman and a witty young man who is unfortunately wearing a ridiculous costume. The reader must imagine the visual
effect, but the audience, seeing it, will certainly be amused. And
now, as Wittipoll himself is very certainly being won over by Mistress Fitzdottrell's eloquence, Manly steps from behind the arras:

                              O friend! forsake not
            The braue occasion, vertue offers you,
            To keepe you innocent: I haue fear'd for both;
            And watch'd you, to preuent the ill I fear'd.

But, since the weaker side hath so assur'd mee,
Let not the stronger fall by his owne vice,
Or be the lesse a friend, 'cause vertue needs him.

(IV, vi, 28–34.)

We are reminded, quite deliberately I think, of the fatuous Bonario leaping from behind the arras to rescue Celia from the foul ravisher. Manly's sudden appearance is not so funny because it is more serious, but unless we can believe that the author of *Volpone,* *The Alchemist,* and *Bartholomew Fair* has suddenly taken leave of his senses we can only assume that our first reaction to Manly is supposed to be one of amusement. A virtuous young woman mightily beset; a witty young man dressed up like a Spanish lady; a sudden materialization from behind the arras. The scene is certainly ludicrous in its design, but it is also serious as Wittipoll in effect recollects himself. He sets out immediately to gull Fitzdottrell by removing his wife from his power.

The situation is complicated and the jest is spoiled i' the retelling; but Wittipoll had been in the house disguised to see Mrs. Fitzdottrell and Manly had been there courting Lady Tailbush. Wittipoll was morally in the wrong, Manly intellectually in the wrong, since he did not at first perceive the true nature of the lady. Manly recognized his friend in disguise and left the room, ostensibly because the ladies had disillusioned him, but really because he wanted to prevent Wittipoll's seduction of Mrs. Fitzdottrell. Manly's intellectual enlightenment virtually coincides with Wittipoll's moral enlightenment. As Wittipoll himself is coming around under the influence of Mrs. Fitzdottrell's virtuous eloquence, Manly steps from behind the arras and Wittipoll becomes the virtuous friend.

Manly is a very minor character in the play; except for the exceedingly brief intrigue with Lady Tailbush he is simply a commentator on his friend's actions. He seems actually to be Wittipoll's symbolic *alter ego* in a situation anticipating that in *The Magnetic*

Lady, where Captain Ironside and Compass are apparently to be regarded as two aspects of one complete figure. Thus Manly represents the moral nature and Wittipoll the intellectual nature of the ideally whole man. When the two are symbolically combined, the moral and the intellectual natures work toward the same end, the rescue of Mistress Fitzdottrell from the foolish tyranny of her husband.

Manly is not, therefore, a clumsily introduced *deus ex machina,* but the emergence of Wittipoll's conscience, the realization of his own potentialities already strongly hinted at in Mistress Fitzdottrell's reference to his mastery of language:

> my hope was then,
> (Though interrupted, ere it could be vtter'd)
> That whom I found the Master of such language,
> That braine and spirit, for such an enterprise,
> Could not, but if those succours were demanded
> To a right vse, employ them vertuously!
> (IV, vi, 10–15.)

Language, the instrument of society, becomes also the potential agent of virtue. Still, though, we have not left the comic world.

Fitzdottrell, as part of his fantastic dealing with Merecraft's office of dependencies, must enfeoff his property, and, having fallen in love with Wittipoll's disguise—appropriate enough in view of his infatuation with clothes—he decides to make it over to Wittipoll, who, however, refuses the honor and suggests that Manly receive the trust. Fitzdottrell is doubtful, but is finally convinced. Wittipoll then reveals his identity and announces that he and Manly will now make the property over to Mistress Fitzdottrell, on the grounds that she will know better how to use it.

This represents a subtle and amusing extension of the situation in *Epicoene.* In that play the collegiate ladies who tyrannized over their husbands were a satirical aspect of a society turned upside-down. In *Bartholomew Fair* Jonson had demonstrated that turning society upside down twice—first in Littlewit's house, then in the Fair—did not make it stand right side up. In *The Devil is an Ass* the second reversal is both comic and salutary: it is a reversal of the normal relationship for Fitzdottrell to make over his property to the Spanish lady; it is a further reversal for the Spanish lady's friend to make it over to Fitzdottrell's wife; and it is an ironic reversal of the comic when the wife is not only better qualified to use the property but will use it to reclaim her idiotic husband.

The society represented by Fitzdottrell is the society into which Pug enters to do evil, a society so bad that the devil fears that his own forces are no match for it and suspects that the citizens of London must have their own stud to breed their own superior vices. (I, i, 108–109.) It is such a chaotic society that virtues are no longer to be distinguished from vices:

> They haue their *Vices,* there, most like to *Vertues;*
> You cannot know 'hem, apart, by any difference:
> They weare the same clothes, eate o' the same meate,
> Sleepe i' the selfe-same beds, ride i' those coaches,
> Or very like, foure horses in a coach,
> As the best men and women. (I, i, 121–26.)

Fitzdottrell epitomizes everything odious in this world. He is concerned only with externals; he longs to see the devil; he goes to plays only to be seen and admired; he considers clothing more significant than what lies beneath; he hires the Spanish lady to instruct his wife in the ways of the world, and impulsively tries to give her his property; he is unable to discern the virtuous nature of his wife. He is avaricious and socially ambitious (he wants to become Duke of Drowned-land); he is incapable of fighting his own battles, for he seeks the advice of Everill, master of the dependences, about how to conduct his quarrel with Wittipoll. And, in addition to being blind, greedy, cowardly, and stupid, he is guilty of beating his wife, the one thoroughly virtuous person in the play.

It is significant of Jonson's moral intention that when Fitzdottrell is thus lifted out of the play and objectively described, he ceases to be amusing. Fitzdottrell then seems to be the dangerous devil in society. Though Satan is Pug's master in hell, Fitzdottrell is his earthly master, giving him orders and punishing him for disobedience. Fitzdottrell's feigned madness in the last scene serves as a symbolic statement of his malady and, since he represents the worst in his society, the malady of that society. As he foams at the mouth and raves, Sir Paul Eitherside says, "That is the *Diuell* speakes, and laughes in him." (V, viii, 29.)

In his fit of madness he is seen as the embodiment of the devil, a kind of devil who, in contrast to the relatively harmless Pug, is potentially dangerous to society and must be checked before he constitutes a genuine danger. As devil Fitzdottrell is also an ass, as his relationship with Merecraft, Guilthead, Lady Tailbush, and the Spanish lady—not to mention his wife—all indicate.

If Fitzdottrell is the sum of the chaotic society of the play, its driving force is the marvelously conceived Merecraft, certainly one of Jonson's triumphs. L. C. Knights has clearly shown how precisely Merecraft represents the early capitalist entrepeneur,[8] and a failure to call attention to this once more would be less than fair to Jonson, who, we are told, was in his forty-three-year-old dotage when he wrote this play. When Merecraft first appears on the stage, he brings with him the consuming vision of the capitalist ethos:

> Sir, money's a whore, a bawd, a drudge;
> Fit to runne out on errands: Let her goe.
> *Via pecunia!* when she's runne and gone,
> And fled and dead; then will I fetch her, againe,
> With *Aqua-vitae,* out of an old Hogs-head!

[8] *Drama and Society,* 214–18.

While there are lees of wine, or dregs of beere,
I'le neuer want her! Coyne her out of cobwebs,
Dust, but I'll haue her! (II, i, 1–8.)

It is hard to imagine anything better than this, the oracle, as it were, of the chief god of Fitzdottrell's society.

The action and argument of the play engage the two contesting groups, the Fitzdottrell-Merecraft group against the Wittipoll-Manly-Mistress Fitzdottrell group. It is the function of this second group, the characters with the strongest symbolic overtones, to bring about at least the possibility of change in the others by opposing a kind of moral norm to their chaos, which is not to say that there will be a perfect masque-like symbolic resolution. *The Devil is an Ass* has clear affinities with the masque, but it is, after all, a comedy. The possibility of a rational life is presented. Now, it is important to recognize that this rational life is, in its essence, highly idealistic. Its achievement lies beyond the powers of most human beings. It is, and for all practical purposes it remains, an ideal. This in no sense implies a denigration of its validity.

As *Bartholomew Fair* indicates, Jonson was quite aware of the fact that human beings are not exactly perfectible; but as the symbolic argument of this play seems to imply, he also knew that an impossible ideal is infinitely preferable to most of its alternatives. As Jonson's mind and art become more and more refined—too refined for most of his critics, who feel the necessity of judiciousness—his sensibilities lead him to the acceptance of impossibly high but spiritually valid goals. In this respect, and in this play, he is being led to conclusions similar, in comic terms, to those reached in the ultra-refined late tragicomedies of Shakespeare and the plays of Beaumont and Fletcher.

The moral argument of this play is Platonic. Against the gross materialism of society it opposes the saving grace of perfect love, which means, of course, disinterested and virtuous friendship, a friendship which sees in the beloved friend the incarnation of the highest spiritual ideals. In oversimplified and hence in distorted terms, the love of virtue is opposed to the love of money; in Jonson's own work the chief precedent occurs in the masque *Love Restored,* performed at court in 1612, in which the theme is the triumph of love over avarice. Its principal thematic argument appears in the long speech of Robin Goodfellow as he unmasks Plutus, god of money, who has been posing as Cupid, god of love.

The revelation of Plutus as bane to society is hardly a new idea, and for Jonson the ultimate source may have been *The Plutus* of Aristophanes. In any case, Fitzdottrell, feigning madness, quotes the amusing words of the ruined informer of Aristophanes' play. Robin Goodfellow's words, which seem to anticipate the argument of *The Devil is an Ass,* follow:

Nay then, we spirits (I see) are subtler yet, and somewhat better discouerers. No; it is not he, nor his brother ANTI-CVPID, the *loue of vertue,* though he pretend to it with his phrase and face: 'Tis that Impostor PLVTVS, the god of *money,* who ha's stolne LOVE'S ensignes; and in his belyed figure, raignes i' the world, making friendships, contracts, mariages, and almost religion; begetting, breeding, and holding the neerest respects of mankind; and vsurping all those offices in this Age of gold, which LOVE himselfe perform'd in the golden age. 'Tis he, that pretends to tie kingdomes, maintaine commerce, dispose of honors, make all places and dignities arbitrarie from him: euen to the verie countrey, where LOVE'S name cannot be ras'd out, he ha's yet gain'd there vpon him, by a prouerbe, insinuating his preeminence, *Not for loue, or money.* There LOVE liues confin'd, by his tyrannie, to a cold Region, wrapt vp in furres like a *Muscouite,* and almost frozen to death: while he, in his enforced shape, and with his rauish'd Armes, walkes as if he were to set bounds, and giue lawes to destinie. 'Tis you, mortalls, that are fooles; and worthie to be such, that worship him: for if you had wisdome, he had no godhead. He should stinke in the graue with those wretches, whose slaue he was. Contemne him, and he is one. Come, follow me. Ile bring you where you shall find LOVE, and by the vertue of this Maiestie, who proiecteth so powerfull beames of light and heat through this Hemispheare, thaw his icie fetters, and scatter the darknesse that obscures him. Then, in despight of this insolent and barbarous *Mammon,* your sports may proceed, and the solemnities of the night be complete, without depending on so earthie an idoll. (170–200.)

In the masque, love is the antithesis of and the answer to avarice. In the play, Cupid, god of love, has been supplanted as ideal by Anticupid, the love of virtue, but the parallel is otherwise remarkably close. Mistress Fitzdottrell is a virtuous woman, and Wittipoll's love for her becomes, naturally enough, but not so patly as I describe it, the love of virtue, safely contained in the comic context and action. The love-avarice themes are almost completely separate at the beginning of the play; they draw more and more closely together as the play proceeds, so that, through his finally ideal love for Mistress Fitzdottrell, Wittipoll gulls both the rogues and fools, a process which implies the possibility of their correction.

There is no Robin Goodfellow to arrive on the scene and conclude the antimasque, drive Plutus into oblivion, and introduce the masque proper—the fully realized symbolic resolution. Instead, Wittipoll himself progresses from one stage of love to a higher which is still implied in the lower; as a result of having achieved the higher stage, he is able to take Fitzdottrell out of the hands of Merecraft and return him, with both comic and seriously symbolic implications, to the authority of his wife, the exemplar of true virtue. Manly's words at the end of the play emphasize the idea of comic correction while simultaneously implying a future ideal resolution:

The few that haue the seeds
Of goodnesse left, will sooner make their way
To a true life, by shame, then punishment.
(V, viii, 172–74.)

In attempting an explanation of the argument of a complex work of art, one necessarily oversimplifies and thus violates the work itself. The ring, for example, which Merecraft gets from Guilt-head has a history that seems to reflect the meaning of the comedy. Fitzdottrell, wishing to enter his wife in the good graces of a group of ladies who will contribute to her education in polite society— the society he will enter when he becomes Duke of Drowned-land —has his friend Merecraft obtain a ring from Guilthead the gold-smith. This ring is to be a gift to the distinguished Spanish lady (Wittipoll in disguise), who in return will, through her polite and worldly conversation, instruct Mistress Fitzdottrell in the ways of the world of high society. Since Merecraft owes money to Guilt-head and is being blackmailed by his own surly counterpart Everill, the price Fitzdottrell pays will be rather high. The price will be jacked up to "hedge in" Merecraft's debts. Then it will be jacked up again for Everill's blackmail.

But of course Merecraft intends to keep the ring himself. Pug, Fitzdottrell's page, is supposed to give it to the Spanish lady (Witti-poll), but is gulled out of it by Trains, Merecraft's accomplice. Then Fitzdottrell complains that the Spanish lady doesn't seem to have it, and so Merecraft finally has to give it to her (him) after all, whereupon she (he) gives it to Mistress Fitzdottrell.

The ring is conventionally ambiguous. It is gold and comes from Guilthead and thus symbolizes the aspirations of the mercantile class. It passes through the hands of Merecraft and thus symbolizes the entrepeneur class. The ring is a conventional sexual symbol, but, being round, it is also—particularly for Jonson—a symbol of moral and artistic perfection. It is a marriage symbol, and hence to be associated with perfect love. In a comedy of pleasant errors, Mistress Fitzdottrell finally gets the ring purchased by her husband, and she gets it from Wittipoll, who, in thus outwitting everyone, has simultaneously brought Fitzdottrell theoretically to his senses.

The ring is thus a central symbol: because of its wealth of associations, it represents a kind of moral norm whose validity and efficacy is predicated on its being rescued from a corrupt and avaricious society—the rogues through whose hands it passes—and on its being given by the reformed Wittipoll to the virtuous Mistress Fitzdottrell. Thus wit—Wittipoll—and virtue are symbolically united through the ring under circumstances which will make it impossible for either to become sullied.

If *The Devil is an Ass* does something new in comedy, it also reiterates, in rather refined terms, a Jonsonian argument which we have seen before. In a distinctly subordinate aspect of the play, Wittipoll seems to glance once again at the figure of the artist, like Ovid in *Poetaster,* the poet who is not a good man, but whose apprehension of beauty and command of language—two qualities specifically attributed to him—imply his potential for achieving the moral virtue necessary to make the good man as well as the good poet. In his role of satiric poet his function is to reform society—Manly's speech at the end of the play suggests the possibility. His effectiveness, like Volpone's, is vitiated by an impure motive, although Volpone's is much more impure than Wittipoll's. His role as satirist continues after his reform as he and Manly announce that Fitzdottrell's deed will be given to his wife, a comic device whose significance we have already discussed. Since the courtly and Platonic themes are at least as literary as they are philosophical, and since Mistress Fitzdottrell's beauty makes a lyric poet out of him, we might say that the power of art has been partly responsible for the change he undergoes. But in *The Devil is an*

Ass this is a peripheral matter, implied in the context but never intrusive.

THE STAPLE OF NEWS

It is perhaps significant that there is a nine-year interval between *The Staple of News* and *The Devil is an Ass*. However, to say with Palmer—to use Dryden's unfortunate term—that this play is "definitely the first of the dotages"[1] and that Jonson "had lost touch"[2] with the stage during this time is to reveal an outright misunderstanding or a gross misreading of one of Jonson's most complex dramatic achievements. This interval does not represent a "wasteland" period or a dark hiatus in Jonson's development as a dramatist, for he continued to write masques. Furthermore, while *The Staple*—and the plays that succeeded it as well—is in a sense a "new" kind of comedy for Jonson, it is linked technically and thematically to his earlier work for the stage. It is both reminiscent and anticipatory, a kind of summation of almost everything in Jonsonian drama to this point and a guide to what will follow.

Unquestionably *The Staple* is a comedy of a different sort from the early "comicall satyres" and from the works of Jonson's great middle period. Yet the "humors" technique has not been completely abandoned in this play; and its allegorical structure, though possibly influenced most immediately by the masque, is also reminiscent of *Bartholomew Fair* and *The Devil is an Ass*. On the thematic level, *The Staple* represents a logical extension of what Jonson had been doing up to this time in the comic mode. It is a highly particularized treatment of a recurring theme in Jonson—avarice and its effect on the values of a whole society. Also, though the over-all tone and satiric effect may be slightly more subdued than they are in some of the earlier plays, Jonson is as usual the con-

---

[1] *Ben Jonson,* 284.
[2] *Ibid.,* 268.

summate master of his pen—with multilevel puns, diverse topical and literary allusions, and transmuted borrowings abounding throughout the play. In both content and method the play is a magnificent composite.

The barest summary of material in the play must include possible references to or borrowings from an earlier English play (*The London Prodigall*), from Roman satire (Horace, in particular), from Aristophanes (*Plutus,* especially, and *The Wasps*), and from Jonson himself (*News from the New World*). In method *The Staple* combines allegorical techniques similar to those of the morality play and the masque with the satiric method common to old comedy and classical and contemporary satire. This special fusion of the allegorical and the satiric, which extends to *The New Inn* and *The Magnetic Lady,* accounts for the play's relatively subdued tone and distinguishes the comic method here from that of Jonson's earlier comedies.

The inevitable question now arises: What kind of comedy is *The Staple of News?* The question may be answered at this point in a general and somewhat ambiguous way by saying that it is a new species of Old Comedy. In its purpose at least it appears to be a type of *Vetus Comoedia,* in the tradition more of Aristophanes than of Menander and Terence. For Jonson is concerned here with a broad social theme, after the manner of Old Comedy; but at the same time the play's resolution and certain other elements in it are more suggestive of the tradition of New Comedy.

It might seem that the combination of satiric and sympathetic treatment of characters and the blend of realistic and symbolic handling of material would make an incongruous and inconsistent mixture; but this is not the case. Though a strange hybrid, the play is structurally organic; and Jonson's success in fusing the rather heterogeneous elements in the play suggests that the broad categories "Old" and "New" are not always the most useful generic subdivisions for classifying comic art. The last two comedies, indeed, represent a thorough fusing of the two modes, and such terms may very well be misleading as applied to *The Staple of News.*

Nevertheless, the strong implication of the ideal and the didactic concern of *The Staple* serve to place it, in purpose, at least broadly in the tradition of Old Comedy. The social theme—the use and abuse of wealth and the distortion of values in a social structure that abuses its wealth—dominates the whole play. It is the center from which everything in the play radiates outward in interrelated strands, even as Pecunia, who symbolizes wealth, is the central character around whom all the other characters move.

The play's didactic purpose is made specific by the Prologue:

> For your owne sakes, not his, he bad me say,
> Would you were come to heare, not see a Play.
> Though we his *Actors* must prouide for those,
> Who are our guests, here, in the way of showes,
> The maker hath not so; he'ld haue you wise,
> Much rather by your eares, then by your eyes . . .
> Great noble wits, be good vnto your selves,
> And make a difference 'twixt Poetique elues,
> And Poets: All that dable in the inke,
> And defile quills, are not those few, can thinke,
> Conceiue, expresse, and steere the soules of men,
> As with a rudder, round thus, with their pen.
> He must be one that can instruct your youth,
> And keepe your *Acme* in the state of truth . . .
>
> (1–26.)

The emphasis here is on the role of the poet as teacher, one who can "Conceive, expresse, and steere the soules" of those who "heare," not merely "see," the play, those who can understand the implications of its theme for their own society. For, as the Epilogue remarks, the poet has the *"double scope,/ To* profit, *and* delight."

Although *The Staple* is like Old Comedy in its social purpose and underlying idealism, unlike Old Comedy it articulates the ideal within the limits of the dramatic context. Furthermore, a transformation of character occurs: through the agency of Penniboy Canter and of Pecunia herself, both Penniboy Senior and Penniboy Junior undergo changes at the end of the play, although Penniboy Junior's early good-heartedness renders his change not at all surprising. The tone of the play is a mixed one, as Jonson must have intended it to be; for the play suggests something of the relationship between the ideal and the actual, between real value and sham value. The expression of the ideal is much more explicit than it is in Jonson's earlier, more ironic comedies, and the modification in comic method here can probably best be accounted for in terms of what was happening to the English audience at this time.

Jonson's development in these later comedies parallels in some ways Aristophanes' later development, especially as it is known from the *Plutus*. Possibly Jonson and Aristophanes turned to the specifically allegorical mode for similar reasons: the change in the temper of the times—the change in the audience itself—may have made it increasingly difficult for both playwrights to say what they had to say in a mode that would be acceptable to the spectators—and for Aristophanes the state—without compromising the integrity of their work. In this type of play Jonson saw fit to express his theme in a more difficult and subtle, less frankly blunt manner than he had used in the earlier comedies.

In modifying his comic technique, Jonson could assume that he would not lose the "fit" audience who would have insight into the play as a complex exploration of his theme. At the same time he would not alienate—even make hostile—other levels of his audience who would view the play more simply. In other words, Jonson is here, as elsewhere, making excellent use of what may be termed the dramatic metaphor of point of view.

The epistemological validity of the artistic illusion, and of experience itself, is grounded upon the metaphysical commitment of the viewer. As reality itself is defined and circumscribed, so is the possibility of learning what is real. This applies to the characters operating within the frame of reference of the experiential reality of the play as well as to the spectator, who must view the play as an image of the larger reality which the total play implies. This is not to say that Jonson is an out-and-out relativist. He is anything but this; in all of his plays, even the most involuted, "doubly" ironical ones like *Bartholomew's Fair,* what is truly real and valuable is clearly articulated, ironically or symbolically or perhaps explicitly, for the encompassing spectator-viewpoint, which must, of course, include all the fragmented, partial points of view within the play.

Jonson, then, is one of the most philosophical of playwrights, assuming as he does a reality—or an ideal—with its concomitant axiological and epistemological implications. Writing as much to "profit" as to "delight," he makes rigid demands of that spectator for whom the play is a catalyst exciting new knowledge or a reassessment of old. The viewer or critic who maintains a complex point of view toward a Jonson play may hope to discover the real implications of the dramatic metaphor of point of view. He may see various levels of illusion in the play—and a corresponding diversity of technique or method by which the theme is objectified. As relations between or among various levels become clear, one can only marvel at the complex, yet tight structure. Almost everything turns out to have a relation to the theme; in *The Staple* even the most insignificant pun is far more than a mere linguistic exercise.

Some critics have remarked that the "realistic" satire concerned with the office of the Staple itself is not integrated successfully with the allegory of Lady Pecunia and the Penniboys. In the light of the play's large intention, these objections seem invalid; for the realistic topical elements and the Pecunia allegory fuse into a complementary expression of one central theme. The intermeans also are a part of this contrapuntal arrangement. There is actually only one "plot" in the play. It is largely his handling of character that enables Jonson to unify the seemingly disparate elements here. The characters function simultaneously as realistic and symbolic personages and should never be seen from one point of view exclusively.

It was remarked earlier that the thematic concern of *The Staple* is a recurring one in Jonson, though it becomes more particularized in the later plays. His immediate concern here, as always, is with social disorder: he shows the devastating and ultimately amoralizing and demoralizing effect which avarice in its many forms may have—indeed, has had—on the total structure of a society, specifically the society of seventeenth-century England.[3] Knights's comments on *The Staple of News* are much to the point. But capitalism itself—represented in this play by the Staple venture and by Penniboy Senior—is symptomatic of an even more fundamental distortion of values for Jonson as humanist.

Ultimately—more essentially—the play objectifies an appearance-reality theme: What is real? What is truly valuable? And how can the truth of reality be articulated and, more important, known and actualized in the setting of a capitalistic society whose values and whose ideals have been confused and distorted? On one level, then, the play is a modern morality—a comic allegory—on the theme of avarice.

---

[3] One of the most valuable commentaries on the economic status of seventeenth-century England and on Jonson's attitude toward the growing emphasis on capitalism is contained in L. C. Knights's *Drama and Society*.

It may seem strange, the result of a curiously distorted perspective, that Jonson seems to subsume all the social evils under the general heading of avarice. But in his day the worship of money for its own sake was still occasionally regarded as immoral; and usury was generally regarded as detestable, although practiced often enough. Penniboy Senior is outraged at the fact that the legal limit on interest has been lowered from ten to eight per cent, a figure now charged by respectable bankers. The practices of modern loan companies, and the gullibility of their customers, would have made him envious indeed. Avarice may still be the root of all evil, but it is now usually equated with a belief in progress and a laudable desire for an accretion of respectability.

The final act suggests a possible resolution of the problem: there is a transformation of character—Penniboy Junior and Penniboy Senior—through the immediate agency of Penniboy Canter and the ultimate agency of Lady Pecunia herself, who comes to function near the end of the play in a Platonic-allegorical fashion similar to that of Lady Lodestone in *The Magnetic Lady*. Thus, only through right use of Pecunia—through a proper evaluation of her—can many of the values which acquisitive capitalism has distorted be restored to their rightful and traditional place. The poet, the military man, and most of the others in the play have forfeited their true function in society in favor of appearance or sham reputation and have distorted truth and virtue themselves. Pecunia as an ideal has a different abstract value for each of them, and thus her various symbolic meanings seem incompatible at times. One of the purposes of the play thus becomes an attempt to define the role of Pecunia, both as an ideal and as an actuality in experience.

The relation of the Pecunia allegory to the Staple itself is clear. As a speculative scheme whose main purpose is to draw money (Pecunia), the office of the Staple reveals avarice in one of its most odious manifestations. For, to draw money, it will defraud the people of truth and foist on them what they want, appearance. It is described as a house of Fame by the Register. In its substitution of current rumor and lies for the truth, the Staple serves to extend the confusion of values in a society where values are already confused. But it looks good on the surface; it has a specious order which appeals immediately to Penniboy Junior, the young heir, who promptly invests in it by buying a clerkship for Tom the barber.

Symbolizing all commercial schemes and ventures which prostitute truth and real value (that of money included), the Staple collapses utterly, and literally, because in any case it would attract only the least significant aspect of Pecunia; indeed, in the play it fails to get her even to "sojourn" there for a while. And as a place where false news—any news—is manufactured, or at least where idle rumors pass for news, it suggests a symbolic concretion of the generalized noise symbolic of the chaotic society of *Epicoene*.

The love of money, which is a perversion of values, is articulated in the vending of noise, the perversion of truth—Catholic news for Catholics, Protestant news for Protestants; both of which, true or false, can be had for money. The perversion of truth is an abuse of language; language is the instrument of society. The perversion of truth for money becomes therefore an assault on society, trivial or pernicious falsehood perpetrated for gain. In this respect *The Staple of News* is Jonson's most prophetic play, particularly for a time when many newspapers make claims not for their accuracy but for the fact that advertising in their columns is lucrative. When the Staple finally collapses, only jeering remains, idle noise without even the profit motive remaining.

Jonson plays on the various meanings of staple. It is a mart or emporium—a storehouse, source, or place of supply—but it is also the commercial commodity itself — the principal commodity of traffic in a market. It is what the people want—according to the law of supply and demand; and, to satisfy this public demand, the emissaries of the Staple delve into all corners of society in their efforts to gather not what is true and lasting but what is vendible, however false and ephemeral. It is significant that Cymbal is the "Governor of the Staple," the "tinkling Captain" of the emissaries, and also a "grand-captain of the jeerers." The Biblical reference is clear ("Though I speak with the tongues of men and angels, and have not charity, I am become as sounding brass, or a tinkling cymbal"), but it extends beyond the allusive level to the thematic.

At the end of the play all ties except those of Love are discharged by Pecunia. It would seem that Jonson is suggesting through the allegory of Pecunia that love itself is the only means whereby the restoration of moral and human values may be effected in the confusion of seventeenth-century English society, an argument he had already made in different terms in *The Devil is an Ass*.

Pecunia is the most difficult and complex character in the play and at the same time she is the most important. Like others in the play she is both a "realistic" and a symbolic character, conceived as an almost completely serious personage. It is not so much the conflict between Pecunia as a real woman and Pecunia as allegorical symbol that poses difficulty in determining her precise role in the play as it is the multiple levels of allegorical meaning which she is assigned.

She is a lady to whom "all the world" are suitors; her most specific allegorical meaning, then, is money, as her name implies and as many references in the play make explicit—Old Penniboy the usurer, her guardian, has kept her locked up, etc. Her drawing all others to her is consistent with her being equivalent to gold, which draws all other metals. She is a kind of goddess whose "grace" is sought by those at the Apollo. There are allusions to her title as the Infanta of the Mines (this is the way she is listed in the Dramatis Personae)—Aurelia Clara Pecunia. This is obviously a topical allusion to the episode of the Spanish marriage at the same time that it suggests thematically that the monarchy itself has been infested with "money" morality.

Towards the end of the play, however, Pecunia seems to become a different sort of ideal, something like the "golden mean" which she herself expresses in the final speech of the play. And in this capacity she becomes at least partly responsible for the transformation of the Penniboys.

Jonson may have overburdened the character of Pecunia. The difficulty is that at times her specific allegorical meanings do not seem consonant with her meaning in this larger, almost Platonic, sense. She never becomes fully actualized as a realistic personage in the play, largely because of her multiple symbolic functions. This is probably intentional on Jonson's part. As money, she has become all things to all men, each seeking to actualize her after the distorted ideal image he has of her. The point of view of each of her suitors determines her material value and her ideal value for him. She is seen as everything from a whore to a princess in the social world of the play, and only after some clarification of her worth in the world does some understanding of her more ideal implications become possible.

As the play's heroine Pecunia is both a real lady who is being prostituted by Penniboy Senior—as a "Flesh bawd"—and a representation of wealth that is being similarly prostituted by old Penniboy as a "money bawd." Her entourage—Mortgage, Statute, Band, and Wax—are also bawds of Penniboy Senior. This dual aspect of character enforces strikingly an equation which the play makes: the prostitution of wealth is a spiritual prostitution of the body politic—and as morally reprehensible as the prostitution of the flesh.

Since she carries a more complex symbolic meaning, Pecunia is less "realistic," and humorous, than her "shadows." She is the sun around whom all the others are "concentricks," as Broker, her secretary, remarks at one point. Thus she is the center of the mad universe in which even the devil Pug proves ineffectual in *The Devil Is an Ass*. Since money has become the sun around which the whole earth revolves, chaos results when the specious order of the Staple is not successfully underwritten by Pecunia; and since money is the mainstay of the hollow "justice" which Penniboy Senior extols, he is metamorphosed into the mad "judge" when he loses Pecunia.

The function of other characters in the drama is made clear through their relationship to Pecunia. Because they have Pecunia in their charge, the Penniboys are extremely important. Pecunia is associated at the outset with Penniboy Senior, the miserly usurer who represents one extreme of the misuse of money or wealth—pure acquisition for its own sake. Although he ostensibly controls Pecunia, he has become a kind of martyr to her Grace (II, i, 10–11), delighting and suffering in his enslavement to her. He is obsessed with the name of justice (II, iii, 40–45, and III, iv, 33) if not the fact of justice, and to him gluttony is the greatest sin (II, iii, 25–31). When he says at one point (III, iv, 42) that he is "mad with this times manners" he is ironically anticipating the famous mad scene later (V, iv) when he metes out justice to his dogs.

His insistence on frugality places him at the opposite pole from his nephew, Penniboy Junior, the young heir and prodigal, who almost loses Pecunia because of his prodigality. The play dramatizes young Penniboy's initiation into the world as he reaches his majority. At the beginning of the play he is waiting for the striking of the clock that will denote his coming of age. When the hour of his manhood arrives, he acquires the outward signs of his identity as a Penniboy by getting properly outfitted by the tailor, the spurrier, and others. He thoroughly upsets his disguised father, Penniboy Canter, by paying these persons without first checking the items on their bills. Hopelessly immature and stupid, although still somehow engaging, he falls in with the Staple scheme and purchases an office for Tom immediately; whereas his more cautious uncle will have no part of the scheme after he learns that it will involve the use of his Pecunia. Dining at the Apollo with Pecunia and the jeerers, he becomes so taken with "canting" that he soon proposes to build the College of Canters.

Penniboy Junior and Penniboy Senior represent extremes in their attitudes toward the use of money. Penniboy Junior is so prodigal and irresponsible that he will surely dissipate his inheritance; while Penniboy Senior, by keeping Pecunia locked up, has misused his wealth also. They both undergo a kind of transformation in the final act, coming at last to some understanding of the real value of money and its proper use—though not before Penniboy Senior has lapsed into madness at the losss of Pecunia and Penniboy Junior has been stripped of his fine apparel and given the patched beggar's cloak by his father.

The process is that of a ritual, both Penniboys being spiritually transformed as they are materially transformed, through the loss of Pecunia. After the scene in which his father has revealed himself, Penniboy Junior remarks, "I now begin to see my vanity/ Shine in this *Glasse,* reflected by the *foile!*" (V, i, 14–15.) And at the conclusion of the play Penniboy Senior gives his lands and goods to his nephew and announces that he will go to cleanse his vices. Both Penniboys have taken on new identities which go deeper than either fine clothing or tatters. This miraculous change has been wrought by Penniboy Canter, who stands between the two men as a mean. Through his own symbolic "rebirth"—disclosure of his real identity—he brings about the transformation of the other two, a transformation not out of keeping with the play's large symbolic intention.

Penniboy Canter provides much of the play's specific commentary on the avaricious vices of the age, his "cant" being the only genuine satire among all the jeering that occurs. Through Penniboy Canter, Jonson makes it clear that he is satirizing the vices that have come to be associated with the positions of society represented by the suitors of Pecunia. He is not concerned here with representatives of their classes who are functioning responsibly in society. In the play those have lost all sense of value, substituting rank and place for virtue. They have perverted language itself, replacing meaningful communication with cant and jargon. They have in effect sold themselves and their traditional functions in society, have sold their virtue or real worth, in favor of the trappings, the externals that a prostituted wealth may bring.

Penniboy Canter's revelation of himself to the others constitutes the play's "catastrophe," or so think the ladies of the chorus, who accuse him of being "a kin to the poet"; and so he is, although not in the way they mean it. A canter is a speaker of cant, but he is also a singer—that is, a poet—an identity readily attributed to him through the fact that he is several times referred to not as Old Canter but as Old Chanter.

The recognition scene is important in the articulation of the appearance-reality theme—the clothes symbolism is significant here —but the fifth act provides a still further working out of the theme. For it is here that Penniboy Junior proves himself to his father, as he saves him from being tricked by the crafty Picklock. Thus he is not so naive as his father has thought; nor is Penniboy Canter so clever as he has thought himself to be in arranging this elaborate test of his son, for he has made an error in judgment that almost results in his real loss of identity as a Penniboy. This of course is consistent with Jonson's general practice with respect to the poet-figure.

In every instance the suitors of Pecunia represent a prostitution of a social position. Almanack, Shunfield, Madrigal, Pyed-Mantle, and Fitton have compromised their function in society in their pursuit of Pecunia. Madrigal, for example, affects the popular form of the madrigal or whatever else appeals to the taste of the times. Doctors such as Almanack, who resort to astrology and other esoteric malpractices, cannot hope to cure their patients, let alone a "sick" society. Fitton, Emissary Court at the Staple, has retained only the outward forms and manners of the courtly tradition. They have lost their lands and securities as they have forfeited their traditional roles in society.

Now they have become jeerers, false satirists who pretend to comment upon society, who pretend to understand real value and virtue. Language itself has been perverted into a game, and they now expend their diseased wit in trivial jeering and canting. Penniboy Senior, who is their favorite object for jeering, calls them "birds of prey"; and Penniboy Canter refers to them as "ulcers" that "infect the times." They act as a corruptive influence on Penniboy Junior, to the extent that he proposes to erect a "Canters College." It is small wonder that at this point Penniboy Canter explodes and reveals himself to the group. They are so intimately involved with the schemers at the Staple that, when the Staple crumbles, Cymbal, its "midwife," becomes the "grand-captain of the jeerers."

Perhaps the most culpable of the lot is Madrigal, the poetaster, for the true poet's mission is to teach society, to steer the souls of men to whatever true value exists in the chaotic world of experience. But the criterion of popular taste has so influenced Madrigal that he readily concedes in his bout with Lickfinger that the cook is the better (because the more "palatable") poet.

One of the most carefully drawn characters is Emissary Westminister, Domine Picklock. Young Penniboy's— and Penniboy Canter's—attorney, he, along with the barber Tom, is a direct link between the Penniboy episodes and the Staple episodes. He is singled out for special punishment—the pillory—because he is the most vicious of the galaxy of unsavory personages. Penniboy Senior equates justice with law, but it is the unscrupulous Picklock who shows the absurdity of pushing this equation to its extreme. He seems to lack even the vestige of moral and social conscience that Penniboy Senior retains. A "petty-fogger" and "a fine pragmatic," he cheats all sides indiscriminately. Putting on the cloak of the Staple he describes himself to Cymbal and Fitton:

> Tut, I am *Vertumnus,*
> On euery change, or chance, vpon occasion,
> A true *Chamaelion,* I can colour for't.
> I moue vpon my axell, like a turne-pike,
> Fit my face to the parties, and become,
> Streight, one of them. (III, i, 34–39.)

Later, when he is attempting to cheat Penniboy Canter, Penniboy Canter describes him in alchemical terms:

> Fore-head of steele, and mouth of brasse! hath impudence
> Polish'd so grosse a lie, and dar'st thou vent it?
> *Engine,* compos'd of all mixt mettalls! (V, ii, 34–36.)

Picklock lives by law and not by truth, and it is only fitting that Penniboy Junior vanquishes him (V, ii) with truth that is supported by legality. Through the character of Picklock, Jonson seems to be saying that the profession of law, with its substitution of legal sanction for morality and of cant and jargon for truly communicative language, serves as the principal means of perpetuating the avaricious vices of the age. This round-head has been involved in every species of villainy shown in the play, and his punishment is an example of true justice rather than mere legality.

Jonson specifically denied any animus toward the legal profession as such, and some distinguished lawyers were his close personal friends. But there can be little doubt that he had limited enthusiasm for a profession whose practitioners have often made it possible for injustice to prevail over justice. Jonson's attitude toward lawyers is a little like that of Aristophanes toward Socrates in *The Clouds,* the man who labors mightily to prove the obvious and whose verbal facility works in such a way as to suggest that it is possible for falsehood to prevail over truth.

Like *Every Man Out of his Humor* and *The Magnetic Lady,* this play has a chorus—the gossips Mirth, Tattle, Expectation, and Censure. They interpret the Prologue at the beginning of the play and comment between the acts upon the action. A very bad audience, they typify the "critical" humors of certain captious persons who might have been expected to be in the real audience in the seventeenth century—or among any group of spectators of the drama. Gossip Mirth assures the Prologue that they are *"persons of* quality" and *"women of* fashion," who have "come to see, and to be seene." (Induction, 8–10.) They are part of an inescapable legacy which playwrights always have with them, "hereditary" descendants of those carping play-goers *"such as had a longing to see Playes, and sit vpon them, as wee doe, and arraigne both them, and their Poets."* (19–21.) They are, then, the inverse of the kind of spectator that the Prologue (both for the Stage and for the Court) pleads for, because they "see" rather than "heare" the play and can never understand the play as the ritual it is intended to be. Their flagrant interruption of the Prologue suggests their general obtuseness.

The Chorus as "audience" is more than a "realistic" perimeter for the action of the play, however. It is a part of the total illusion of the play, a structural and thematic "play-within-the-play" device that helps to illuminate the total meaning of the drama. Gossip Mirth remarks in the Induction that she is *"the daughter of* Christmas, *and spirit of* Shrouetide," (11–12), referring to the time of year when *The Staple* was originally performed. She has been to the *"Tiring-house"* to see the "Actors *drest,"* and the Poet's *"sweating to put me in minde of a good Shrouing dish . . . a stew'd* Poet." (61–66.) Her remarks here prepare the reader or viewer for subsequent food references during the play—the numerous "Butter" references and the culinary-poetic descriptions by Lickfinger. But these topical allusions, both to Lent itself and to the newsmonger Butter, suggest in a comic-chorus manner something of the larger import of the play.

In the richly symbolic presentation of its theme, the play is like a masque. It is a Lenten occasion calling for ritualistic fasting and a period of penance. Specifically, *The Staple,* as a kind of comic morality, calls for thinking and revaluation on the part of the spectator. As the Court Prologue expresses it, the play is offered as a "Rite,/ *To* Schollers, *that can iudge, and faire report/ she senses they heare, aboue the vulgar sort/ Of Nutcrackers, that only come for sight."* (5–8.) After Shrovetide, the period of confession and festivity, come Ash Wednesday and Lent, the time of penance. *The Staple of News* is a festival and it is also society's confessional, to be followed, no doubt, by a penance predicated on the terms of the confession. Thus Jonson presents, against the background of a Christian tradition, an aspect of the mythological situation in *Bartholomew Fair.*

But the members of this foolish antimasque regard the play as a kind of Feast of Fools, and Mirth evidently considers herself its Lady of Misrule when she calls herself the "daughter of Christmas, and spirit of Shrovetide." However, the irony is that they are real fools rather than mock fools. Always looking for the wrong things in the play, they are constantly being disappointed—as when they find no devil or fool, for example. They rarely penetrate beyond the accidental to the essential: Tattle looks for news that will be "new, and fresh" and "untainted, I shall find them else, if they be stale, or flye-blowne, quickly!" Even Mirth, their leader, though she has some insight into the play as allegorical representation, misses the point. The author is finally moved to address the reader directly, explaining the function of the Staple ("wherein the age may see her owne folly") and remarking that these "ridiculous Gossips that tattle between the Acts" have been wholly mistaken about the meaning of the allegory. (To the Readers, end of Act II.)

These gossips, then, are more than a device for getting the play under way and providing it with a realistic framework. Their more essential and significant function in its total context is to dramatize another facet of the appearance-reality/value theme with which the play is ultimately concerned: What is truly real and valuable? And how can it be known? Their limitations suggest the double-edged nature of point of view, which, as a metaphor for the epistemological potential, represents the possibility of both circumscription and expansion. The Chorus has the limited, circumscribed point of view, the inverse of that complex viewpoint that is demanded of the spectator who would discern, through the play's alchemical action, the metaphysical and epistemological implications underlying it—who would distinguish appearances from reality. The use of the chorus enables Jonson to make a final devastating ironic comment on the society of his own time: How can the myth, the real fable of the play, be understood by an audience such as these, whose sense for the perception of value in art as well as in life is limited and confused?

The most persistent objection to this play has been that there is an apparent disparity between the allegorical and the realistic action, a disparity that centers in the figure of Pecunia. In the main she is an abstract figure, but from time to time she seems to speak and act as though she were realistic. She is introduced at the beginning of II, i, in strictly allegorical terms; in II, ii, she is specifically money; in II, iv, the jeerers have come to see her, they say, and Penniboy Senior, her guardian, tells them he has no money to lend them. In II, v, she is described as "The *Venus* of the time, and state." (34.) And when she appears she is described in the stage direction as sitting in state. (at l. 44.)

She talks briefly, however, almost like Dol Common:

> p. se. Vouchsafe my toward kinsman, gracious *Madame,*
> The fauour of your hand. pec. Nay, of my lips, Sir,
> To him. p. iv. She kisses like a mortall creature,
> *Almighty Madame,* I haue long'd to see you.
>
> (46–49.)

The thought of Penniboy Junior, the prodigal, has brought life to her veins:

> And I haue my desire, Sir, to behold
> That youth, and shape, which in my dreames and wakes,
> I haue so oft contemplated, and felt
> Warme in my veynes, and natiue as my blood.
> When I was told of your arriuall here,
> I felt my heart beat, as it would leape out,
> In speach; and all my face it was a flame,
> But how it came to passe I doe not know. (50–57.)

This is an extension and a renewal of the Jonsonian technique of attributing symbolic value to an essentially realistic character. He is here attributing a measure of realistic value to an allegorical character, and the humor arises not from the realistic but from the allegorical personality, as the figure of money feels itself coming to life at the thought of an irresponsible young prodigal. The abstraction speaks almost like a human being.

In Penniboy Junior's reply, the human being speaks almost like an abstraction, or rather like a parody of an abstraction, a non-existent romantic lover whose language is ludicrously inappropriate:

> My passion was cleare contrary, and doubtfull,
> I shooke for feare, and yet I danc'd for ioy,

> I had such motions as the Sunne-beames make
> Against a wall, or playing on a water,
> Or trembling vapour of a boyling pot— (63–67.)

As the similes begin to accumulate, Penniboy Senior brings Pecunia back to reality:

> That's not so good, it should ha' bin a *Crucible,*
> With molten mettall, she had vnderstood it. (68–69.)

Pecunia as money should have effected an alchemical transformation in Penniboy Junior.

When Penniboy Senior tells his nephew that she will go with him wherever he pleases, Penniboy Canter observes that the money-bawd is also a flesh-bawd. (98–100.) This introduces the theme of Pecunia as whore, which is amplified considerably in IV, ii, where the encomium of Pecunia is punctuated by general kisses, and represents an extension of the references to money as a whore in *The Devil is an Ass*:

> Sir, money's a whore, a bawd, a drudge;
> Fit to runne out on errands: Let her goe.
> *Via pecunia!* (II, i, 1–3.)

The similarity of theme does not alter the fact that the technique is different. Merecraft's speech says money is a whore, while in *The Staple of News* money, allegorized as the lady Pecunia, is implicitly described as a whore and made to act like one, in keeping with her morally indifferent nature. Jonson does not, it seems to me, permit us to view her as a realistic character. Thus when she finally rejects Penniboy Senior, she does so in language which insistently directs our attention to her allegorical nature:

> But once he would ha' smother'd me in a chest,
> And strangl'd me in leather, but that you
> Came to my rescue, then, and gaue mee ayre.
>   (IV, iii, 41–43.)

The allegorical figure is given realistic overtones that do not destroy the allegorical basis. At the end of the play, now in the possession of the reformed Penniboy, she can refer to herself as the golden mean, not because she is, but because this is now Penniboy Junior's understanding of her, as it is also the understanding of the other Penniboys.

The problem is far from simple. I have attempted to describe it in terms of the masque and the morality play. Another analogy suggests itself: Pecunia may be described as a figure out of Spenserian allegory appearing in a comedy which, in the main, is not allegorical. The analogy is obviously imperfect, but it is suggestive. In the masque, allegory and realism are not allowed to come directly together. In allegory generally there is of course no realism unless we can describe the great majority of Jonson's comedies as realistic allegories, in which case the term itself would account for the situation. In realism there is no allegory, unless it is all allegory, although there may be symbolism, which, however, will not violate the realistic tone.

But in *The Staple of News* there is an allegorical figure moving about in a realistic world—really allegorical, not symbolic, because she remains consistent and has her own world: Broker, Mortgage, Bond, Statute, Wax; Penniboy Junior's clothes are symbolic—they *represent* folly; Pecunia is allegorical because as Pecunia she *is* money and as money she stands for the object of society's irrational ambition. The allegorical figure representing something other than itself finally is or becomes what it represents, as we can deduce from Spenser's practice. The great virtue of this is that each becomes a metaphor for the other. At first Pecunia is money; at the end money is Pecunia who, now in the outright possession of Penniboy Junior, represents, by virtue of that fact, the golden mean.

Does the allegorical figure become intrusive when it appears in a realistic context? For many readers the answer, obviously, is yes.

But Jonson is concerned here with problems of appearance and reality. With customary verve he has presented a society turned upside down, engaged in the pursuit of false and ephemeral values. The reality that this society pursues is actually appearance, an appearance that becomes reality only when society, centered in Penniboy Junior, is able to perceive the true nature of the object of its pursuit.

THE NEW INN

The Devil is an Ass and *The Staple of News* have found a few vigorous defenders; *The New Inn* has been more cordially damned than any other single play by Jonson. No play, of course, is without some defenders, but this has fewer than any of the others. The reason may be that the play is really as bad as most critics think it is; or it may be that its argument has eluded the critics; or it may be, as Mr. Partridge has suggested, that it failed in its first stage presentation, that the author bitterly attacked the first audience, and that Dryden dismissed it, along with the other late plays, as a dotage.[1]

Among the serious objections which have been voiced, the main ones are that its plot is monstrous and labored and that the play is dull.[2] The first ought not to represent a subjective judgment, but the second may. With respect to the first objection, the word *monstrous* apparently means supremely improbable, with the added implication "offensively so." The charge is an interesting one, for Jonson, with virtually no precedent in his own earlier work, supplied, in the first printed text, a complete summary of the action with an explanation of what we are to understand preceded it. Thus the author has specifically directed attention to a plot rejected by most critics. Either Jonson had lost all critical sense in thus pro-

---

[1] *The Broken Compass*, 189.
[2] C. H. Herford, Vol. II, 193–94.

ducing such a plot and then writing a summary of it, or it has a significance which has been overlooked.

Since the view is almost unanimous that this play is indeed a dotage, it might be well to observe that the author took the greatest care in preparing it for the press, that it contains some of Jonson's best writing (a point conceded even by Castelain[3]), and that in those comic scenes which have elicited such an outraged clamor because of their elaborate and multitudinous puns, he has, for better or for worse, displayed a virtuoso command of language. None of these three facts proves that the play is good, but they may be suggestive.

Even one who asserts that the puns are bad—and I must confess that I find many of them amusing—should admit that the author has not violated decorum: *he* is not using them, his low characters are. Falstaff's "were it not here apparent that thou art heir apparent" has been joyfully, and perhaps justly, greeted as an example of its author's fertile wit. But when Jonson has his characters outrageously associate fencing with geometry, philosophy, mythology, and literary criticism, all through the names of famous fencing masters or systems of fencing, he is accused of something like paralyzing stupidity—to paraphrase Edmund Wilson on Jonson's puns in general.[4] But punning has never been popular among great intellects—except Chaucer, Shakespeare, Jonson, and Swift, perhaps. Dr. Johnson spoke of the pun as Shakespeare's "fatal Cleopatra," something he could not resist and something that always got him into artistic difficulties. It may be that in voicing this complaint the great lexicographer was speaking merely as a

---

[3] Maurice Castelain, *Ben Jonson: L'homme et l'ouevre*, 422 ff.

[4] "Morose Ben Jonson," 216. Wilson's phrase is "stunning stupidity." The alliteration is not effective. It is characteristic of Wilson, in this essay, that he should paraphrase Dryden on Jonson's puns without pointing out that Dryden regarded *Epicoene*, a play Wilson dislikes, as being very close to the most perfect comedy ever written. Wilson is very careful in his use of other critics.

harmless drudge. But I come neither to praise Jonson's puns nor to bury them; I hope to explain them.

I feel reasonably confident in my assertion that adverse criticism of this play, whether it is ultimately right or wrong, has not been predicated on an understanding of the play's argument, its scene, or its characters, or, in fact, of its tone, something that Mr. Partridge examined with characteristic perceptiveness, a perceptiveness that led him to a salutary and exemplary reassessment of its literary and dramatic value.

In the first place, why has the scene of the play been so generally ignored—except insofar as it has been called ridiculous? And why has no significance whatever been attributed to the very sharp distinctions made between the two principal groups of characters— those below stairs and those above? And why has it been assumed that the love-plot, and particularly Lovell's discourses on love and valor, was intended with complete and unrelieved seriousness? Why did Dr. Tennant, for example, in his absurd attack on the play, assume that Jonson was trying to write something like *Twelfth Night,* merely because it includes love and mistaken identity?[5] *The New Inn* is far from simple, and many of the attacks have been the results of errors of oversimplification.

To begin, then: the action of the play occurs in the New Inn, The Light Heart, at Barnet, which is presided over by its light-hearted host, Goodstock, and his major-domo, Fly. As the play begins, the principal guest of the inn is one Lovell, who is retired and melancholy because of unrequited love for a Lady Frampul, a love which, however, he has never declared to the lady. One feels constrained to ask, in view of the fact that all the action occurs in this inn, whether it is possible that the inn itself may have some special significance, since Rome, Smithfield, and the Blackfriars all

[5] In his edition of the play, Yale Studies in English, XXXIV, (New York: Henry Holt, 1908.)

seem to have some special significance in the plays for which they provide the setting.

In the first scene, the Host says that the inn of The Light Heart is for lighthearted people. He is offended that Lovell should persist in his melancholy retirement. In the second scene he reiterates and re-emphasizes his irritation and expostulates with Lovell. In the third scene he indicates that he himself is living in retirement from the immorality and licentiousness of the world. Lovell wants the Host's son for a page, but the Host observes that all the great houses of England have degenerated. So far from being the breeding grounds of all the virtues, they are nurseries of vice:

> Instead of backing the brave Steed, o' mornings,
> To mount the Chambermaid; and for a leape
> O' the vaulting horse, to ply the vaulting house:
> For exercise of armes, a bale of dice,
> Or two or three packs of cards, to shew the cheat,
> And nimblenesse of hand; mistake a cloake
> From my Lords back, and pawne it. (I, iii, 72–78.)

Lovell is equally unenthusiastic about the trade of innkeeper:

> . . . me thinkes, a man
> Of your sagacity, and cleare nostrill, should
> Haue made, another choise, then of a place
> So sordid, as the keeping of an Inne:
> Where euery *Iouial* Tinker, for his chinke,
> May cry, *Mine host, to crambe, giue vs drinke;*
> *And doe not slinke, but skinke, or else you stinke.*
> *Rogue, Baud,* and *Cheater,* call you by the surnames,
> And knowne *Synonyma* of your profession.
>
> (I, iii, 109–17.)

The nature of the Host's isolation and the significance of his trade and of his inn are revealed implicitly in his reply to Lovell:

But if I be no such; who then's the Rogue,
In vnderstanding, Sir, I meane? who erres?
Who tinkleth then? or personates *Thom*. Tinker?
Your weazill here may tell you I talke baudy,
And teach my boy it; and you may beleeue him:
But Sir at your owne peril, if I doe not:
And at his too, if he doe lie, and affirme it.
No slander strikes, lesse hurts, the innocent.
If I be honest, and that all the cheat
Be, of my selfe, in keeping this Light Heart,
Where, I imagine all the world's a Play;
The state, and mens affaires, all passages
Of life, to spring new *scenes,* come in, goe out,
And shift, and vanish; and if I haue got
A seat, to sit at ease here, i' mine Inne,
To see the *Comedy;* and laugh, and chuck
At the variety, and throng of humors,
And dispositions, that come iustling in,
And out still, as they one droue hence another:
Why, will you enuy me my happinesse?

(I, iii, 118–37.)

Now, though a recognition of the fact that the new inn of The Light Heart symbolically represents the comic stage may or may not lead one to the view that this is a good play, any critical assessment must be based on knowledge of the play. One of the things that Jonson has done is to make the comic stage the metaphorical scene of his comedy, and its action "the state, and mens affaires, all passages/ Of life. . . ." One of the things that happen in this comedy is that the Host, the proprietor of the New Inn, experiences a change as a result of observing and finally participating in the action which is played on his stage.

Why has Jonson chosen an inn to represent the stage? On the realistic level an inn is a place of resort, frequented by all kinds of people from all walks of life. Thus the inn can at once become symbolic, as, in a sense, another famous inn, the Tabard at Southwark, had become symbolic.[6] Indeed, Chaucer's description of one of the guests in *that* inn has already been quoted by Lovell in I, iii, 68. Jonson's intentions are not Chaucer's, but reverend Chaucer, as Lovell calls him (69), has assembled almost all of his pilgrims in an inn before sending them on their way to Canterbury.

The inn-yard, of course, had been the scene of theatrical performances, of morality plays, for example, and it was still used for theatrical performances in the country in Jonson's day. Furthermore the inn, like the tavern, was a place of drinking and feasting—of *symposia*. The Apollo room had been the scene of an amusingly debased Symposium in *The Staple of News,* and in the New Inn riotous drinking below stairs occurs in counterpoint with a Symposium on love and valor above. Without taxing either ingenuity or credulity, then, it is important that the action of this play occurs in an inn.

That the New Inn is the comic stage specifically is indicated when the Host says that he sits at ease in his inn to see the comedy. It is elaborated in Lovell's hyperbolic language as he laments the lot of the unsuccessful lover and expresses his chagrin at having had his secret found out by an inn-keeper:

> O loue, what passion art thou!
> So tyrannous! and trecherous! first t'en-slaue,
> And then betray, all that in truth do serue thee!
> That not the wisest, nor the wariest creature,
> Can more dissemble thee, then he can beare
> Hot burning coales, in his bare palme, or bosome!
> And lesse, conceale, or hide thee, then a flash
> Of enflam'd powder, whose whole light doth lay it
> Open, to all discouery, euen of those,

---

[6] On this point, see also R. J. Kaufmann, *Richard Brome, Caroline Playwright,* 43.

Who haue but halfe an eye, and lesse of nose!
An Host, to find me! who is, commonly,
The log, a little o' this side the signe-post!
Or, at the best, some round-growne thing! a Iug,
Fac'd, with a beard, that fills out to the ghests,
And takes in, fro' the fragments o' their iestes?
But, I may wrong this, out of sullennes,
Or my mis-taking humor? Pray thee, phant'sie,
Be layd, againe. And, gentle-Melancholy,
Do not oppresse me. I will be as silent,
As the tame louer should be, and as foolish.

(I, iv, 1–20.)

"Hot burning coales" and "enflamed powder" are of course amorous hyperbole, seriously intended by Lovell, but somewat ludicrous to others.

The host, the round-grown thing, the jug faced with a beard, that serves the guests and takes in from the fragments of their jests, sounds suspiciously like the author. Lovell has a "mistaking humor" and resolves to be "as silent,/ As the tame louer should be, and as foolish." Hyperbole, Jonson the comic poet, a humor, a tame lover, and folly are all to be found in the Host's New Inn, all of which would seem to suggest that the Host stands in part for Ben Jonson—specifically, not the comic poet generally—and that *The New Inn* is a new kind of comic play with an even broader range of characters than we have seen before, with new situations and new argument, but with the same host, the round-grown thing, who had been filling out to the guests now for over thirty years and who perhaps still had one or two surprises for adventurous palates.

As usual, the first act is concerned with presenting the principal characters more or less revealingly and with getting the action under way or indicating how it will get under way. The arrival of Lady Frampul and her company almost drives Lovell out of the house, but his presence has been detected, and Pru persuades him to take part in the festivities. Lovell now confesses to the Host his passion for Lady Frampul and explains why he has not revealed it directly to her.

It is appropriate that the man who will discourse on love and valor should himself be languishing with love, like his medieval counterpart, the courtly lover. But unlike Chaucer's Aurelius, for example, Lovell has kept silent not out of fear and despair, but out of loyalty to the young Lord Latimer, whose father's page he had been. Respecting the virtuous father, he will not attempt to win the son's beloved. Still he is not to be completely separated from the figure of the courtly lover:

> I oft haue bene, too, in her company;
> And look'd vpon her, a whole day; admird her;
> Lou'd her, and did not tell her so; lou'd still,
> Look'd still, and lou'd: and lou'd, and look'd, and sigh'd;
> But, as a man neglected, I came of,
> And vnregarded— (I, vi, 108–13.)

He is, in other words, a courtly lover whose reticence is grounded not in fear of the cruel beloved, but in affection and loyalty to a benefactor, and responsibility to the benefactor's son.

Jonson's practice, introduced in *The Deuil is an Ass,* of imposing comic overtones on an essentially serious speech, appears again in this play. Lovell tells the Host that his entire life is consumed in love. "There is no life on earth, but being in loue!" (I, vi, 84.) But he is the tame lover, as he has said, and he is as foolish as the tame lover.

> But it is Loue hath beene
> The hereditary passion of our house,
> My gentle host, and, as I guesse, my friend. (97–99.)

Now Lovell is serious, but his words are ludicrous, and to the student of Jonson they may suggest the genealogy of the La-Fooles. Lovell is a lover who will be foolish, and he comes from a family of lovers. That the situation is partly comic is shown by the posing of the epistemological question:

> But is your name *Loue-ill,* Sir, or *Loue-well?*
> I would know that. LOV. I doe not know't my selfe,
> Whether it is. (95–97.)

But the epistemological question is also an axiological one: what, in fact, is the precise value of Lovell's love?

The central episodes of the play are the discourses on love and valor that Lovell delivers to Lady Frampul in the presence of the entire company, with just a sufficient number of interruptions to make the scenes dramatic. Mr. Partridge has called attention to the fact that these scenes are comic, a conclusion at which he arrives by observing that Lady Frampul's reactions are ludicrously hyperbolical, which of course they are.[7] There is something absurd in Lovell's situation as well. He delivers a highly Platonic discourse on disinterested and perfect love while he himself is consumed with passion. That is to say he is unable to act in accordance with the theory of love he propounds. He delivers a highly articulate Senecan discourse on valor (which here means Stoic fortitude), convincing everyone in the room of the truth of what he is saying, and then, in an agony of unrequited love, takes to his bed like Troilus or Aurelius, with the difference that his language shows that he knows how he should act, while theirs does not.

There is, therefore, an inconsistency between the appearance and the reality. It appears that Lovell knows how to act; the reality is that he cannot do so. Mr. Partridge has indicated the presence of the appearance-reality theme in Jonson's use of clothing images, particularly in the scene involving Nick Stuff the tailor and his

---

[7] *The Broken Compass,* 190 ff. See particularly 194–98.

wife Pinnacia. This theme, however, has already been implied in the identity of the New Inn as the comic stage: it appears to be a wayside inn, but in reality it stands for something else. Lovell appears to be in complete command of his faculties, but in reality he is not. Pru becomes sovereign of the festivities in the inn, but in reality she is Lady Frampul's maid. The Host appears to be a professional innkeeper, but in reality he is not. The nurse appears to be an Irish beggar, Frank appears to be a boy, etc., etc.

In the illusory world of the New Inn, nothing, in fact, is what it appears to be, and yet the appearance has considerable relevance to the reality. This is illustrated most clearly in the multiple identities of Frank, the supposed son of the Host. He is borrowed by Lady Frampul, to be disguised as Laetitia, because there is a shortage of women in the party. Beaufort falls in love with and marries him. Then Frank's true identity is revealed, to Beaufort's discomfiture, whereupon the nurse reveals that Frank is in reality the lost Laetitia. Thus the disguise has the function not of concealing but of revealing the true identity.

Ironically, when her identity is revealed, Beaufort does not want her after all, assuming that she is the daughter of a beggar or innkeeper. He takes her when he learns that the Host her father is really Lord Frampul, but in the meantime, as a morally and intellectually defective character on the comic stage, he has clearly preferred the appearance to the reality. And, to return to Lovell's discourses, the fact that he is unable to act in accordance with the principles which he propounds in no way detracts from their validity as principles. He is, in fact, expressing an ideal not completely dissimilar to that expressed in *The Devil is an Ass,* and again, the impossible ideal is preferable to its baser alternatives.

In this play the distinctions between appearances and reality comprehend the differences between principles and actions. The appearance reveals the reality, the action comments on the principle, and the principle comments on the action. Pru the chambermaid so well fulfills her role as queen that from a maid she is transmuted into a lady, marrying Lord Latimer. At the end of the play she is wearing the dress that Nick Stuff made for Pru and that he had his wife Pinnacia wear as part of the indecent ritual of his abnormal lust. The dress is becoming to Pru, as it had not been to Pinnacia, because Pru is, in spite of her material station, a lady, whereas Mistress Stuff is not—her language gives her away:

> PRU. Yo' haue a fine sute on, Madam! and a rich one!
> LAT. And of a curious making! PRU. And a new!
> PIN. As new, as Day. LAT. She answers like a fish-wife.
>   (IV, iii, 29–31.)

It seems to me that the gallants and ladies in this play do not, as Mr. Partridge suggests,[8] make the same assumptions about clothing that Nick Stuff and his wife do. Nick Stuff's peculiar mode of sexual gratification is predicated on the idea that it is more pleasurable to sleep with a countess than a tailor's wife—an assumption which may or may not be true. The assumption—or at least the gratification—is complicated by fetishism, or something like it. Since there are no countesses available to him, he will dress his wife like one and himself like a footman.

Freud would have been quite satisfied with this, but Jonson's foray into the realm of abnormal psychology makes a social point: in satire and therefore, one supposes, in life, countesses have been known to be interested in footmen—there is a similar situation in Book III of *Gulliver's Travels,* where it is strictly a matter of social satire. When Pinnacia Stuff is dressed like a countess, she acts like the very worst kind of countess imaginable and calls poor Nick her "protection." This situation represents a greatly intensified example of the blurring of distinctions which made up such an im-

8 *Ibid.,* 198–205.

portant part of the thematic argument of *Epicoene*. Nick imagines he is sleeping with a countess; Pinnacia imagines she is a countess lying with a footman. And since Pinnacia imagines she is acting like a countess, Lady Frampul and her friends are outraged that such behavior should be attributed to people of their own social class.

The Stuffs, therefore, get no pleasure from honest connubial bliss, which for them would be mere drudgery: they prefer symbolic fornication. They have deserted their own social status for a non-existent one, and are thus left nowhere. The tediousness, as many critics have called it, of this comic situation, delivers, in very few lines, a telling thrust at distorted moral and social values: when Pinnacia and her husband first appear in the inn, Sir Glorious Tiptoe, Hodge Huffle, and Bartholomew Burst all accost her, thinking her to be a "lady gay." (IV, ii, 52, 65–66.) As a real lady she is taken upstairs to the ladies and gentlemen, and as a lady she is received until she begins to talk, thus revealing herself. Sir Glorious and his friends hear her talk and assume she is a whore in spite of her fine clothes; Lady Frampul and her friends are momentarily misled by the clothes. And they throw her out, not because her behavior is unladylike and disgusting, but because it implies disgusting behavior on their part.

Lovell's rescue of Pinnacia from the gallants below stairs represents a different level of comically inverted values. She was of course perfectly in her element, an element from which she was rescued by Lovell acting the part of the chivalrous hero effecting the salvation of a lady in distress. Lady Frampul describes it affectingly:

> I nere saw
> A lightning shoot so, as my seruant did,
> His rapier was a *Meteor,* and he wau'd it
> Ouer 'hem, like a *Comet!* as they fled him!
> I mark'd his manhood! euery stoope he made

Was like an Eagles, at a flight of Cranes!
(As I haue read somewhere.) (IV, iii, 11–17.)

The tragic simile is ludicrously inappropriate to the situation, since Lovell has merely rescued an inglorious tart from a group of drunken louts.

The drunken louts and their placing in the comedy present a problem because they appear not to be clearly integrated into the major action of the play—that involving Lovell, the Host, and the others. As I have already suggested, it seems odd that no one has paid particular attention to the seemingly divided nature of the dramatis personae—one group above stairs and one below. This is a new arrangement in Jonson, unless one would use *Poetaster* as an example; but in that play there are comic and serious actions, brought together in the last act, while here there are two kinds of comic representation: ribald low comedy in low places and a highly refined version of New Comedy upstairs.

The refinement upstairs has something to do with the ribaldry below stairs. The apparently nonsensical drunken conversations between Fly, Sir Glorious Tiptoe, and the others occur more or less in counterpoint with the discourses on love and valor that are the chief ornaments of the major action. It is obvious that Jonson felt that a comedy even of refined sensibilities required some linguistic violence, and the drinking scenes supply it. Yet this does not supply a really satisfactory explanation in terms of the artistic intention.

Actually each of the two threads of action is concerned—as is usual with Jonson—with the presentation of social themes, while at the same time both reinforce the art-theme implicit in the Host's metaphorical identification of his inn as the comic stage. Realistic comedy below stairs carries symbolic meaning; idealized discourses above stairs are punctuated sharply by contrapuntal returns to reality. And the symbolic action implied in all of the mistaken identities in the main plot culminates in a return to reality that is also a ritual— "... our sacrifice/ Of *loue* to night," as the Host calls it. (V, v, 153–54.)

One's first impression is that the nonsensical conversations between Fly and his friends represent the kind of social commentary implicit in the representation of language as noise in *Epicoene*. Sir Glorious Tiptoe is the *miles gloriosus* reduced to his ultimate absurdity: he is both coward and ignoramus, fooling no one and completely impotent from the beginning. Bobadill affected to be a talented soldier; Sir Glorious affects only to be an authority on fencing. He has no plans to save the commonwealth, his interest in fencing is purely formal—geometrical—and in fact he is not even good at fencing, as his rout at the hands of Lovell shows. But the language of fencing, which supplies those "purely nominal" jests so offensive to early critics, is significantly more double edged than Sir Glorious' sword. There is some point also to the references to the household as a militia.

At the center of almost all the talk downstairs are Fly and Sir Glorious Tiptoe. Fly is the quartermaster of the inn. He is "a Creature of all liquors, all complexions,/ Be the drinke what it will, hee'l haue his sip." (II, iv, 13–14.) He was part of the inventory when the Host "came to take the Inne, here." (16–17.) He is jestingly described as a scholar, and it is with his nominal scholarship that he manages to produce directly and indirectly the outrageous puns on fencing and mathematics in II, v. As a scholar he wears black "And speakes a little taynted, fly-blowne *Latin*,/ After the Schoole." (22–23.) His calling is to "enflame the reckoning . . . Bring vp the shot i' the reare, as his owne word is." (26–27.) And he is visitor-general of all the rooms.

> Some call him Deacon *Fly*, some Doctor *Fly*,
> Some Captaine, some Lieutenant. But my folkes
> Doe call him Quarter-master, which he is. (33–35.)

At the end of the play the Host turns the inn over to Fly:

> *Fly,* prouide vs lodgings,
> Get beds prepar'd: yo' are master now o' the Inne,
> The Lord o' the light Heart, I giue it you.
> *Fly,* was my fellow *Gipsey.* All my family,
> Indeed, were *Gipseys,* Tapsters, Ostlers, Chamberlaines,
> Reduced vessels of ciuility. (V, v, 124–29.)

There is certainly more than a bare suggestion that Fly is symbolically associated with the Host either as an aspect of the Host's own identity or, like Face, as a figure representing the comic spirit. As Fly he is a familiar spirit beloved by the Host. As quartermaster he provides sustenance for the guests of the inn, and cheats them when he can. He came as part of the inventory of an inn that has already been identified as the comic stage. He speaks Latin and forces Sir Glorious Tiptoe to reveal the many facets of his varied and profound ignorance. And he was the Host's fellow gypsy, one of the reduced vessels of civility with whom he had associated during his career as an innkeeper, just as the other gypsies—tapsters, ostlers, chamberlains—are also associated with the inn.

If Fly is to be identified as comic spirit, it should perhaps be more precisely as the spirit of satirical comedy, since he seems designed to draw out the most ludicrous in the characters below stairs. In this connection it is interesting that neither of the gallants, Beaufort and Latimer, is more than mildly interested in Fly's activities and that in II, v, they assume that he is no more clever than Sir Glorious Tiptoe. The gallants represent the new audience, no longer interested in the richly various commodity their host the playwright had been vending with such success for so long. Thus the activities carried on in the two levels of the inn represent the Old Comedy, with Fly, Sir Glorious, and the others, and the New Comedy, with Lovell, Lady Frampul, and their train. And Beaufort and Latimer stand for the audience being educated in the inn.

If this necessarily tentative identification of the two main groups of characters is at all accurate, it must be said that in spite of the apparently simple arrangement, the play is complex and the complexity must be examined in detail. It is obvious that the action above stairs reflects on that below; it is less obvious that the action below also reflects on that above, in a fairly elaborate way. The characters below stairs represent, on the first level, a society in which nothing seems to mean anything; the riotous misuse of language is the central symbol. The characters above stairs represent a society in which the very real meaning of language can be grossly misunderstood, a society that has intellectual principles on which it is unable to act.

But the misuse of language below stairs is also directed toward a larger end. Fencing becomes a kind of debased geometry and the inn a militia. The puns on fencing as geometry are introduced in II, v, by Sir Glorious Tiptoe's comments on the Host's being in *cuerpo*—not properly dressed. This is a reiteration of the appearance-reality theme: the Host is not a satisfactory one for Sir Glorious because he is not dressed well enough. He observes that your Spanish host is never seen "without his *Paramento's,* cloake, & sword." (73.) But Fly retorts that his master has in fact a long sword, "To note him a tall-man, and a Master of fence." (77.)

He teaches not the Spanish system of fencing, however, but the Greek, that of the Greek master, Euclid, the nominal jest depending on one's knowledge of the fact that the Spanish system of fencing taught by Don Luis Pachero de Narvaez was sometimes called the geometrical or Euclidean because of its extreme formality:[9]

> He do's it all, by lines, and angles, *Colonel,*
> By parallels, and sections, has his *Diagrammes!* (92–93.)

Sir Glorious is astonished to learn that Euclid is a fencer now in

[9] Herford and Simpson, Vol. X, 311.

Elysium. The Host is thus identified with Euclid, which inspires Sir Glorious to observe,

> Fart vpon Euclide, he is stale, & antique,
> Gi' me the modernes. *Fli.* Sir he minds no modernes,
> Go by, *Hieronymo!* (80–82.)

Those who congenitally dislike puns will no doubt deplore the fact that Hieronymo was not only the hero of Kyd's play but also a noted contemporary Italian fencing-master. The Host, identified with Euclid and hence with the ancients, has no use for a modern fencing master whose name also suggests a relatively modern play. The associations here are clear enough if one has the Simpsons' notes at hand; but why should the Host be identified as a playwright thus obliquely through the fancy fencing references? The answer lies in Jonson's *impress,* with the figure of the compass.

For Jonson, the compass, a mathematical and geometrical instrument, stood also for the artist, as is clearly indicated in the figure of Compass, the scholar-mathematic (who is also the poet) in *The Magnetic Lady*. The appearance-reality theme has been reintroduced in the references to the Host's clothes—he is not what he appears to be, or he is something that he does not appear to be. It has been rendered both diffuse and intense in the fencing-geometry references, which have at least a double function in identifying the Host—or re-identifying him—and revealing the familiar wit of Fly and the obtuseness of Sir Glorious Tiptoe.

The military references have a similar function. Jonson had always admired the true soldier. In *The Staple of News* he had praised him highly:

>   ... a *true Souldier,*
> He is his *Countryes strength*, his *Soueraignes safety,*
> And to secure his peace, he makes himselfe
> The *heyre* of danger, nay the *subiect* of it,
> And runnes those vertuous hazards, that this Scarre-crow
> Cannot endure to heare of. (IV, iv, 144–49.)

In *The Magnetic Lady,* Captain Ironside, the soldier, is the *alter ego* of Compass the poet-figure, just as Manly has a similar relationship to Wittipoll in *The Devil is an Ass.* In *The New Inn* the references to the staff of the inn as militia, taken in conjunction with the figure of the Host as mathematician-poet, serve to round out, allusively and ironically, the identity of the inn. Ironside, as *alter ego* of Compass, represents the moral nature necessary to the poet. The inn-mates as militia represent a comic inversion of the moral ordering power of comic art. The symbolism is elaborately double edged, working in roughly the same way as the fencing-geometry references: it identifies an aspect of the inn, and it reveals a blurring of standards through ludicrous misuse of language.

However, since the identity of the soldier with moral order is not definitely made until *The Magnetic Lady,* one cannot make a positive identification here—although one might recall Brainworm's disguising himself as Fitz-Sword. Instead, an essentially disorderly situation on the realistic level, the plot of Fly's militia, as Sir Glorious calls it (III, i, 1), is described as though it presented a perfect military order:

> I like the plot of your *Militia,* well!
> It is a fine *Militia,* and well order'd!
> And the diuision's neat! (III, i, 1–3.)

Sir Glorious then describes the whole arrangement in detail, only lamenting that it is not quite so good as the Spanish. And, according to Sir Glorious, Fly will preside over this militia both as commander and as an exact professor. (33.)

Thus two symbols of order—geometry and the military—insistently make their appearance in the scenes below stairs, ironically reflecting on the disorder in which they occur, while at the same time, through the identity of Fly and the Host, they imply an order that subsumes comic disorder. The crew below stairs in the inn has its own existence, which is simultaneously and in a number of different ways related not only to the larger life of the play but to the embracing life of the comic stage.

Beaufort and Latimer, it seems to me, are really deficient not only in their mistaken assumption about Fly, but also in not being amused at the panorama of ignorance that they view in the second act. In this respect they are rather like Winwife and Quarlous entering the Fair for the wrong reasons. The Fair was a tremendous affirmation of both life and art. If the same thing cannot be said about the cellar in the New Inn, it is surely significant that Fly will remain in charge after the Host and the others have left. The louts in the cellar disappear from the action after the middle of the fourth act, but presumably they are permanently attached to the place. Their absurd folly, depicted as occurring in the cellar on the ground floor, is apparently the permanent legacy of the New Inn.

Like all double-plot plays, *The New Inn* presents two thematically related situations, with, in this instance, a third one added by virtue of the nature of the inn itself. What happens in the refined comedy upstairs is not quite so refined as it may appear to be at first glance. Downstairs, language has become strictly meaningless except in so far as it has symbolic value: the realistic language is chaos; the symbolic language is not. Upstairs, exalted language is regularly deflated by realistic verbal pinpricks and by the reader's recollection of what is going on in the real world below.

The two principal groups of characters represent two sides of the same coin, but in another sense each is a coin with two sides of its own, one aspect of which we have seen in connection with the realistic group that is also symbolic. The symbolic group is also realistic. For example, there seems to be little doubt that the discourses on love and valor, occurring in an inn endowed with all the wealth of metaphorical meaning that we have seen, constitute both real idealism and realistic satire. The fact that Lovell speaks so well of love and valor when he cannot act in accordance with his own understanding of either must surely be a comment on the refined sensibilities and more than occasionally gross behavior of members of the court of Charles and Henrietta Maria.[10] In the first chorus of *The Magnetic Lady* the Boy observes that *The New Inn* was concerned with "some recent humours still, or manners of men, that went along with the times." (102–104.) The manners below stairs were not recent, but those above were.

Jonson is not only satirizing courtiers who do not act in accordance with principle; he is also suggesting that if a principle or an ideal is beyond the powers of human beings to realize in their own behavior, then its very nobility lessens its value. In *The Devil is an Ass* he drew on the masque to suggest an idealized resolution of a real problem and to imply that a noble ideal is better than most of its alternatives. In *The Staple of News* he varied the technique by making a symbolic object assume different identities in the minds of different characters. In *The New Inn* a frankly Platonic ideal is resolved in a frankly ritualistic manner: *Bartholomew Fair* ended ritualistically in an invitation to a feast: *The New Inn* ends ritualistically in a sacrifice to love. At the court of Henrietta Maria a disquisition on Platonic or courtly love was capable of ending in fornication. In *The New Inn* the noble idealism is superseded by something better, by marriages and reconciliations.

And, as in the three preceding plays, tragicomedy is averted by placing the idealistic and the sentimental in a comic context. For example, the discourse on love is preceded by a particularly fine display of inconsequentiality in the cellar. During the discourse there are some sharply deflationary comments by young Beaufort that have the function of bringing the high-flown Platonism back to earth:

> I relish not these *philosophicall* feasts;

[10] Herford saw the connection, but not as satire. (Vol. II, 196–199.)

> Giue me a banquet o' sense, like that of *Ovid*:
> A forme, to take the eye; a voyce, mine eare;
> Pure *aromatiques,* to my sent; a soft,
> Smooth, deinty hand, to touch; and, for my taste,
> *Ambrosiack* kisses, to melt downe the palat.
>
> (III, ii, 125–30.)

And yet Beaufort's comment is far from beastly: the form to take the eye and the voice to take the ear could easily start one up the Platonic ladder. More distinctly anti-Platonic is his later retort to Lovell's insistence that the end of love is to have two people made one in will and affection, with the minds "inoculated," not the bodies: "Gi' me the body, if it be a good one." (155.) The irony of this comment is characteristically elaborate: it is designed to deflate Lovell's Platonic statement; Beaufort is assiduously making love to a person everyone thinks is a boy; but the person is really a girl after all, so that his preference for the body is not so naive as it first appears.

Lady Frampul's reaction is comic in a somewhat different sense. She claims to have been translated by an alchemy of love or language; she feels a transmutation of her blood, "And all he speakes, it is proiection!" (171–77.) No doubt there is a pun on projection. Later she compares Lovell not only to Plato, which would be appropriate enough, but also to writers of romance—Heliodorus, Tatius, D'Urfé, and Sidney, of whom Jonson had expressed guarded disapproval in the conversations with Drummond.

Under the inspiration of Lovell's speech she becomes a devotee of the religion of love and says that heretofore she has been a heretic. She wonders what penance she should perform to be received into the church of love:

> Goe on procession, bare-foot, to his Image,
> And say some hundred penitentiall verses,
> There, out of *Chaucers Troilus, and Cresside?*

Or to his mothers shrine, vow a Waxe-candle
As large as the Towne May-pole is, and pay it!
(218–22.)

She says she could begin to be in love with him even though he is old enough to be her father. Mr. Partridge has demonstrated the comic nature of Lady Frampul's reactions and points out that Pru delivers the superlative comment: "Beware, you doe not coniure vp a spirit/ You cannot lay." (251–52.) Even this almost superfluous piece of advice has its extra ironic twist, in view of the fact that they all go to bed at the end of the play to beget a new generation for the New Inn.

Act III, which, as the poet says in the argument, opens the *epitasis,* or business, of the play, begins below stairs, where the talk keeps pace with the drinking. It has only two scenes, the second, quite brief, being given over to Lovell's first discourse. It concludes with Fly's announcement that a "newer lady," Pinnacia Stuff, has appeared at the inn.

With Act IV we are below stairs once more where a different kind of love is the subject of conversation, so that Lovell's discourse has been placed in counterpoint with a less refined sort and has also been punctuated by Beaufort's own views on the subject, less exalted than Lovell's and considerably more so than those of Sir Glorious Tiptoe, Hodge Huffle, and the rest. The effect is not to make Lovell an island of virtue in a sea of lust, for his actions show that he too is imperfect, but to indicate that the rarefied Platonism of his discourse ought to be attached to reality without being debased by realistic grossness. This point, I think, is anticipated by Beaufort's irritation when the nurse asserts that he intends to "leap" the supposed (and real) Laetitia: "Leape her? I lip her, foolish Queene at Armes." (III, ii, 117.)

The first two scenes of Act IV involve drinking and quarreling in the cellar and the appearance of the Stuffs. The third scene presents their peculiar vice and their rejection by the outraged company. The fourth scene is devoted to Lovell's discourse on fortitude, the truth of which is apparent to everyone, including the young gallants. The two discourses establish ideal standards of behavior in love and in the vicissitudes of social life that, for all their generally accepted truth, are almost impossible of realization—so much so that the verbal Stoic Lovell retires with an imperfect Idea of his Platonic mistress in his heart and no fortitude whatever to ease the pain. As the catastrophe impends, appearance and reality remain two rather different things.

Whatever its defects may be, the play thus far has been marvelously put together. It is like other double-plot plays in that the action and language of each part comment symbolically on the other, a fact that is perhaps more obvious than its ultimate significance. But Jonson's imitations become characteristically Jonsonian, and this is a double-plot play in which both plots are comic, a departure from the usual procedure. If it seems to have some resemblance to the situation in *The Devil is an Ass,* the parallel is only approximate, because the serious business of Wittipoll and Mistress Fitzdottrell, which offers an idealized answer to the gross follies of the comically-envisioned world, becomes more and more closely associated with that world. In *The New Inn* the two worlds as such remain separate: they are finally joined symbolically, but not in the realistic action. Through the first four acts a perfectly balanced tension has been established between the worlds above and below stairs, with a few symbolic links implied.

Because of the symbolic nature of the inn in which all the action occurs, and because of the structure of the play, it is necessary to examine the nature of the two worlds more precisely than we have done so far, as a necessary preliminary to an exposition of the catastrophe. At this point a little oversimplification will perhaps be welcome.

The comic world represented by the louts below stairs is essentially the world of realistic, satiric comedy with a few overtones of Shakespearean rusticity, as when Pierce Anon the drawer observes, apropos the expounding of some truth by Fly, "We are all mortall,/ And haue our visions." (III, i, 129–30.) It is a world in which values have been inverted and distinctions blurred, a world which makes sense only in so far as we understand its true nature. It is a world in which all traces of normal order have been unsystematically but consistently perverted. It is a world characterized by bawdy language and bawdry, elaborate puns, and absurdity, an inverted reflection, in the steel glass of satire, of the chaotic society outside. It contains no moral norms but those existing vestigially in the minds of the spectators, minds formed by traditions that are themselves falling into disuse. It is an insanely reversed image of what should ideally be sane.

It is, therefore, the traditional artistically conceived world of Old Comedy that Jonson has presented so well and so often before. Still, it is different from that world, in that it includes all the externals but not the essential intellectual substance. In the great comedies of the middle period the Aristophanic world was complete and self-contained, with moral and social principles implicit in their dramatized negation. The world of *The Alchemist* exists in persistent reference to the society that in large measure helped produce it: the world of Sir Glorious Tiptoe exists in contrapuntal reference to the world of Lovell and Lady Frampul.

It clearly reflects aspects of a chaotic society, but as we watch the play we are less concerned with reflections of a real society, more concerned with reflections *on* another comic society, a society which, as I have suggested, reflects certain preoccupations of the court of Charles and Henrietta Maria.

Jonson seems to have had relatively few misgivings about the court of James as a model of its kind, contenting himself with a few satiric barbs here and there; in the middle plays he had been content to direct his attention to society and present his instructions for the court in the epitome of courtly entertainment, the masque. I would assume that by 1628–29 he had come to the conclusion that society was beyond the reach of redemption through laughter. Twice in *The Staple of News* he explained specifically the very meaning of social satire, and, perhaps revealingly, he suffered a stroke two years later. I would say that by now he felt that the court was the only hope for a return to anything like a sane and reasonable social order. (I am not concerned here with history's verdict on James and on Charles, only with Jonson's.)

But the court was hardly presenting the perfect example to society that Jonson had always felt it should. Thus for four acts of this play the two estates symbolically reflect each other's follies and absurdities. After the fourth act the satirical presentation of a comically ruinous society is dropped and attention is directed to resolving the moral and intellectual problems of the other realm. The old real world remains, but in a state of hopeless distinegration—or almost hopeless. The only thing that can revive it will be the regeneration of the world upstairs.

The comedy in the cellar represents in detail the externals of Old Comedy; it is a reflection of the empty social world outside; its main dramatic significance lies in its relationship to the comic world upstairs, the satirical representation of the court.

The society of the comic world above stairs consists of ladies, gentlemen, gallants, and servants. It is essentially domestic, and its action concludes with marriages and reconciliations. The world thus presented is the world of New Comedy, but as domestic New Comedy it alludes satirically to a very important segment of the social world at large—the court. Therefore, while it dramatically represents the world of New Comedy it also has overtones of Old Comedy, since the satire goes beyond a domestic situation in its scope and embraces the very fountainhead of society. It might be argued also that since the Old Comedy world below stairs is domiciled in the New Inn and thus constitutes a kind of family, it carries overtones of New Comedy.

The two comic worlds of *The New Inn* thus represent two social worlds and two kinds of comedy, associated in the play through symbolic and thematic cross-references. They are associated also through the fact that Jug and Trundle act as criers, Ferret as clerk, and Jordan as usher for the court of love at the beginning of III, ii, which, in terms of the art-theme of the play, suggests Old Comedy ushering in and introducing New Comedy. And finally they are associated via the fertility ritual that ends the play, a ritual said to be implied in the marriages that characteristically end New Comedy and which was most certainly central to the Dionysian rites which immediately preceded Old Comedy, significant vestiges of which remained in the figure of the priest of Dionysus who presided over the comic presentations in the Athenian theater. Thus the jests below stairs are more than purely nominal and the action above stairs not entirely monstrous.

"The fifth, and last *Act* is the *Catastrophe,* or knitting vp of all." (Argument.) There is a good deal to be knit up. Lovell has delivered his discourses, profoundly affecting Lady Frampul, but has retired in a fit of desperate melancholy, convinced, after describing fortitude so eloquently, that his case is hopeless. Lady Frampul, having listened eagerly to discussions of ideal love and noble fortitude, is wildly in love with Lovell. Beaufort has behaved in a somewhat more rational way: he has retired to the stable and married the supposed Laetitia, a fact that the Host predicts will cause considerable amusement. Pru appears in the new suit which has been retrieved from Pinnacia Stuff and is sent to get Lovell, who the Host thinks will be cheered up by Beaufort's expected discomfiture. Beaufort appears, issues some eagerly anticipatory orders, and is somewhat disturbed to learn that he has apparently married a boy, something not included in his plans.

The nurse then bursts in and reveals that the boy is really a girl after all. More misunderstandings are resolved when it turns out that the nurse is really the lost wife of the lost Lord Frampul and that the Host is Lord Frampul no longer lost. The marriage of Beaufort and Laetitia is on again, the Host is reunited with his wife, Lovell is to marry Lady Frampul, Latimer will marry Pru, and Fly inherits the inn.

The theme and substance of the last act is metamorphosis. Nothing can happen until literal identities are revealed and symbolic identities perceived—the audience does not even know that the supposed Laetitia is the real Laetitia and can only anticipate that if Beaufort persists in his wooing he will be embarrassed. The catastrophe just described is surprising in every detail. Its logic depends upon the revelation of both the literal and the symbolic identities heretofore unsuspected.

It has been often asserted that the last act is preposterous, that is, that it is unbelievable, or that things like this don't really happen. Stated thus simple-mindedly, the point no doubt has merit, particularly if one is prepared to assume that literature is just like life, that self-deception never occurs, that each of us understands fully the nature of everyone else, and that disguises, real and metaphorical, have no place in comedy. *The New Inn,* of course, is not like Jonson's other plays—nor, for that matter, are the other plays all alike: its technique is comic, but its situation is something like that of *The Winter's Tale* and *The Tempest.*

The problem now, therefore, is to explain the catastrophe, to draw together the threads of action and metaphor, to define the significance of the revealed identities.

As the last act develops—and it does so very rapidly—it becomes apparent that the realistic action has suddenly slipped into the background and that the symbolic structure that remains represents the heart of the play. The realistic action does indeed continue, since the scene and the characters are the same as they were during the preceding four acts, but its main significance has little to do with realistic comedy as such. There are apparent New Comedy resolutions: Beaufort, the young rake, is reclaimed and marries the girl, almost like an engaging prodigal; Latimer will marry Pru for her virtue; Lovell and Lady Frampul are finally joined; the host is reunited with his wife. There is nothing new in these situations. They are as old as Menander, and I describe them as "realistic"—although of course they are not—merely as a means of distinguishing their bald representation from their various levels of meaning and significance.

I have already discussed the development of the appearance-reality theme in the relationship between Beaufort and Laetitia, first a boy, then a girl, then apparently a boy again, and finally not only a girl but the daughter of Lord Frampul. If one insists on regarding this kind of play as realistic, then this situation is necessarily absurd. But the terms of the action prevent our thinking of it as realistic. It seems to me that Jonson has here adopted something like the later Shakespearean technique of presenting an action in such a way that we are, at every critical point in its development, thrown back on the necessity of regarding it in symbolic terms. I have suggested that Beaufort, along with Latimer, is, on the symbolic level, to be equated roughly with a segment of the audience being educated in the comic theater.

The action of the last act represents the culmination of this process. As prodigal, Beaufort is reclaimed through the knowledge of the true identity of Laetitia—that is, the marriage, when it is finally formalized, represents a sacramental union under the terms of which the prodigal has been brought home. But the marriage of Beaufort as guest and audience in the New Inn will also represent something else, as is indicated in V, iv, when Beaufort appears, after his marriage in the stable that has become a church, the ceremony having been performed by a priest Fly had fetched from his lodging in the next inn:

> HOST. Haue patience, *Pru,* expect, bid the Lord ioy.
> PRU. And this braue Lady too. I wish them ioy.
> PEI. Ioy. *Ior.* Ioy. *Iug.* All ioy. *Hos.* I, the house full of ioy.
> FLY. Play the bels, Fidlers, crack your strings with ioy.
>
> (V, iv, 20–23.)

On the realistic level, all this joy is predicated on the expectation of mirth from Beaufort's impending embarrassment. But its verbal expression passes almost from comedy to ritual: joy reiterated seven times in four lines, with an invocation of music, bells and fiddles. In effect Beaufort has been married to joy, here identified by her Latin name, Laetitia; this kind of joy is an essential quality of the inn, as the Host has indicated in the first act, when he complains about Lovell's melancholy:

> It is against my free-hold, my inheritance,
> My *Magna charta, Cor laetificat,* . . . (I, ii, 23–24.)

The Host's *magna charta* is that the heart of man must be made joyful. The quotation is from Psalm civ in the Vulgate: *"Et vinum laetificet cor hominis."*

One of the ends of comedy is a religious end, a point reiterated in the solemn but joyful ceremony at the end of the play. Laetitia is thus an essential part of the New Inn, but not to be enjoyed casually. Beaufort does not properly possess her until she has been formally given to him by her father the Host, and after he has been castigated by her mother as a "young lord of dirt" for the hasty marriage and equally hasty rejection.

The New Comedy attachment between Beaufort and Laetitia thus becomes also, on the symbolic level, a statement of a proper approach to comedy and, I believe, an approach to life, an understanding of the nature of joy. The quality itself is ambiguous, like the nature of Pecunia. True understanding lies in the minds of its observers. Joy may be either modest or immodest, so that we see Laetitia undergoing experiences roughly parallel to those of Pecunia. The association with New Comedy is made when, as Frank, she appears in I, iii, quoting the *Andria* of Terence. As a comic quality Frank will be kept in the inn by his supposed father to avoid the debasement inherent in the world outside. As the supposed Laetitia she is courted by Beaufort during Lovell's discourses. And as the real Laetitia she is given to Beaufort by her father, whose full significance we shall examine shortly.

Once the possibility of true understanding has been established, the union of Latimer and Pru can be effected more briefly. Latimer seems to be the same kind of person as Beaufort except that he has not been so struck by the charms of Laetitia. His moral nature is initially somewhat higher than Beaufort's. Thus when the Host and Beaufort supply Pru with a large dowry, Latimer takes her for herself. The identity of Pru as the "best deseruing/ Of all that are i' the house" (V, v, 130–31) has been implied in the elaborate pattern of clothing images with which she is surrounded. On the more or less realistic level she is best deserving because her true moral nature has exalted her above her merely social station, a mode of presentation which restates in a slightly new context an old Jonsonian theme. On the symbolic level the statement is new, and in attempting to relate Pru to the art-theme, one is led ultimately to identify her with a strikingly new version of the crafty slave of Roman comedy, with typically Jonsonian refinements.

As crafty slave she has the function of aiding and abetting not the headstrong young master but the headstrong young mistress, furthering her aims while at the same time exposing and implicitly correcting her follies. The young gallant in Plautus and Terence is characteristically in love with a theoretically marriageable or apparently unmarriageable young woman, and it is the slave's function to help make this marriage possible and to frustrate the old domineering father. The outline of the situation remains here, with details significantly changed in keeping with Jonson's moral argument and in accordance with his own more complex technique. The slave has become a maid, the young gallant a young woman.

The father—of the girl, this time—actively aids the marriage. And he is not defeated but rewarded. And, to plunge deeper into the metamorphosis Jonson has effected, the girl's beloved is not a young gallant but a man old enough to be her father. The potential Oedipus situation is resolved in a marriage between two people who have finally become mature. Pru is the prime mover in bringing this about. As such, she is, as the Host says, the "best deseruing/ Of all that are i' the house, or i' my Heart" (V, v, 131)—best deserving because she has been the charming and efficacious agent of virtuous reconciliation, an end she has attained by simultaneously revealing the best and the most absurd in the two characters with whom she is mainly concerned.

The Host as comic poet is no doubt well aware of the satirical reconciling role of the slave of Roman comedy, a really indispensable figure who has appeared brilliantly in Jonson's own plays. Brainworm, Mosca, Face, and Humphrey Wasp are variations on the same theme. The virtues of the redeemed young man joined with the wit, loyalty, and cleverness of the manumitted slave, after a ritual marriage derived from the metamorphosis and revelation of the two characters, will, therefore, implicitly be carried out into society as they leave the New Inn. At the same time, Pru, as metamorphosed slave, has helped her master metamorphosed-into-mistress attain her heart's desire by arranging matters so that the heart's desire is a worthy one. Lady Frampul is of course still frampul, but soon her name will be Lovell, and the Host's question, "But is your name *Loue-ill,* Sir, or *Loue-well?*" will be answered.

Jonson has chosen to use a modified version of New Comedy because it admits of reconciliation and marriage, something almost totally foreign to Old Comedy and to almost all of Jonson's earlier plays. Why he should wish reconciliation and marriage now, in violation of his earlier practise, is a question I shall attemt to answer in terms of the reconciliation of the Host, Lord Frampul, with his long-lost wife, the old nurse.

It is essential to recognize that by the last act the two figures of the Host and the nurse have become almost totally symbolic, and frankly so. The nurse stops talking as though she were drunk and removes a patch she has worn over one eye for seven years. The Host removes his cap and a false beard, and is once more Lord Frampul. The situation is preposterous, no doubt, to anyone who imagines he has been reading a realistic comedy—or something intended as such. (Surely someone must have seen the Host shaving, or the nurse peeping.) Critics have also wondered how Leonatus managed to get from Celtic Britain to Renaissance Italy, a feat less credible than the present situation.

The problem of the Host and the nurse can be resolved only by a consideration of their identities. As usual, the disguise reveals rather than conceals. The identity of the Host as comic poet and proprietor of the New Inn which is also the comic theater has already been suggested. The cap and false beard are designed specifically, I think, to redirect our attention to his symbolic role. The sudden and striking removal of the disguise reminds us precisely of the role he has been playing as host of an inn that he now gives to Fly, a development of the parasite of Roman comedy who also stands for the spirit of satirical comedy.

The suggestion has also been made that as comic poet the Host

stands particularly for the comic poet who wrote the play. A speech
in the last scene tends to reinforce this identification and to suggest
its large significance:

> I am Lord *Frampull,*
> The cause of all this trouble; I am he
> Haue measur'd all the Shires of *England* ouer:
> *Wales,* and her mountaines, seene those wilder nations,
> Of people in the *Peake,* and *Lancashire;*
> Their Pipers, Fidlers, Rushers, Puppet-masters,
> Iuglers, and Gipseys, all the sorts of Canters,
> And Colonies of beggars, Tumblers, Ape-carriers,
> For to these sauages I was addicted,
> To search their natures, and make odde discoueries!
>
> (V, v, 91–100.)

The passage reads almost like an autobiography, personal and literary, with its references to *The Masque of Gypsies, The Staple of
News,* the youthful wanderings, and the perpetual avid interest in
searching the natures of "these savages" and making "odd discoveries," discoveries about human motives presented with such force
and such grace over a period of thirty years. Like Prospero leaving
the island where he had practised his sublime magic for so many
years, the Host leaves the inn where he had "filled out" to the
guests. Like Prospero giving Ariel his freedom, the Host gives Fly
his freedom and the inn as well. But Prospero will return to Milan
briefly, and then to earth. The Host will go we know not where;
he will be "like *Mecaenas,* hauing but one wife." (V, v, 155.) Since
the wife of Maecenas was a notorious shrew, the Host, unlike Prospero, retains his identity as a comic prototype.

But who is the Host's wife with the uncouth disguise? The
drunken old seeming-Irish beggar with the patch over her eye?
The Host calls her Shelee, or variants thereof, often enough to

force us to remember that the name is Gaelic for Celia, the heavenly. She, deserted by her husband in a fit of peevish eccentricity, has been living with him in the inn these many years, each one's identity unknown to the other. Her disguise represents the symbolic form assumed by the ideal when it is put to the service of the comic poet. It becomes ludicrous without losing its formal designation.

And it is a sharp reminder of how much more Jonson did than write "realistic comedy." It recalls the exalted dedication to *Volpone,* where the comic poet is invested with divine inspiration and noble idealism. Shelee removes her disguise in order to prevent her daughter Laetitia's prostitution by Beaufort, a prostitution she fears has been effected through the agency of Fly. It *would* have been a prostitution if Beaufort had not come ultimately to understand her full nature rather than a part of it. Joy, as the true daughter of Celia and the comic poet, retains a purity which finally purifies her imperfect young husband, although, as Jonson has suggested more than once, she is capable of prostitution and debasement if she is put to imperfect uses.

The Host is now reunited with his wife, and his children are not only well married, but symbolically married. He has done all he can do. His inn becomes the property of Fly; he himself has only had a lease. He leaves his adopted family, the "reduced vessels of civility," who may now be identified as Brainworm, Mosca, Corbaccio, Sir Amorous La Fool, Sir Epicure Mammon, Wasp, Knockem, Merecraft, the Penniboys, Sir Glorious Tiptoe, and the rest. And they, one might add, are to be identified with the legacy of another Host—a pardoner, a monk, a miller, a reeve, and their descendants, Hodge and Diccon the Bedlam, Matthew Merrygreek, Tib Talkapace, and Sir John Falstaff.

As the play ends, Lovell's song is sung, his vision and dream of beauty. With a stroke of incomparable grace we are brought back to the world of comedy:

'Twill be an incense to our sacrifice
Of *loue* to night, where I will woo afresh,
And like *Mecaenas,* hauing but one wife,
Ile marry her, euery houre of life, hereafter.
They goe out, with a Song.

Jonson could invest even a stage direction with poetry.

THE MAGNETIC LADY

Jonson's last comedy is, as C. H. Herford said, very far from contemptible,[1] a view that is very far from universal. In tone it is the most Chaucerian of all his plays—the Chaucer of the Prologue. It presents an unusually tidy action—the neatest of all Jonson's plots—while at the same time it reads almost like a treatise on comic character and, to a certain extent, on comic argument. Unlike *The New Inn,* this play does not constantly force one to examine and re-examine the symbolic argument, although it does present such an argument.

One cannot describe *The Magnetic Lady* as a better work of art than its predecessor, but, to use a rather unfortunate word, it is more "successful." That is, it can be enjoyed even if one does not know precisely what it is about. It is not "better" because it does not say as much, but what it does say is communicated with ease, economy, and discipline. That the notably lessened artistic intensity of this play has nothing whatever to do with "declining powers" is easily inferred from the fact that it was followed by the fragmentary *Sad Shepherd,* a work of surpassing beauty, in which the old poet, like Verdi at the end of *his* career, embarked on a wholly new venture, well on its way to success when it was cut short by the poet's death.

In *The Magnetic Lady,* there is a feeling of intellectual relaxation not so apparent in *The Alchemist* or *Bartholomew Fair,* al-

---

[1] Vol. I, 99.

though it would be impossible to demonstrate that they are lesser plays on that account. There are fewer learned jests, and some of them are amusing even if only partially understood. One is not perpetually under the uneasy impression that he is missing something—although he may be, of course. The action is relatively simple and the characters do not require symbolic identification. Herford spoke of the art that conceals art in *Bartholomew Fair;* it is so strongly present in *The Magnetic Lady* that one is likely to overlook it entirely.

In *The New Inn* Jonson had shifted his artistic base from a version of Old Comedy with variations to a version of New Comedy, in accordance with his desire to effect symbolic reconciliations and marriages. *The Magnetic Lady* seems to involve a perfect fusion of the two modes. As in New Comedy, the scene is domestic, an important revelation of identity occurs, and the play ends with marriages. There are young gallants who want to marry an attractive young woman and an old man who would like to prevent their doing so. The young gallants are, however, unsuccessful, and the old man is a usurer and the girl's uncle rather than the father of one of the gallants; the situation is roughly comparable to that in *The New Inn* and to that in most New Comedy. But, as usual, only roughly so.

In terms of the basic situation in this play, the social world outside is also engaged: there are a lawyer, a usurer, a soldier, a parson, a courtier, and a politician; and their conversation effectively brings their world into the world of Lady Lodestone's household. If it is true that the defeat of the *senex* involves a triumph of fertility over age and impotence, such a triumph occurs here when Compass finally encompasses Pleasance. Again the world of society is involved, because the *senex* is not only an old man defeated by youth (without the help of a crafty slave), he is also a usurer, defeated by Compass, the "scholar mathematic." His world is defeated with

233

him, the world of Bias, Practice, Parson Palate, and Sir Diaphanous Silkworm.

Since these figures represent satirical versions of aspects of the real world of the body politic, the traditions of Old and New Comedy have again been brought together, more closely and directly than in *The New Inn,* not necessarily through superior art, but because of different intentions. The rather different artistic worlds of Old and New Comedy are joined in such a way that, as in *The New Inn,* each retains its peculiar values and virtues and both together engage the full range of society, public and domestic.

As I have already suggested, another artistic world is engaged here also, that of the Prologue to *The Canterbury Tales,* as is true to a lesser degree in the preceding play. If the range of social characters in this play is characteristically Jonsonian, its presentation is almost Chaucerian; at least Jonson recognized that good humor is an admirable comic vehicle, that reverend Chaucer had carefully calculated the effect of each of his descriptions in the Prologue, and perhaps that each of the tales represents a distinct, and partially dramatized, point of view. In this respect Chaucer's art is not unlike Jonson's or that of any other competent dramatist.

In most of his plays, Jonson has presented an almost Chaucerian range of character. But in *The Magnetic Lady* the process goes even further than it had in *The New Inn.* I have already suggested that the inn of The Light Heart has something in common with the Tabard. But the perimeter of Lady Lodestone's circle is more all-encompassing: a lady, a gossip, a waiting woman, a nurse, a midwife, a scholar, a soldier, a parson, a physician, an apothecary, a courtier, a lawyer, a usurer, a subsecretary, and a steward-tailor. *The Magnetic Lady,* in spite of its small cast, is remarkably inclusive.

Chaucerian characters have been changed by Jonson in accordance with his satirical purposes. Thus Parson Palate has nothing in common with Chaucer's parson, but a great deal in common with his friar. There are fewer than nine-and-twenty in this company, and the change is a pointed one: the parson is an ideal, the friar a reality. Jonson's parish-pope as parson reminds us of the real virtues of the other parson while revealing an amusingly unpleasant reality. Doctor Rut is partly identified with Chaucer's doctor of physic, but he also has something in common with a scurrilous satiric poet like Carlo Buffone.

The references to Jonson himself, particularly the one in the first act, are not self-conscious jests by the old poet seeking to regain his audience; they are amusingly self-deprecatory, like similar references in *The Canterbury Tales*. One of the references seems to indicate that Jonson is deliberately associating himself with Chaucer. When Compass finishes his description of Parson Palate, Ironside asks, "Who made this EPIGRAMME, you? *Com.* No, a great Clarke/ As any'is of his bulke, (*Ben: Ionson*) made it." (I, ii, 33–34.)

The epigram, by one of the greatest masters of the form in English, is written in perfect Chaucerian couplets, it echoes Chaucer's description of the friar, and it is by the great clerk Ben Jonson, although spoken by Compass, who, as his name shows, does have something in common with the bulky clerk. He is not Ben Jonson, of course; he is Compass, but as we examine the symbolic argument, the figure of Ben Jonson is always in the background.

An aspect of Jonson's technique that particularly pleased Dryden was his practice of describing certain characters before they appear on the stage. This has the function of familiarizing us with them while it stimulates our desire to see them. This is Chaucer's technique also; *The Canterbury Tales* would have been effective as stories even if we did not know the characters telling them. But they happen to be, almost without exception, gauged to the nature of the characters described in the Prologue. The *protasis* of Jonson's play is like the Chaucerian Prologue in the way it carefully introduces characters and establishes the scene, and for at least two of the characters the technique is clearly Chaucerian, formal vignettes, one of them using the Chaucerian couplet.

Another Chaucerian element is present in this play. In *The Staple of News* Jonson had indicated that certain kinds of people provided a greater burden than the body politic could bear. Penniboy Canter's justification for his gibes is that his victims are intolerable, although the play ends with symbolic regeneration. But before the tremendous and typically Jonsonian humaneness of *Bartholomew Fair* there had always been a strong infusion of moral indignation. We are bound to laugh, if a bit uneasily, even at *Volpone,* and the pure hilarity of *The Alchemist* will not blind us to the unpleasantness of parasites on a willing body politic: the plague has been raging in the background, and Jeremy is a kind of comic Jeremiah. But of one of his most grotesquely repulsive—and fascinating— characters, Chaucer will hardly permit himself to say more than "But of his craft, fro Berwyk into Ware,/ Ne was ther swich another pardoner." One could hardly say that Jonson is less humane than Chaucer, but his humaneness takes a different form.

In *The New Inn,* however, and emphatically in *The Magnetic Lady,* the inclination is to be much more tolerant. Jonson has come a long way from the Juvenalian ambition to print wounding lashes in the iron ribs of vice and folly. The satirical figures in this play have the same real counterparts in society that they had in the earlier plays, yet the poet has compassed them all, as it were, in a tone much closer to indulgence than to savage indignation.

To his last day Jonson may have had no more love for the human race as such than Swift had (nor is there any reason why he should), but the anger that informs the comical satire of *Every May Out* and appears in vestigial form as late as *The Staple of News* has given way to resigned and rather amused acceptance in the last two plays. This is partly a change in Jonson and partly the result of artistic exigencies.

It would be foolish to overlook the fact that he experimented and changed constantly. No two plays are alike. The early interest in Plautine new comedy displayed in *Every Man In,* and earlier in *The Case is Altered,* is revived and altered in the direction of elaborate symbolism in the last two comedies. The symbolic reconciliations are partly the result of his revived interest in New Comedy; the revived interest in New Comedy is partly the result of a mellowing of his own attitudes toward life and art. In the earlier plays no vice is so bad that it cannot also be amusing. This remains true in the last plays with the added implication that no one is so foolish that he cannot be controlled or even reclaimed.

No character in Jonsonian comedy is so irredeemably bad as Antonio or Sebastian in Shakespeare's most humane and sympathetic play. In Shakespeare there is always an edge—a Demetrius who is *such* an ass, an Angelo whose redemption we must accept while we wish he were being hanged, a Don John who is *such* a bastard. In part this represents the difference between comedy and tragicomedy, but not entirely, as *The Sad Shepherd* indicates. Jonson, indeed, never wrote anything so shattering as *King Lear.* This is partly because *King Lear* is one of the most stupendous tragedies ever written, partly because Jonson and Shakespeare had very different ways of looking at the world. *Sejanus* insists that we look at men as they are; *Lear* forces us to see them as either better or worse. Shakespeare violates only the most pedantic kind of decorum,[2] but Jonson doesn't violate decorum at all.

So far from being the simple child of nature he was once thought to be, Shakespeare is a consummate artist who never asks us to look at nature as it is. So far from being the *surly* moralist, Jonson asks us, except in the tragedies, to look at society, to laugh and be ad-

[2] *Cf.* Rymer's comments on Iago.

vised. There was always something incipiently Chaucerian as well as Aristophanic in Jonson's ability to make us laugh at vice as well as at folly. Those critics who have argued that Jonson's characters are not "alive" or that Jonson is all art and Shakespeare all nature— thus misrepresenting Shakespeare and Jonson, art and nature, all at once—have simply forgotten the nature of dramatic characterization. Readers who imagine that Hamlet's problems are theirs are giving themselves airs. The famous scholar who announced, within the memory of man, that King Lear is just like the headstrong old man next door should really think about moving to a different neighborhood: he lives in dangerous surroundings.

I have said that *The Magnetic Lady* can be enjoyed by one who does not understand it. The realistic action is inherently amusing if not uproarious. There is a problem: who will marry Lady Lodestone's niece Placentia? There are several candidates, all of them foolish, opportunistic, or otherwise deficient. Lady Lodestone is undecided, and various friends and members of her household attempt to help her make up her mind. There is a complication in the fact that Lady Lodestone's brother Sir Moth Interest, a usurer, holds the dowry, which through his usurious practices has become tremendous. Because of this, he claims the right to have a main voice in the decision.

Then another complication develops: it seems that Mistress Placentia, about whom some suspicious observations have been made by Dr. Rut, has just given birth to a fine if somewhat obscure son. This very considerably dampens the enthusiasm of the suitors. The problem is resolved when Compass overhears a conversation between Mistress Polish and the nurse, Goody Keep, revealing the fact that Mistress Placentia is really the daughter of Mistress Polish and that her supposed daughter Pleasance is the real niece. Compass quickly marries Pleasance (at an uncanonical hour, which suggests that the marriage is after all only symbolic), Sir Moth

Interest is humiliated through a Chaucerian practical joke, and Compass' friend Ironside the soldier marries Lady Lodestone.

Ironside had precipitated the premature birth by frightening Placentia when he drew his sword and quarreled with the courtier Sir Diaphanous Silkworm, for the very good reason that Sir Diaphanous was in the habit of mixing water with his wine, a despicable practice that Ironside rightly detested. Lady Lodestone marries Ironside because his offense caused the unexpected birth, which led to the discovery, which led to the reconciliations.

This plot is, for Jonson, astonishingly simple and lighthearted. If, like Damplay, we have any questions about its logic or its structure, they are answered by the Boy in the chorus. In view of the nature of the chorus—two playgoers and a boy employed by the theatrical company—we are justified in assuming that the play is intended at least partly as an illustration of comic structure, with enlightening comments between the acts.

But the subtitle is *Humors Reconciled,* and we are told in the first chorus that the author is "now neare the close, or shutting up of his Circle," as a result of which he "hath phant'sied to himself, in *Idaea,* this *Magnetick Mistris.* A Lady, a brave bountiful Housekeeper, and a vertuous Widow: who having a young Neice, ripe for a man and marriageable, hee makes that his Center attractive, to draw thither a diversity of Guests, all persons of different humours to make up his *Perimeter.* And this hee hath call'd *Humors reconcil'd."* (104-111.)

If any reader of Jonson has overlooked the possibility of a symbolic argument in the play itself, these words of the Boy will certainly suggest that he has made a mistake. The description of Lady Lodestone recalls the figure of Demeter, if not precisely that of Ursula, although the significance of her identity must be seen in relationship to the identities of the other principal characters. Her widowhood does not precisely jibe with the condition of Demeter, but it is close enough. Demeter had a missing daughter, Lady Lodestone has an unidentified niece. The brave bountiful housekeeper is closer. This of course is not Demeter as fertility specifically but as nature. Her house has a function similar to that of The Light Heart in the preceding play. It is the center attractive of a varied household and a wide diversity of guests for whom she apparently holds perpetual open house.

The beginning of *The Magnetic Lady* is completely unlabored and disarming: two friends meet in the street, *in foro* (as characistically happens in Roman comedy), and one invites the other to join him at Lady Lodestone's house, where his friend can be assured of good entertainment. Jonson has done this sort of thing so many times before that, for the audience or reader who has been paying attention all along, there is no need to labor the point—on Jonson's part or ours.

> Welcome good Captaine *Ironside,* and brother;
> You shall along with me. I'm lodg'd hard by,
> Here at a noble Ladies house i' th' street,
> The Lady *Loadstones* (one will bid us welcome)
> Where there are Gentlewomen, and male Guests,
> Of severall humors, cariage, constitution,
> Profession too: but so diametrall
> One to another, and so much oppos'd,
> As if I can but hold them all together,
> And draw 'hem to a sufferance of themselves,
> But till the Dissolution of the Dinner;
> I shall have just occasion to beleeve
> My wit is magisteriall; and our selves
> Take infinite delight, i' the successe. (I, i, 1–14.)

Compass calls Ironside brother, and in his reply Ironside calls Compass brother. Since Ironside is captain, we know he is a soldier, just as by glancing at the dramatis personae we know Compass is a "scholar mathematic." The name and the occupation suggest Jonson's *impress,* and we are free to assume that perhaps Compass has something in common with Jonson as artist, just as the term *brother,* reiterated several times during the play, once indicating that the relationship has existed for twenty years, suggests that Compass and Ironside, like Wittipoll and Manly, are two aspects of a total personality. Nothing that happens subsequently does anything to upset this view.

Compass is lodged at a noble lady's house in the street where there are gentlewomen and male guests of different humors, manners, constitutions, and professions. They are all very different from one another, but if he can hold them together until after dinner he will think his wit is magisterial, and he and his friend will be infinitely pleased with the result. The noble lady's house we can take to be a new but quite recognizable version of the theater symbol presented as an inn full of guests in *The New Inn.* Since Compass wishes to hold the diverse guests together and draw them to a sufferance of themselves "but till the Dissolution of the dinner," he is the comic poet presiding over the comic ritual. *Magisterial* as applied to his wit carries its customary meaning and also its alchemical meaning: the magisterium is the philosopher's stone. Compass as alchemist will encompass the banqueters, an action in which, if it is successful, he and his friend will take infinite delight.

Jonson has wasted no time in establishing a comic situation—preparing us for a comic banquet, a feast of fools—while simultaneously setting up his symbolic situation. Ironside's identity becomes clear almost as quickly. Compass's "brother," he nevertheless is not interested in the invitation:

> I love not so to multiply acquaintance
> At a meales cost, 'twill take off o' my freedome
> So much: or bind me to the least observance. (16–18.)

The implication that he represents the serious side, or the moral nature, of the witty Compass, is made clear by all of his subsequent actions in the play. He is constantly moved to eloquent but somewhat ludicrous moral indignation, as when he breaks the wineglass across Silkworm's nose.

The witty man and the moral man are brothers now, at the beginning of the play, and by the end they will be involved in a more elaborately metaphorical union when Ironside marries Lady Lodestone and Compass marries Pleasance—*her* name, at least, hardly requires comment. It is so similar in intent to Laetitia, and the natures of Compass, Ironside, and Lady Lodestone are so similar to those of the Host, Lovell, and a combination of Lady Frampul and the nurse, that one gets the impression that Jonson has here set out to repeat certain aspects of his earlier argument with unmistakable clarity, so that even the kind of audience that detested *The New Inn* would finally get the point.

This is a less complex and difficult version of *The New Inn,* making very similar points with less of the insistently autobiographical. Compass is to be identified with Jonson, but with Jonson as comic poet, not as Jonson retiring from the stage. *That* matter is taken care of in the chorus. In the play itself the references to Ben Jonson preserve a mock anonymity. When Chaucer, Compass, and Jonson assume a common identity in the exchange over the epigram, the figure of Compass becomes identified with a comic tradition extending from Geoffrey Chaucer to Ben Jonson.

As is usual in the late plays, there are two groups of characters, the customary realistic figures and a group of symbolic figures, Compass, Ironside, Lady Lodestone, and Pleasance. My impression is that the two groups are brought even more closely together in this play than in the three plays which preceded it. Indeed, we seem to be getting back to a slightly revised version of the great plays of the middle period, with the difference in tone already noted, a difference reflected in the sympathetic poet-figure and, as in *The New Inn,* in the combining of the techniques of Old and New Comedy. As is also usual in the late plays, the experiences of the symbolic group provide an implied resolution of the moral and intellectual chaos represented by the others.

At this point in the present study of Jonson, the realistic figures hardly seem to require comment. In detail, their absurdity is different from that which we have seen before, but its general outline is familiar. The symbolic characters are familiar, too, but since they are the movers, their significance had better be examined. Compass-Ironside combine to form the poet-figure, Compass representing the craft or skill—the manipulative powers—and Ironside the moral nature. Lady Lodestone is nature and her house the comic theater. She is the object that Compass points to—the compass is an instrument of navigation as well as of geometry—and she must be enlightened by him: Jonson argues implicitly, in play after play, that it is the function of the poet to reduce nature to its quintessential order, form, and coherence. The true Pleasance, like the true Laetitia, represents the quality without which the comic poet is seriously deficient. She is essential to his existence, and he marries her.

Compass observes, overhears, manipulates, comments on, and finally controls the inhabitants of the perimeter of Lady Lodestone's circle, but he does so with the aid of his friend Ironside the soldier. The reason for the symbolic association of these two figures is clear enough. Jonson had been a soldier once, and he always respected the soldier's office. Ironside is the moralist of the play, and by and large he is an angry moralist. Breaking a wineglass on Silkworm's nose or drawing his sword on the assembled idiots at Lady Lodestone's dinner table, he is merely doing what Jonson himself was no doubt often tempted to do; while Compass, exposing the fools and reconciling the reasonably virtuous, does what Jonson the poet regularly does in the late plays.

As we have seen, Compass and Ironside represent fragmented versions of a single figure, the comic poet complete. For Jonson, the comic poet is a moralist, but the moral is pointed through laughter, as the prologues to *Volpone* and *The Alchemist,* to cite obvious examples, suggest. The moral indignation that so clearly informs *Every Man Out* and *Poetaster,* and is present but not oppressive in the middle plays, is here presented as a necessary adjunct of the comic poet.

Lady Lodestone's ménage is a kind of microcosm, and she is the center attractive around which a diversity of guests, all persons of different humors, make up the perimeter. The microcosm will thus represent a nature of which Lady Lodestone is the goddess. Compass, the artist, directs Lady Lodestone, nature, an idea emphasized by Parson Palate's statement that Compass is the instrument she should sail by.

The relationships implied in the marriages planned at the end of the play are interesting and complex. Compass marries Pleasance after the false Pleasance has been exposed. The comic artist, that is, is joined with that which is pleasing and agreeable. Ironside, morality, marries Lady Lodestone, nature. Ironside and Pleasance represent the constant view that poetry should instruct (Ironside) and please (Pleasance). Lady Lodestone and Compass represent the proper relationship between nature and the artist, in the sense that Compass's revelations and manipulations correct and enlighten Lady Lodestone. But Compass doesn't marry Lady Lodestone and Ironside doesn't marry Pleasance. So this pattern emerges: Morality-Nature are balanced off against Artist-Pleasance.

Within this framework there is another relationship: Lodestone and Pleasance are aunt and niece, guardian and ward; and Compass and Ironside are brothers. These four, during the course of the play, have moved to the artistic and thematic center, while the gulls and sharpers have been at the perimeter, or have been moved to the perimeter. Nature, corrected by art and married to morality, is thus able to cast off the accidents of nature represented by most of her household and diverse guests, and is able to distinguish the true Pleasance from the false Placentia. Jonson's revival of the old game of infants switched in the cradle reminds us of the true identity of Frank-Laetitia and of her symbolic value, and suggests that he is doing here in apparently simple terms what he had done in the earlier play in extremely complex terms. In *The Magnetic Lady* the impure pleasure (Placentia) is rejected and the pure (Pleasance) retained.

Ironside, Compass, Lady Lodestone, and Pleasance are four separate figures, but their identities merge at various significant points, and none of them is self-sufficient. Art, nature, morality, and pleasure finally become parts of a unified whole, joined in marriage, which is not only a representation of unity, but a sacred relationship. The two couples are paired off as they are because nature is chaotic without morality; pleasure is chaotic without knowledge. Nature and pleasure are the ground of comedy; morality and art give it form.

Jonson therefore presents, in terms dictated by the realistic action, a symbolic synthesis of the elements essential to his comic art. The four elements are joined in a real and symbolic marriage of four characters who are themselves at once realistic and symbolic. If this is to be seen as a New Comedy denouement reaffirming the ideals of life and fertility, it is symbolically a moral and intellectual fertility which is reaffirmed. But the affirmation of fertility as such is essentially meaningless. It must derive significance from its representation on the stage, as in *Bartholomew Fair, The New Inn,* and *The Magnetic Lady.* Comedy itself is not ordinarily ritual, no matter how much of the ritualistic it may contain.

In *The New Inn* the distinction between the worlds above and below stairs implies the distinction between the realistic and the symbolic. The situation in *The Magnetic Lady* is similar but different: *The New Inn* requires us to make distinctions if we would make sense of the play. *The Magnetic Lady* does not; the play will be amusing, if far from weighty, if we leave it at something like realistic satirical comedy. The workmanship through which the secondary theme is communicated is of a very high order, like that of *The Alchemist,* but without the tremendous intellectual energy apparent in every line of the earlier play. Even the puns on Compass, Steel, and Lodestone work satisfactorily on the two levels ordinarily occupied by puns. The typically Jonsonian third level is engaged with our apprehension of the symbolic argument.

It must be admitted that, for all the fine workmanship, *The Magnetic Lady* is far less impressive on the realistic level than is *The Alchemist.* Still, this is, as Herford said, no contemptible play. Everything works, which is rather more than can be said for many plays; the parts are perfectly disposed by the hand, quite literally, perhaps, of a past master.

Chapter Six

Epilogue: *The Sad Shepherd*

||||||||||||||||||||||||||||||||||||||||||||||||||||||||||||||||||||||||||||||||||||||||||||||||||||||||||||||||||||||||||||||

ALTHOUGH THERE HAS BEEN some speculation that *The Sad Shepherd* may be a relatively early work abandoned and never finished, the consensus, with which I emphatically agree, is that it is a very late work, not abandoned but actually in progress at the time of the poet's death. If it is the product of his last months, as I think it is, it eloquently bears out the statement in the epilogue to *The New Inn* that his sickness had not impaired the powers of his brain:

> *That's yet vnhurt, although set round with paine,*
> *It cannot long hold out. All strength must yeeld,*
>   *Yet iudgement would the last be, i' the field,*
> *With a true Poet.* (10–13.)

The "judgment" that had served him so well for so many years was not only completely in his power in his last years, but at the very end of his life it was capable of exploring with wonderful success an almost new field.

I say almost, because Jonson had apparently done something remotely like this much earlier, in the lost entertainment called *The May Lord,* which will concern us briefly a little later on. *The Sad Shepherd* may also be described as the logical artistic result of the increasing interest in the theme of reconciliation in the later comedies. The play is pastoral; pastoral drama is almost without exception tragicomic; and reconciliation is the essence of tragicomedy. Having explored comedy fully and successfully, he now turned to pastoral tragicomedy, and the poet who wrote his swan song in 1629 attempted to begin what looks almost like a new career in 1637. In the prologue he announced that if this play pleased, there would be more.

The play presumably has a single setting, the scene described as a landscape of forest, hills, valleys, cottages, a castle, a river, pastures, herds, flocks, all full of country simplicity; Robin Hood's bower, his well, the witch's dimble, the swineherd's oak, the hermit's cell. This masque-like scene is the world of the play, stylized, ideal, inclusive. It is too inclusive to be strictly conventional; it admits evil; it includes low, as well as delicately exalted, rusticity. It is not so much the world of Marlowe's passionate shepherd, or even of *The Shepherd's Calendar,* as it is the *expanded* pastoral world of *The Faerie Queene* or *Comus.*

It is, indeed, the green world of fertility, regeneration, and triumph, but it includes figures not always associated with that idyllic and ideal world, and the characters do not move in and out of it, but are born and die in it. Its inhabitants include not only the shepherds and shepherdesses of pastoral, but a woodman and master of the feast, his lady, hunters, a chaplain, troubles unexpected (and serious), and a devout hermit, the reconciler. Its fixtures include not only the conventional ones, but a witch's dimble, a hermit's cell, and a castle, all apparently simultaneously visible to the audience. All of these persons and places may properly appear in genuine pastoral, but they seldom appear in a single pastoral unless it is of great magnitude, as *The Faerie Queene is*—and as pastoral that poem is far from conventional.

In spite of its inclusive nature, or perhaps because of it, the pastoral world of *The Sad Shepherd* is completely ideal, in its artistic conception totally divorced from conventional reality. If there is such a thing as pastoral realism it appears in such details as Robin's jests about those parts of the deer which Marian will find most attractive (I, vi, 6–9), but this is not the kind of rusticity one finds in a rural work like *A Tale of a Tub*. And while Lorel is an authentic lout, his situation prevents our taking him as realistic. There are no deeds and language such as men do use, but an ideal transmutation and heightening of these things in a world which, completely separated from ours, implies a higher rather than a lower mode of being than that enjoyed by nominally civilized men in organized human society. By obliterating the distractions of society the pastoral poet takes a different view of the sources and the nature of human activity.

Pastoral has often been regarded as trivial—or at least as less serious than other literary forms. Sometimes, no doubt, it is. But it very often involves something much more serious than shearing clean sheep to the sound of well-tuned oaten reeds in or near a bower of roses. If an ideal world is essentially unreal (as it is certainly unrealistic), this by no means deprives it of significance for the lives of real men in a real world. Colin Clout is a shepherd, and as such he is a singer; but his songs are about politics, religion, and art, as well as about sheep and unrequited love. *The Faerie Queene* is not strictly a pastoral, but it has its roots in pastoral, and it is sung by the same shepherd "whose Muse whylome did maske,/ As time her taught, in lowly shephards weeds."

It should hardly be necessary to remind ourselves at this point in history that pastoral need not be trivial, but if it *is* necessary we can always refresh our memories by rereading *Lycidas,* a poem written in the same year as *The Sad Shepherd,* which draws together its author's views of art, nature, and human experience with stunning brilliance. Jonson's departure from the literary world coincides almost precisely with Milton's arrival in it, and the departure and the arrival are attended by works in a mode which, at its best, is superbly adapted by its stylized form to lead symbolically to the heart of human experience. This is equally true in pagan, Hebrew, and Christian cultures. The *Hymn to Demeter* is essentially pastoral, as are many of the Psalms. Christ as the good shepherd is also a pastoral figure. In *Paradise Lost,* the fall of man and the prediction of his redemption both occur in perfect pastoral surroundings.

As pastoral is far from trivial, so also is tragicomedy, and the play with which we are now concerned was clearly designed as a pastoral tragicomedy. The popular use of the word tragicomedy is, to say the least, misleading. A tragicomedy may indeed be a play which combines tragic and comic elements; or it may want deaths, which is enough to make it no tragedy, yet bring some near it, which is enough to make it no comedy. It is a play which lacks a tragic catastrophe or a conventionally comic denouement; it is essentially symbolic, often allegorical; it is concerned with the affairs of the spiritual rather than the material world; it proceeds, unlike comedy and tragedy, on the basis of laws of meaningful improbability rather than of logical probability; and it leads to reconciliation through progression on the part of one or more principal characters from a lower to a higher mode of being.

Obviously, certain kinds of nondramatic pastoral have the same characteristics. The relationship derives from the essential unreality of both forms and from the symbolic nature necessarily associated with the unreality. That is to say, a representation that is unreal will be essentially meaningless if it is not symbolic or at least highly metaphorical. We have a form called pastoral tragicomedy because pastoral and tragicomedy are similar. *Lycidas* is symbolic, and its progression is basically tragicomic.

Before any rational discussion of *The Sad Shepherd* is possible, it is necessary to conjecture how the poet intended it to end. Francis Waldron in the eighteenth century and Alan Porter in the twentieth both wrote continuations of the play in which Maudlin, the witch, who is the center of the troubles unexpected, is reformed. Although I greatly admire Waldron's continuation, it seems to me that this was a mistake. Maudlin is not only the envious one, she is really a witch, not only an unexpected trouble, but a real evil, as are her daughter, Douce the proud, her son, Lorel the rude, and Puck-Hairy, their servant.

Briefly, it seems to me that, in view of what happens in most of the three completed acts, it was Jonson's intention that Maudlin and Puck-Hairy will be stripped of their magical powers, thus rendering them impotent as sources of future evil; that through the agency of the sage Alken, Earine will be able to experience the ritual rebirth implicit in her escape from the tree; that through the agency of Alken and perhaps of the hermit, Aeglamour will be restored to his senses and reunited with Earine; and that Robin and Marian will be represented as ruling henceforth over an undisturbed and ideal pastoral world.

The only point, therefore, on which I would be inclined to disagree seriously with Waldron and Porter is that involving the disposition of Maudlin. We can predict the reconcilations without difficulty. The problems presented in the action are problems to be solved in the customary tragicomic way, and while we cannot specify in detail how the *catastasis* and catastrophe would work, we can safely predict the outcome.

The central situation in the play is the loss by Aeglamour, the sad shepherd, of his beloved, Earine, who he thinks has been drowned in the Trent, but who has been imprisoned in a tree by the witch Maudlin. Aeglamour's deep melancholy drives him to despair and anger, and almost to madness. Maudlin also attempts to introduce discord into the relationship between Robin and Marian, and, through her supernatural ability to change shapes, is almost successful, being defeated only by Robin's common sense, which leads him to conclude that the sullen and disagreeable Marian (Maudlin as Marian) is really not Marian at all. Complicating elements are introduced in the persons of Lorel, for whom Maudlin has stolen Earine, and Puck-Hairy, Maudlin's thoroughly disagreeable servant.

Puck-Hairy is actually Maudlin's devil, as he himself points out in III, i, 7, a figure who intensifies her evil and attempts to insure its success. Another complicating element is the love of Amie and Karolin—not a complication really, but a representation of total innocence balanced between the mature virtue of Robin and Marian on the one hand and the foreboding evil of Maudlin and her train on the other. Alken the sage informs the shepherds and hunters of the true nature of Maudlin and offers to show them how to capture her.

Meanwhile, disguised as Marian, the witch tells Lionel and Karolin that the good old woman Maudlin has cured Amie, who lies sick in the grip of innocent love, the nature of which she does not understand. Aeglamour, distracted, in "A Cogitation of the highest rapture" (III, ii, 37), predicts the apothesis of Earine, whose spirit will ascend to the heavens,

> tempring all
> The jarring Spheeres, and giving to the World
> Againe, his first and tunefull planetting!
> O' what an age will here be of new concords!
> Delightfull harmonie! to rock old Sages,
> Twice infants, in the Cradle o' Speculation,
> And throw a silence upon all the creatures!
>
> (III, ii, 30–36.)

Robin recognizes Maudlin even in the form of Marian and attempts to apprehend her. He is unsuccessful, but he does get the magic girdle which has enabled her to assume Marian's form. Puck-Hairy promises to help Maudlin achieve her evil ends and avoid capture by Robin Hood . . . and the fragment ends. We may assume that Maudlin and her train will be rendered impotent, Earine released and reunited with Aeglamour, and Robin and Marian restored to calm pastoral peace.

The occasion for bringing together all the figures in the play is the feast planned by Robin and Marian, a feast interrupted by sorrows and unexpected troubles. That being so, it probably has its customary symbolic function, as at the end of *Bartholomew Fair* or *Every Man In,* as the chaste revelry of chastened people. Before the feast can take place, therefore, the events or characters which threaten or delay it must be rendered incapable of doing so. Maudlin, disguised as Marian, has had the venison sent to herself. When it is recovered by Scathlock, the witch curses both the roast and the cook.

Since the play opens with a symbolic situation anticipated, the apparent significance of the characters should be examined.

As the play opens, Aeglamour describes the lost Earine:

> Here! she was wont to goe! and here! and here!
> Just where those Daisies, Pincks, and Violets grow:
> The world may find the Spring by following her;
> For other print her aerie steps neere left.
> Her treading would not bend a blade of grasse!
> Or shake the downie *Blow-ball* from his stalke!
> But like the soft *West-wind,* she shot along,
> And where she went, the Flowers tooke thickest root,
> As she had sow'd 'hem with her odorous foot.
>
> (I, i, 1–9.)

The language suggests clearly that Earine symbolizes spring and fertility, the source and center of life. Later on, in Aeglamour's enraptured cogitation, she is represented as capable of reducing the jarring spheres to order. Presumably, then, she represents ideal nature and hence, in the Jonsonian context, moral perfection.

Aeglamour, the lover of Earine, has been separated from her by Maudlin (envy), Douce (pride), and Lorel (loutishness). It is to be the function of Alken the sage to render these three figures impotent so that Aeglamour and Earine can be reunited. Earine is glossed by Jonson as the beautiful, and the name comes from Greek *earinos,* maiden of spring. Stated simply, the pattern is: love deprived of life by envy. The problem is thus a moral one.

This is the central situation. Presumably the problem presented here will be resolved through the agency of Alken, through his understanding of the nature of Maudlin, which will finally lead to her being rendered impotent. The reconciliation apparently was to take place with the blessing of Reuben, the devout hermit. We must therefore consider the symbolic value of Alken.

In II, vii, Alken indicates that he knows where the hunters may find Maudlin and take her, and Clarion replies,

> You speake
> *Alken,* as if you knew the sport of Witch-hunting,
> Or starting of a Hag. (19–21.)

In II, viii, John asks Alken where they can hope to find the witch, and before Alken tells them, he makes an observation about himself:

> I have ask'd leave to assist you, jollie huntsmen,
> If an old Shep'herd may be heard among you;
> Not jear'd or laugh'd at. (8–10.)

Much earlier Alken has been described by Clarion as

A good sage Shepherd, who all-tho' he weare
An old worne hat and cloake, can tell us more
Then all the forward Fry, that boast their Lore.
(I, iv, 80–82.)

These short passages, it seems to me, are autobiographical. Alken is a wise old shepherd—in pastoral language, a poet—appreciated by some of the younger shepherds and hunters, out of favor with others. He has apparently been jeered at, although his main intention all along has been to assist the jolly huntsmen. The passages are very brief, because self-pity was hardly one of Jonson's infirmities. It is not inappropriate, however, for him to suggest, toward the end of his life, that perhaps he may still have something of value to say.

We have evidence for regarding Alken as a version of Jonson and hence for regarding him as a poet-figure. For the latter identification, the most important evidence comes in the stupendous speech in which he describes the witch's dimble. (II, viii, 15–68.) This is clearly a vision of hell. Indeed, just before this speech, Alken asks Scarlet if he knows the witch's dell, and Scarlet replies, "No more then I do know the walkes of Hell." (14.) Alken is conceived in the light of the ancient tradition of the poet as possessing not only universal knowledge but also secret knowledge, and is thus a new version of the Jonsonian commentator who now is endowed with knowledge of heaven and hell and yet remain consistent with his surroundings.

It is this figure of the poet, represented here as a wise old shepherd with special and secret knowledge, who was apparently to be instrumental in reuniting Earine and Aeglamour. It is significant, I think, that Alken's advice is directed specifically to the hunters, and that the language of his advice is put more often than not in the language of hunting. Hunting had special significance for

255

Jonson, as it did for Ascham, as the closing chorus of the masque
Time Vindicated shows:

> Turne Hunters then,
>   agen,
> But not of Men.
> Follow his ample,
> And just example,
> That hates all chace of malice, and of bloud:
> And studies only wayes of good,
> To keepe soft Peace in breath.
> Man should not hunt Mankind to death,
> But strike the enemies of Man;
> Kill vices if you can:
> They are your wildest beasts.
> And when they thickest fall, you make the Gods true feasts.
>
> (524–36.)

The information and advice that Alken gives the hunters is, in
its own context, similar in intent to the advice given by the chorus
in the masque. In effect they are being told how to strike the
enemies of man and kill vices. Alken thus fulfills the poet's highest
function, as Jonson saw it, by offering detailed and artistically conceived moral instruction. Alken's long speech is not only fascinating in its invocation of a poetically conceived vision of evil; it is
also and at every point a work of art, an imaginative and skilfully
wrought description which relates allusively but definitely to the
affairs of men. Love and life, driven apart by envy, are to be reunited by the poet.

Robin Hood and Maid Marian, although susceptible to temporary deception and unable directly to help Aeglamour find his Earine, are morally secure and virtually impervious to the threat posed
by Maudlin and her devil Puck-Hairy. Maudlin assumes, without
achieving her ends, the bodily form of Marian; and Puck-Hairy,

as a woodland spirit of evil, like Spenser's "evil Pooke," has an indirect association with Robin; Robin and Puck-Hairy have their own provinces in the forest. Maudlin and Marian, in fact, represent two fragmented aspects of what was originally a single figure, as do Robin and Puck-Hairy. Robin and Marian are safe because they have in effect left their evil natures behind them. The evil nature, being what it is, attempts to conquer the virtuous, but the virtuous, being what *it* is, resists successfully.

Apparently the two figures of Marian and Maudlin derive from the somewhat inconsistent figure of Maid Marian in the popular Robin Hood literature. In the folklore Marian was a "Lady of Misrule" at the Christmas revels. In this guise she deserts Robin, the chief deity of the Robin Hood religion, for his rival, a rather elaborate combination of Chronos-Saturn-Bran. At the end of the festivities, Robin ritualistically kills the rival; but because of Marian's role in the festivities she is often referred to not as Maid Marian but as Maud Marian, *i.e.,* Mary Magdalene, who repents her earlier unchaste role. Maudlin in *The Sad Shepherd* is sometimes called Maud, sometimes Maudlin. The name Maudlin, meaning tearfully repentant, is profoundly inappropriate to the envious witch of Papplewick except insofar as it suggests Magdalene. And Maudlin meaning Magdalene *is* appropriate if we assume that Jonson has taken the incipiently sinful Maud Marian and made her wholly evil, and the theoretically virtuous Maid Marian and made her wholly good.

The same kind of process has been followed with Robin and Puck-Hairy. In early tradition Robin Hood was identified with Merddin, who later becomes Merlin, born of the union between an incubus and a mortal. Robin was also euphemistically known as Robin Goodfellow, who, as we know from Shakespeare, was identified with Puck. Puck was not always simply a mischievous sprite; he was sometimes an evil spirit, as Spenser describes him in the

Epithalamion and as Jonson portrays him in Puck-Hairy. A pamphlet called *Robin Goodfellow, his Pranks and Merry Gests* was published in 1639, in which Robin is depicted as an ithiphallic god of witches. In an illustration he is shown as having young ram's horns and ram's legs. The Somerset witches called their god Robin. The ram figure, associated with Robin, or Robin Hood, is thus also to be associated with the devil. In Cornwall, the word *robin* often meant phallus. It would appear, therefore, that Jonson's Puck-Hairy is a real agent of the devil, while his Robin Hood is the other aspect of the hero of folklore, tidied up considerably.[1]

Jonson's pastoral method is strikingly illustrated in the arrangement of characters just described. These represent idealizations of potentialities for good and evil, while the other characters, in pastoral isolation, represent innocence, or, on occasion, virtues sullied but not destroyed; for example, Earine and Aeglamour show the influence of evil envy, pride, and loutishness—humanity purged of all sensibility—on perfectly innocent, hence perfectly helpless, figures. Maudlin, Douce, Lorel, and Puck-Hairy on the one hand, and Earine and Aeglamour on the other, represent something of which Robin and Marian have divested themselves. Earine and Aeglamour will divest themselves of envy, pride, and brutality, or their effects, through the agency of Alken, or knowledge, in combination with Reuben, or holiness.

If the lost *May Lord* had survived, the working out of the mythological and legendary details would possibly have been easier, since it may have dealt with a tradition much older than the popular Robin Hood stories. In that ancient tradition, the May Lady was identified with St. Mary of Egypt, or Mary Gypsy, or Mary Gyp, also known as Marian, Miriam, Mariamne, Marina, a sea goddess and patroness of poets and lovers;[2] while the May Lord would

[1] For the foregoing material on Maid Marian and Robin Hood, I am indebted to Robert Graves' brilliant book, *The White Goddess*, 438–43.

probably have been based on the figure of an ancient prototype of Robin Hood.

On the other hand, *The Sad Shepherd* may be a revision of *The May Lord*. The early pastoral had included an enchantress; and, as Drummond reports, "contrary to all other pastoralls, he bringeth the Clownes making Mirth and foolish Sports." (400–401.) Jonson was to justify something like this in the prologue to *The Sad Shepherd*. In any case, the remarkable fragmenting of characters in the surviving pastoral suggests that Jonson knew a good deal about the tangled Robin Hood folklore and its traditions and ramifications, whether or not he was equipped to take a Jungian tour into the racial unconscious. And he was certainly no less competent than Spenser to give symbolic values to his pastoral figures.

If *The Sad Shepherd* is seen as a play in which the foundations of life itself are joined and reasserted in the figures of Earine and Aeglamour, through the assistance of Alken, the wise poet, and in which models of sane virtue are balanced against archetypes of evil, in it Jonson provides some very specific commentary on these abstract themes. In doing so he has returned, in pastoral terms, to one of the recurring themes of *Bartholomew Fair* while once more taking the Puritans to task, in a new way. Percy Simpson points out the clear connection between *The Sad Shepherd,* I, iv, 18–21, and Spenser's May Eclogue, 39–50.[3] Robin Hood greets his friends who have come for the feast. It is June, and he asks,

> Why should, or you, or wee so much forget
> The season in our selves: as not to make
> Vse of our youth, and spirits, to awake
> The nimble Horne-pipe, and the Timburine,
> And mixe our Songs, and Dances in the Wood,

[2]*Cf.* Graves, *op. cit.,* 438.
[3] Vol. X, 368.

And each of us cut downe a Triumph-bough?
Such are the Rites, the youthful *Iune* allow.

(I, iv, 11–17.)

And Clarion replies:

They were, gay *Robin,* but the sowrer sort
Of Shepherds now disclaime in all such sport:
And say, our Flocks, the while, are poorely fed,
When with such vanities the Swaines are led.

(18–21.)

The speakers in the May eclogue are Palinode and Piers, according to the gloss a Catholic and a Protestant pastor respectively. Palinode speaks favorably of a May festival and wonders why "we" are not merrier, like the others, "girt in gawdy greene." (4.) The young shepherds have gone to the greenwood to fetch home May and his queen, Flora, with their music, and Palinode asks Piers if he doesn't envy the pleasures that they gain with so little labor. Piers is not interested in their pleasures; instead, he pities their foolishness, and, in a passage anticipating part of the St. Peter passage in *Lycidas,* says that they are irresponsible, letting their sheep run at large and passing their time "In lustihede and wanton meryment." (42.) There is no question that Clarion's statement is intended partly as an answer to Piers, who is, by Clarion's standards, exactly as sour a shepherd as Spenser may have been by Jonson's.

Simpson says that Piers answers Palinode "in words that were undoubtedly in Jonson's mind."[4] This is true, but there was more than this in Jonson's mind, as Friar Tuck's comments on "the sower sort/ Of Shepherds" demonstrates:

Would they, wise *Clarion,* were not hurried more
With Covetise and Rage, when to their store

[4] *Ibid.*

EPILOGUE: *The Sad Shepherd*

They adde the poore mans Eaneling, and dare sell
Both Fleece, and Carkasse, not gi'ing him the Fell.
When to one Goat, they reach that prickly weed,
Which maketh all the rest forbeare to feed.
Or strew *Tods* haires, or with their tailes doe sweepe
The dewy grasse, to d'off the simpler sheepe;
Or digge deepe pits, their Neighbours Neat to vexe,
To drowne the Calves, and crack the Heifers necks.
Or with pretence of chasing thence the Brock,
Send in a curre to worrie the whole Flock.

(22–33.)

Spenser's (and Milton's) good shepherds are Jonson's bad shepherds. Friar Tuck's speech is directed against bad shepherds who decry innocent pleasure and feign virtue while they are themselves covetous and destructive. Lionel observes that Friar Tuck's speech describes concealed vices, while the alleged vices of the shepherds of Sherwood are well known:

O Friar, those are faults that are not seene,
Ours open, and of worst example beene.
They call ours, *Pagan* pastimes, that infect
Our blood with ease, our youth with all neglect,
Our tongues with wantonnesse, our thoughts with lust;
And what they censure ill, all others must. (34–39.)

One remembers Zeal-of-the-Land Busy tearing down the idols in the Fair.

Robin Hood's reply suggests a pastoral return to sanity:

I doe not know, what their sharpe sight may see
Of late, but I should thinke it still might be
(As 'twas) a happy age, when on the Plaines,
The Wood-men met the Damsells, and the Swaines
The Neat'ards, Plow-men, and the Pipers loud,

261

And each did dance, some to the Kit, or Crowd,
Some to the Bag-pipe, some the Tabret mov'd,
And all did either love, or were belov'd. (40–47.)

Even in the ideal world of Robin Hood there are divisive elements, and their identity suggests that this play of Robin Hood
is concerned as much with the present as with the past. The sour
shepherds are the symbols of discord marring the idyllic. Jonson
must have known perfectly well in 1637 that they would soon be
the dominant element in the society of his own time. The retreat
to the ideal past would seem, therefore, to be a deliberate attempt
to comment on a present situation in such a way as to indicate the
coming of a crucial if not catastrophic change in the old traditions.
His views here are put in much more general terms than they had
been in the comedies, and the tone is one of regret for the passing
of real pleasures and real virtues. Sherwood Forest is not so much
a place of retreat as an evocation of ideal order and sanity.

The discussion of the shepherds ends with the remembrance of a
sad occasion that mars the mirth and music of the day. Earine has
been drowned, they think, and Aeglamour her lover is in danger
of a frenzied insanity as a result. The general gives way to the
particular, and the recollection of Aeglamour renders concrete the
dangers that they apprehend from the sour shepherds. The activities of Maudlin as witch may be roughly equated with those of the
bad shepherds who, out of envy and malice, kill the simple sheep,
vex their neighbors' cattle, drown the calves, crack the heifers'
necks, or set dogs loose to torment the flock.

Jonson has kept his social commentary well within the bounds
of the pastoral framework, more so even than Milton or Spenser.
His comments on the bad shepherds take up far less space in the
play than they do in this study of the play, but they are there, they
do reply to Spenser in the May Eclogue, and they do culminate
in the reappearance of Aeglamour lamenting his lost love. He has

been stricken by Maudlin, and his mood is envy: he will shed salt
tears by the margin of the Trent and "Quite alter the complexion
of the Spring." (I, v, 12.)

> Or I will get some old, old Grandam, thither,
> Whose rigid foot but dip'd into the water,
> Shall strike that sharpe and suddaine cold, throughout,
> As it shall loose all virtue; . . .
> Or stay, a better! when the yeare's at hottest,
> And that the *Dog-starre* fomes, and the streame boiles,
> And curles, and workes, and swells ready to sparkle:
> To fling a fellow with a Fever in,
> To set it all on fire, till it burne,
> Blew as *Scamander*, 'fore the walls of *Troy;*
> When *Vulcan* leap'd in to him, to consume him.
>
> (I, v, 14–26.)

In sharpest contrast to this is the representation of the love of
Robin Hood and Maid Marian. Their meeting at the beginning of
Act I, scene vi, is one of the most charming and significant passages
in the play:

ROB. My *Marian,* and my Mistris! MAR. My lov'd *Robin!*

MEL. The Moone's at full, the happy paire are met!

MAR. How hath this morning paid me, for my rising!
First, with my sports; but most with meeting you!
I did not halfe so well reward my hounds,
As she hath me to day: although I gave them
All the sweet morsels, Calle, Tongue, Eares, and Dowcets!

ROB. What? and the inch-pin? MAR. Yes. ROB. Your sports then
pleas'd you?

MAR. You are a wanton. ROB. One I doe confesse
I wanted till you came, but now I have you,

Ile growe to your embraces, till two soules
Distilled into kisses, through our lips
Doe make one spirit of love. MAR. O *Robin! Robin!*

(I, vi, 1–13.)

This may be rather like sporting with Amaryllis in the shade, but it does seem that the delightful Platonic reference in the midst of the playful sexuality displays the sane man's humane view of love. Robin Hood thus becomes not only a legendary pastoral figure out of the past but the evocation of an ideal that has the great advantage of not being beyond the powers of real men to achieve. There are a series of moral gradations in the play that represent its symbolic argument.

We can arrive at no final conclusions from examining the action, because the action is incomplete, if tentatively predictable. But we can say with certainty, I think, that Maudlin and her train represent forces of genuine evil, not comic vice; that Earine and Aeglamour represent innocence upset and tempted by evil; that Robin and Marian represent virtue separated from evil; that Alken represents the wisdom which can defeat evil; and that the hermit will represent the holiness which overcomes evil by reconciling those who have been tempted by it.

Robin and Marian are the most potent characters in the play of the sad shepherd, because they represent the rational and moral ideal. If my analysis of their relationship to Puck-Hairy and Maudlin is correct, they represent what probably ought to be called free spirits who, like Tolkien's elves, have not been contaminated by evil. They derive from the old days when, says Clarion, it was possible for a shepherd to wrestle "with a Lasse:/ And give her a new garment on the grasse." (I, iv, 50–51.) And, says Lionel, "all these deeds were seene without offence,/ Or the least hazard o' their innocence." (53–54.) Robin's explanation is that "those charitable times had no mistrust./ Shepherds knew how to love, and not to

lust." (55/56.) Percy Simpson points out that to give a new garment on the grass derives from the saying, to give a green gown[5]
(which hardly requires a gloss).

Puritanism is seen in this play as specifically opposed to May
games, which represent fertility. Like Rabbi Busy, it frowns on
those who will not frown themselves. Jonson's view is equivalent
to that of Spenser's Palinode, with the important difference that
it is presented sympathetically. Jonson had long since left the
Catholic church, and he would undoubtedly have laughed at the
suggestion that it was more inclined to charity than was the Anglican church, or vice versa. But he could hardly have been amused,
and he was not amused, at a theological system which seemed to
say that God's gifts should be regarded as cause for sorrow, rather
than joy. This is not to say that Jonson would have argued that
the Catholic or the Anglican church should sanction public and
non-nuptial bliss in the meadow, only that viewed charitably such
sports are not necessarily the work of the devil.

Jonson's ideal pastoral world, however, is not simply pre-Puri-
tan Britain, or even pre-Protestant Britain; the sentimental me-
dievalist had hardly been invented in his day. As represented by
Robin Hood, it is not a specific time before or after the Fall, but
a time transcending it and impervious to it, when "all these deeds
were seene without offence,/ Or the least hazard o' their innocence."
It is a world in which Amie can freeze and burn with love without
experiencing lust, a world in which sporting with Amaryllis in the
shade will soil her gown but not sully her virtue. And finally, it is
a world in which, since God's gifts are not surrounded by "no
trespassing" signs, no guilt ensues when one seizes them. In this
world nature and fertility are not denied by the virtuous, only by
the wicked and the envious.

At the end of his life, Jonson must have had ample cause for

5 Vol. X, 369.

disappointment. His career as a comic writer demonstrates that he had passionately believed that society could reform itself if it studied well the image of its follies and absurdities on the comic stage. And yet he was much too sane a man to think that it would ever really do so. Certainly he must have known, with Pope, that "no creature smarts so little as a fool." There was a time, indeed, when he hated fools, but it is obvious that by the time he wrote *Bartholomew Fair* he realized that there are worse things in the world. Savage indignation was never a Jonsonian trait, really, and when it appeared, it was a literary, not a psychological, manifestation; in any case, it soon gave way to laughter and then a degree of sympathy.

In 1637 the social scene provided little material for either sympathy or laughter, and perhaps the most wonderful thing about *The Sad Shepherd*—and its author—is that it is a reaffirmation of life, fertility, and joy, written, in a country about to be convulsed by civil war, by a comic poet on his deathbed, but with his wits about him still. It is almost as though that wonderfully taut and admirably pugnacious mind had finally permitted itself to relax a little, withdrawing the steel glass in favor of the crystal mirror, no longer aloof, but safe, one hopes, "from the wolues black iaw, and the dull asses hoofe."

Selected Bibliography

||||||||||||||||||||||||||||||||||||||||||||||||||||||||||||||||||||||||||||||||||||||||||||||||||||||||||||||||||||||||||||||||||||||||||||||||||||||||||||||

ABBREVIATIONS

ELH   *A Journal of English Literary History*
HLQ   *Huntington Library Quarterly*
JEGP   *Journey of English and Germanic Philology*
MLN   *Modern Language Notes*
MLQ   *Modern Language Quarterly*
MLR   *Modern Language Review*
MP   *Modern Philology*
PMLA   *Publications of the Modern Language Association*
PQ   *Philological Quarterly*
RES   *Review of English Studies*
SN   *Studia Neophilologica*
SP   *Studies in Philology*
SQ   *Shakespeare Quarterly*

For criticism and other relevant material, see items listed in bibliography, as follows:

THE EARLY PLAYS: Baskervill, Berringer, Campbell, Gilbert, Gray, Kernan, King, McEuen, Nash, Potts, Redwine, Small, Snuggs, Talbert, Waith.

THE MIDDLE PLAYS: Barish, Dryden, Goldberg, Goodman, Heffner, Levin, McCullen, Maurer, Nash, Pachter, Partridge, Perkinson, Putney, Scheve, Sternfield, Weld.

THE TRAGEDIES: Bryant, Duffy, Gilbert, Honig, Nash, Ornstein, Ricks.

Bartholomew Fair AND THE LATER PLAYS: Barish, Graves, Heffner, Partridge.

Several of the general studies of Jonson contain detailed and valuable analyses of individual plays, as do the various editions cited.

EDITIONS

Ben Jonson. Ed. by C. H. Herford and Percy and Evelyn Simpson. 11 vols. Oxford, The Clarendon Press, 1925–52.

Jonson, Ben. *Bartholomew Fair.* Ed. by E. A. Horsman. ("The Revels Plays.") London, Methuen, 1960.

———. *The New Inn.* Ed. by G. B. Tennant. ("Yale Studies in English—English," xxxiv.) New York, Henry Holt, 1908.

———. *Poems.* Ed. by Bernard H. Newdigate. Oxford, Blackwell, 1936.

———. *Poetaster* (with Dekker's *Satiromastix*). Ed. by Josiah H. Penniman. ("Belles Lettres Series.") Boston and London, D. C. Heath, 1913.

———. *The Sad Shepherd* (with continuation by Alan Porter). New York, The John Day Company, 1944.

———. *The Sad Shepherd* (with continuation by F. G. Waldron). London, J. Nichols, 1783.

———. *The Sad Shepherd, with Waldron's Continuation.* Ed. by W. W. Greg. ("Materialien zur Kunde des Alteren Englischen Dramas, Vol. XI.") Louvain, A. Uystpruyst, 1905.

———. *Sejanus.* Ed. by W. D. Briggs. ("The Belles Lettres Series.") Boston and London, D. C. Heath, 1911.

————. *Selected Works*. Ed. by Harry Levin. New York, Random House, 1938.

Aristophanes. Trans. by B. B. Rogers. ("The Loeb Classical Library.") 3 vols. London, Heinemann, 1927.

Oates and O'Neill. *The Complete Greek Drama*. 2 vols. New York, Random House, 1938. (For Aristophanes.)

Beaumont, Francis, and John Fletcher. *Works*. Ed. by Arnold Glover and A. R. Waller. 10 vols. Cambridge, Cambridge University Press, 1905–12.

Chapman, George. *The Plays and Poems*. Ed. by Thomas Marc Parrott. 2 vols. London, Routledge, and New York, Dutton, 1910.

Dryden, John. *Essays of John Dryden*. Ed. by W. P. Ker. 2 vols. Oxford, The Clarendon Press, 1900.

Ford, John. *Works*. Ed. by William Gifford. 3 vols. London, Toovey, 1869.

Marlowe, Christopher. *Works*. Ed. by R. H. Case. 6 vols. London, Methuen, 1930–33.

Marston, John. *The Plays*. Ed. by H. Harvey Wood. 3 vols. Edinburgh, Oliver and Boyd, 1934–39.

Middleton, Thomas. *The Works*. Ed. by A. H. Bullen. 8 vols. London, Nimmo, 1885.

Middleton, Thomas and William Rowley. *The Changeling*. Ed. by N. W. Bawcutt. ("The Revels Plays.") London, Methuen, 1958.

Plautus, Titus Maccius. *Plautus*. Trans. by Paul Nixon. 5 vols. ("The Loeb Classical Library.") London, Heinemann, 1924–38.

Terentius Afer, Publius. *Comedies*. Trans. by J. Sargeaunt. 2 vols. ("The Loeb Classical Library.") Cambridge, Harvard University Press, 1947–53.

Tourneur, Cyril. *Works*. Ed. by Allardyce Nicoll. London, Franfrolico Press, 1930.

Webster, John. *Complete Works*. Ed. by F. L. Lucas. 4 vols. London, Chatto, 1928.

GENERAL STUDIES

ARTICLES

Bacon, Wallace A. "The Magnetic Field: The Structure of Jonson's Comedies," *HLQ,* XIX (1955), 121–53.

Hayes, H. R. "Satire and Identification: An Introduction to Ben Jonson," *Kenyon Review,* XIX (1957), 267–83.

McGalliard, John C. "Chaucerian Comedy: *The Merchant's Tale,* Jonson, and Moliere," *PQ,* XXV (1946), 343–70.

Redwine, James D., Jr. "Beyond Psychology: The Moral Basis of Jonson's Theory of Humour Characterization," *ELH,* XXVIII (1961), 316–24.

Simpson, Percy. "The Art of Ben Jonson," *Essays and Studies,* XXX (1944), 35–49.

Snuggs, Henry L. "The Comic Humours: A New Interpretation," *PMLA,* LXII (1947), 114–22 (Primarily for *EMO,* but with general application.)

Wilson, Edmund. "Morose Ben Jonson," in *The Triple Thinkers,* 2nd ed. New York, Oxford University Press, 1948.

BOOKS

Barish, Jonas A. *Ben Jonson and the Language of Prose Comedy.* Cambridge, Harvard University Press, 1960.

Baskervill, Charles Read. *English Elements in Jonson's Early Comedy.* Austin, University of Texas Press, 1911.

Baum, Helena Watts. *The Satiric and the Didactic in Ben Jonson's Comedy.* Chapel Hill, University of North Carolina Press, 1947.

Bradbrook, M. C. *The Growth and Structure of Elizabethan Comedy.* Berkeley and Los Angeles, University of California Press, 1956.

Campbell, Oscar James. *Comicall Satyre and Shakespeare's Troilus and Cressida.* San Marino, The Huntington Library, 1938.

Caputi, Anthony. *John Marston, Satirist.* Ithaca, Cornell University Press, 1961.

Castelain, Maurice. *Ben Jonson: L'homme et l'oeuvre.* Paris, Librairie Hachette et Cie., 1907.

Chute, Marchette. *Ben Jonson of Westminster*. New York, Dutton, 1953.

Doran, Madeleine. *The Endeavors of Art*. Madison, University of Wisconsin Press, 1954.

Dunn, Esther Cloudman. *Ben Jonson's Art*. Northampton, Mass., Smith College, 1925.

Ellis-Fermor, Una. *The Jacobean Drama*. 3rd ed. London, Methuen, 1953.

Enck, John J. *Jonson and the Comic Truth*. Madison, University of Wisconsin Press, 1957.

Frye, Northrop. *The Anatomy of Criticism*. Princeton, Princeton University Press, 1957.

Graves, Robert. *The White Goddess*. New York, Vintage Books, 1958.

Kaufman, R. J. *Richard Brome, Carolina Playwright*. New York and London, Columbia University Press, 1961.

Knights, L. C. *Drama and Society in the Age of Jonson*. London, Chatto and Windus, 1937.

Linklater, Eric. *Ben Jonson and King James*. London, J. Cape, 1931.

McEuen, Kathryn. *Classical Influence upon the Tribe of Ben*. Cedar Rapids, Iowa, Torch Press, 1939.

Palmer, John. *Ben Jonson*. New York, The Viking Press, 1934.

Partridge, Edward B. *The Broken Compass*. London, Chatto and Windus, 1958.

Sackton, Alexander H. *Rhetoric as a Dramatic Language in Ben Jonson*. New York, Columbia University Press, 1948.

Small, Roscoe A. *The Stage-Quarrel between Ben Jonson and the So-Called Poetasters*. Breslau, M. and H. Marcus, 1899.

Smith, G. Gregory. *Ben Jonson*. London, Macmillan, 1919.

Swinburne, Algernon Charles. *A Study of Ben Jonson*. London, Chatto and Windus, 1889.

Symonds, J. A. *Ben Jonson*. London, Longmans Green, 1886.

Wheeler, Charles Francis. *Classical Mythology in the Plays, Masques, and Poems of Ben Jonson*. Princeton, Princeton University Press, 1938.

Woodbridge, Elizabeth. *Studies in Jonson's Comedy*. ("Yale Studies in English, Vol. V.") Boston and New York, Lamson, Wolffe and Co., 1898.

STUDIES OF PARTICULAR PLAYS AND GROUPS

Barish, Jonas A. *"Bartholomew Fair* and its Puppets," *MLQ*, XX (1959), 3–17.

——. "The Double Plot of *Volpone," MP*, LI (1953), 83–92.

——. "Ovid, Juvenal, and *The Silent Woman," PMLA*, LXXI (1956), 213–24.

Berringer, Ralph W. "Jonson's *Cynthia's Revels* and the War of the Theatres," *PQ*, XXII (1943), 1–22.

Bryant, Joseph A., Jr. *"Catiline* and the Nature of Jonson's Tragic Fable," *PMLA*, LXIX (1954), 265–77.

——. "The Significance of Ben Jonson's First Requirement for Tragedy: 'Truth of Argument,'" *SP*, XLIX (1952), 195–213.

Duffy, Ellen M. T. "Ben Jonson's Debt to Renaissance Scholarship in *Sejanus* and *Catiline," MLR*, XLII (1947), 24–30.

Gilbert, Allan H. "The Eavesdroppers in Jonson's *Sejanus," MLN*, LXIX (1954), 164–66.

——. "The Function of the Masques in *Cynthia's Revels," PQ*, XXII (1943), 211–30.

——. "The Italian Names in *Every Man out of His Humour," SP*, XLIV (1947), 195–208.

Goldberg, S. L. "Folly into Crime: The Catastrophe of *Volpone," MLQ*, XX (1959), 233–42.

Goodman, Paul. *The Structure of Literature*. Chicago, University of Chicago Press, 1954. (On the structure of *The Alchemist*, 82–100.)

Gray, Henry D. "The Chamberlain's Men and the *Poetaster," MLR*, XLII (1947), 173–79.

Heffner, Ray. "Unifying Symbols in the Comedy of Ben Jonson," in *English Stage Comedy*, ed. by W. K. Wimsatt, Jr. ("English Institute Essays.") New York, Columbia University Press, 1955, 74–97 (*Epicoene* and *Bartholomew Fair*.)

Honig, Edwin. *"Sejanus* and *Coriolanus*: A Study in Alienation," *MLQ*, XII (1951), 407–21.

Kernan, Alvin. *The Cankered Muse*. New Haven, Yale University Press, 1959. (Primarily for the comical satires.)

King, Arthur H. *The Language of Satirized Characters in Poetaster: A Socio-Stylistic Analysis, 1597–1602*. ("Lund Studies in English," Vol. X.) Lund, C. W. K. Gleerup, 1941.

Levin, Harry. "Jonson's Metempsychosis," *PQ*, XXII (1943), 231–39. (*Volpone.*)

McCullen, Joseph T., Jr. "Conference with the Queen of Fairies: A Study of Jonson's Workmanship in *The Alchemist*," *SN*, XXIII (1951), 87–95.

McEuen, Kathryn A. "Jonson and Juvenal," *RES*, XXI (1945), 92–104. (Primarily significant for the comical satires.)

Maurer, David W. *The Big Con*. Indianapolis, Bobbs Merrill, 1940. (For confidence games, particularly relevant to *The Alchemist*.)

Nash, Ralph. "Ben Jonson's Tragic Poems," *SP*, LV (1958), 164–86.

———. "The Comic Intent of *Volpone*," *SP*, XLIV (1947), 26–40.

———. "The Parting Scene in Jonson's *Poetaster* (IV, ix)," *PQ*, XXI (1952), 54–62.

Ornstein, Robert. *The Moral Vision of Jacobean Tragedy*. Madison, University of Wisconsin Press, 1960. (For Jonson's tragedies.)

Pachter, Henry M. *Paracelsus: Magic into Science*. New York, Henry Schuman, 1951. (For its relevance to *The Alchemist*.)

Partridge, Edward B. "The Allusiveness of *Epicoene*," *ELH*, XXII (1955), 93–107.

———. "The Symbolism of Clothes in Jonson's Last Plays," *JEGP*, LVI (1957), 396–409.

Perkinson, Richard H. *"Volpone* and the Reputation of Venetian Justice," *MLR*, XXXV (1940), 11–18.

Potts, Abbie F. *"Cynthia's Revels, Poetaster,* and *Troilus and Cressida,"* *SQ*, V (1954), 297–302.

Putney, Rufus. "Jonson's Poetic Comedy," *PQ*, XLI (1962), 188–204. (Fine appreciations of *Volpone* and *The Alchemist*.)

Ricks, Christopher. *"Sejanus* and Dismemberment," *MLN,* LXXVI (1961), 301–308.

Scheve, D. A. "Jonson's *Volpone* and Traditional Fox Lore," *RES,* I.n.s. (1950), 242–44.

Snuggs, Henry L. "The Source of Jonson's Definition of Comedy," *MLN,* LXV (1950), 543–44.

Sternfield, F. W. "Song in Jonson's Comedy: A Gloss on *Volpone,"* in *Studies in English Renaissance Drama,* ed. by Josephine W. Bennett, Oscar Cargill, and Vernon Hall, Jr., New York, New York University Press, 1959. 310–21.

Talbert, Ernest William. "The Classical Mythology and the Structure of *Cynthia's Revels,"* *PQ,* XXII (1943), 193–210.

———. "The Purpose and Technique of Jonson's *Poetaster,"* *SP,* XLII (1945), 225–52.

Waith, Eugene M. "The Poet's Morals in Jonson's *Poetaster,"* *MLQ,* XII (1951), 13–19.

Weld, John S. "Christian Comedy: *Volpone,"* *SP,* LI (1954), 172–93.

Index

275

DATE DUE

AUG 15 '66	FACULTY		
AP 23 '66	NOV 24 '80		
JY 18 '67	DEC 19 '80		
AG 25 '70	FACULTY		
APR 20 '71			
MAY 11 '71			
NOV 7 '72			
MR 31 '74			
MR 07 '75 RETURNED			
MR 8 '76			
MR 25 '76			
NO 26 '76			
DE 21 '76			
NOV 29 '77			
DEC 21 '77			
DEC 19 1982			
GAYLORD			PRINTED IN U.S.A.